Lives of the Renaissance

Lives of the Renaissance

☙

PEOPLE WHO SHAPED THE MODERN AGE

Robert C. Davis & Beth Lindsmith

34 illustrations

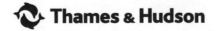

ROBERT C. DAVIS is emeritus professor of Mediterranean History, Ohio State University. He is the author or co-editor of eight books on Mediterranean Renaissance History, including a survey textbook of European history: *Story and History: Western Civilization since 1550.*

BETH LINDSMITH is a writer and editor who has lectured on composition and creative writing at Ohio State University. She has edited numerous academic titles on history, philosophy and anthropology, and her essays have been widely published.

On the cover: see *Sources of Illustrations*

Lives of the Renaissance © 2011 and 2019 Thames & Hudson Ltd, London

Text © 2011 and 2019 Robert C. Davis and Beth Lindsmith

Published in 2019 in the United States of America by Thames & Hudson Inc., 500 Fifth Avenue, New York, NY 10110
www.thamesandhudsonusa.com

Previous edition published in the United States of America under the title *Renaissance People* (Getty Publications, 2011)

Library of Congress Control Number 2018956155

ISBN 978-0-500-29506-9

Printed and bound in the UK by CPI (UK) Ltd

Contents

☙

Capturing the Renaissance

Half a millennium after first lighting up Europe's cultural landscape, the Renaissance still evokes the springtime of Modernity, when medieval fears and follies were discarded for new hope. The cultural rebirth started on the Italian peninsula, where the rediscovery of forgotten Latin letters led to a renewed interest in the Classical study of humanity and its place in the natural world. Its disciples called themselves humanists, and soon they spread their message over the Alps. Never quite forgetting the medieval imperatives of salvation and God's plan, they still shifted the goals of human knowledge, rejecting superstition and custom for new literature, new science, new societies and, finally, the New World itself. After germinating for nearly a century, the Renaissance then burst forth in its full glory around 1500, with the inventions of Leonardo da Vinci, the artistry of Michelangelo and Dürer, the scholarship of Erasmus and the discoveries of Columbus, Vesalius and Copernicus.

Such, at least, is the Renaissance usually taught in schools. Like the humans who made it, however, Europe's time of rebirth also had its dark side. Just a year after Sandro Botticelli painted his *Birth of Venus*, a German priest named Heinrich Kramer published the first comprehensive manual for witch-hunting. Witchcraft and sorcery were actually quite real to many educated Europeans, as were such pseudo-sciences as astrology and alchemy. Pogroms, the Inquisition and millenarian religious movements all flourished more vigorously than they had during the Middle Ages. Few spoke out against such excesses of faith, and fewer still protested as, from the 1490s on, the Universal Church imploded, states slid into dynastic or religious war and their soldiers spread carnage and syphilis among civilians. Europeans who ventured abroad mixed fascination with new climates with imperial ambitions and leftover (but fondly held) notions of holy war – a divine mission to subdue, convert and often enslave those native peoples they encountered.

The failure of Renaissance men and women to apply Classical learning to the troubles of their own day says something about the lessons available from the ancient Greeks and Romans – and about the conflicted knot of ideals, beliefs and sentiment present in European minds. In their writings (if not in their art), they seem less intellectually self-confident than their medieval ancestors or their Enlightenment descendants, but the humanist discourse spreading out from Italy was more method than answers. They offered a state of mind with which to approach the world, not an orthodoxy to provide all the answers.

Those who embraced humanism made of it what they wanted, or what they could. The range with which they experienced the Renaissance was vast, and the aim of this volume is to present that range, through the life and works of ninety-four individuals – men and women, saints and sinners, scholars and artists. Many are familiar names today: the centuries between 1400 and 1600 were embarrassingly rich with truly epochal personalities, and it would be unthinkable to leave out Michelangelo, Columbus, Luther or Copernicus. Yet there are many lesser lights in here as well: those who lived and laboured in comparative obscurity and who also, in their way, personified this reawakening, moved it forward or somehow fell foul of it.

We explore these lives in seven sections, avoiding the approach of surveys that group their subjects by nationality. Instead, each section ties the era's intellectual currents to its dominant political and social concerns, since for us the Renaissance was not a state or a people, but a people's state of mind. We begin with fifty years (1400–1450) that set the stage, featuring ten (mostly Italian) individuals whose remarkable interests and Europe-wide mobility helped establish and spread the new humanism.

Then follows the Renaissance proper – a century of discovery and tumult running from 1450 to 1550. This core of our study breaks down naturally into five sections, each revolving around a grand theme and each marking a stage in Europe's evolving rebirth. Since the cultural shifts we are exploring did not reach all parts of Europe at the same time, there is some overlap between the sections, even as they plot out a continuous narrative thread. Our Renaissance begins abruptly with the remarkable 1450s, witnessing in the space of just three years the fall of Constantinople (1453), the end of the Hundred Years' War (1453), the Peace of Lodi in Italy (1454) and Gutenberg's 42-line Bible (1455). Whatever the long-term impact of these important events, the immediate result was comparative peace and prosperity in much of Europe. We detail these years in two sections, outlining first the possibilities of self-realization (1450–75) and then the national consolidation (1470–95) that such an era made possible.

In time, such peace and prosperity spawned ambitious over-reaching that led, almost inexorably, to the end of both. Our fourth section examines fifteen lives from the ensuing years (1490–1515) of shifts and discontinuities, as princes sought to extend their dynastic reach in Europe, threw vast sums into military modernization and set out on imperialist adventures. Weakened by contention and economic upheaval, the shared Renaissance values of the late 15th century eventually broke down altogether. In our next section (1510–35) we present sixteen Europeans forced to cope with, among other uncertainties, the spreading collapse of the Universal Church and the rise of Spanish power. Only gradually were new norms established from the wreckage of the old social and political ones. We close our presentation of the Renaissance proper with a section devoted to men and women who flourished from 1530 to 1550, during the emergence of princely and Protestant cultures that their grandparents could never have imagined. We then conclude with a valedictory section: fourteen lives from the years 1550–1600. These were the Europeans who had to come to grips with the early-modern world, those for whom the optimism and excesses of the Renaissance were fading in the backward-glancing mirror of history.

❧

1. Old Traditions and New Ideas

1400–1450

The year 1400, when this story begins, was not an especially promising one for Europeans. The bubonic plague, after its devastating arrival in 1348–50, had returned every generation thereafter, driving the population into an exceptionally long demographic trough that bottomed out with a devastating outbreak in 1400–1. The Holy Roman Empire, at the heart of the continent, was split with a particularly bitter leadership crisis in 1400, with one emperor deposed, another murdered, a third deserted by his army and much of Germany falling into banditry and chaos. Europe's two leading monarchies were equally crippled. In 1399 the English king, Richard II, had been removed in a coup d'état whose repercussions echoed for nearly a century, while the part of France unoccupied by English troops was ruled by a thoroughly insane monarch known, appropriately, as Charles the Mad. Finally, the papacy, potentially the continent's moral compass, was hopelessly split between rival claimants in Rome and Avignon – one of them illiterate and the other abandoned by most of the cardinals who had elected him – in what a later historian called 'one of the saddest chapters in the history of the Church'. Believing that this papal decline presaged or even invited God's imminent retribution, in 1399 penitent laymen began wandering from city to city in Catalonia, Provence and Italy, flagellating themselves, gathering in great throngs and predicting the collapse of society.

The decay of such venerable institutions as the Holy Roman Empire and the papacy was not permanent, of course, and, despite being quintessential medieval creations, they eventually found the road to modernization and rejuvenation, as did the still feudal monarchies of England and France. Europe also emerged, albeit slowly, from its demographic slump, and even during the population crisis of the early 15th century some economic advantages emerged from the wreckage. Although there were far fewer Europeans in 1400 than in 1300, the available wealth in some ways remained constant, meaning that individual survivors were demonstrably wealthier, with more and better farmland to feed the cities, which were no longer so crowded and fetid. The artisans who came seeking work, being fewer in number and more in demand, found significantly higher wages, along with cheaper housing. As long as they could avoid the plague, the upper classes too did better for themselves, with undiminished patrimonies going to a reduced number of heirs. The increasingly complex finances of these elites gave rise to more nimble and efficient systems of banking and trade, while their desire to stand out from their peers and enjoy whatever life they were given created an explosive demand for luxury crafts, palaces and works of art.

This demographic and economic confluence especially benefited Europe's two most urbanized centres – the Low Countries and northern Italy. The wealthy textile and trading cities of Flanders and the Netherlands, under the benign if not always enlightened rule of Philip the Bold, entered an era of particular prosperity, expressed through building, land reclamation and the innovative work of such artists as Jan van Eyck. The essentially autonomous towns of northern Italy, linked only tenuously to a negligent Holy Roman Empire, also enjoyed a period of growing wealth, and if most of these free communes had by 1400 found themselves usurped by local lords, a few oligarchic republics still maintained some of the trappings and much of the intellectual ferment of populist rule.

In much of northern Italy this ferment expressed itself in the rediscovery of the peninsula's Classical heritage. Uniquely among major European societies, the Italians could confidently embrace their own past – the Roman Republic and Empire – as a culturally superior era. Extensive, if often enigmatic, ruins had existed for centuries, but by the late 14th century the writings of Latin masters were increasingly being copied and disseminated. As educated Italians uncovered these remnants of their national legacy, many experienced a quasi-religious enthusiasm, dreaming up family trees that reached back to Aeneas or seeking to identify every public building in Republican Rome. This passion for Classical roots had a way of spilling out beyond the preserve of scholars, however, as wealthy merchants asked their architects to design palaces based on the teachings of Vitruvius, military commanders studied the experiences of Caesar and Pompey, and Republican apologists applied Cicero's notions of public service to their own programmes of education and government.

From the late 14th century on, Italians made great use of their Classical past, but their enthusiasm for purging Latin of neologisms, discovering original texts and applying what they found to their own cities, buildings and families could easily have remained a localized, parochial movement. Europeans beyond the Alps, especially those whose past connections with Imperial Rome had been hostile, tenuous or forgotten, had little reason to rush to embrace the study of Latin letters. The Church, which might have provided a conduit to take Latin studies beyond the Alps, was too firmly set against the great majority of Roman pagan authors.

In the years just before 1400, however, the Italians broadened their Classical studies, as the Florentines invited Manuel Chrysoloras to come from Constantinople to teach them Greek. Cicero and other Romans had convinced Italians of the debt that they wed their Greek predecessors, but it was not certain that Italians would take the step of mastering Greek themselves: the language was both difficult and largely forgotten, and the culture more alien than those past influences would make it seem. That they did so was not just to their own intellectual credit. By embracing Greek, Italian scholars and antiquarian enthusiasts shifted their studies from their own, Latin past to create the notion of a larger world of the Classics, one that encompassed the entire ancient world rather than just their Roman ancestors. Between 1400 and 1450, as they mastered Greek and secured its key texts, Italians also launched a genuine, European Renaissance, one proposing the rebirth of a Classical past broad enough to become a movement across the continent.

CR

Manuel Chrysoloras

A GREEK BEARING GIFTS

c. 1350—1415

One of the most charismatic figures of the early Italian Renaissance was not Italian at all but Greek. Born into an ancient family of Constantinople, Manuel Chrysoloras mastered the Greek Classics while still a youth. A bright light of the Byzantine court and personal friend of Emperor Manuel II Palaeologus, Chrysoloras was a natural choice as Byzantium's ambassador to the West. In 1390–91 he went looking for allies to help defend his fading homeland against Turkish encroachment and, although he never managed to elicit any meaningful military or financial support, he did uncover a tremendous, unfulfilled thirst among Italians for Classical Greek letters.

Although rediscovery of the Classics – the great enterprise that made up the core of the Italian Renaissance – was already well under way by the late 14th century, scholars remained handicapped by their inability to read Greek, the knowledge of which had all but died out in the West by the year 1100. The Classical Greek and Hellenist canon – Homer, Plato, the Athenian dramatists, the lyric poets, the satirists and the great scientists – was consequently lost to scholars, who suffered all the more since their favourite Latin authors often proclaimed their literary debt to their Greek forebears. Those wishing to experience this ultimate source of Western culture could only make do with bad translations out of Arabic or struggle over Greek originals on their own. Petrarch owned a copy of Homer, which he found tantalizingly inaccessible, while Boccaccio had a go at translating the *Iliad*, but the results were neither literary nor especially accurate.

In 1391 Chrysoloras was in Venice, where he met the Florentine Roberto Rossi, who wrote enthusiastically of the Byzantine's broad knowledge of Classical Greek letters to the chancellor of Florence, Coluccio Salutati. Mustering support from some of the wealthiest and most cultured Florentines, Salutati sent an emissary off to Chrysoloras, who had already returned to Constantinople, offering him a professorship at the University of Florence and giving him a long shopping list of Greek works, both to use as teaching tools and to lay the foundation of a Greek library in Florence. Chrysoloras took his time negotiating over his salary and did not arrive until 1397, but once he took up his post he readily grasped that his primary duty was to make ancient Greek literature available to Italian students. Training pupils to read and comprehend a dead language was, at this time, a novel undertaking. Chrysoloras saw that turning Classical Greek into Latin – the common language of Florence's literate elite   was something of an art form, requiring his students to master the spirit of the ancients as well as their literal words, to produce texts that were all faithful to the original while still elegantly translated.

During his stay in Italy, Chrysoloras gave hundreds of aspiring Classicists their first exposure to the Greek letters. An inner circle of his best students remained excited and united for the rest of their lives by the knowledge, as Leonardo Bruni put it, that they were the first Italians in over 700 years to have mastered Classical Greek. Inspired by their master, they produced innumerable translations that made Florence the centre of 15th-century humanism and placed it at the very heart of the Renaissance.

Chrysoloras himself remained just three years in Florence, and then, in typical academic fashion, he was poached by Florence's great rival, the duke of Milan, to teach at the University of Pavia. Before long, however, Chrysoloras was again on the move, visiting universities in Bologna and Padua. Eventually his masters back in Constantinople drafted him away from teaching and assigned him to diplomatic missions. He travelled to Paris, Rome and Germany, seeking (though rarely finding) funds and support for the failing Byzantine Empire. Chrysoloras's ecumenical inclinations also allied him with the papacy in its attempt to reconcile the Greek and Latin

Churches. It was while on his way to the Council of Constance, as the Greek Orthodox Church's representative, that he died suddenly in 1415.

During the century that followed, other Greeks, some more able scholars than Chrysoloras, came to Italy. None stirred up quite the excitement that he had, however, either in the few years of his active teaching or in the decades after his death. Although he was not a prolific writer, his translations into Latin of Homer and of Plato's *Republic* immediately became seminal works in the Greek Classics, used by Italians as models for their own efforts. Years after his death, in 1484, his *Erotemata* ('Questions'), arguably the first Greek grammar, was published in Venice and won pre-eminence among scholars of both Classical literature and the New Testament.

⌗ Christine de Pizan

DEFENDER OF WOMEN

c. 1364–*c.* 1430

'And I who was formerly a woman, am now in fact a man,' wrote Christine de Pizan in *The Book of Fortune's Transformations*. The line could come from a modern newspaper headline, but is actually from a 15th-century allegory, an autobiographical tale of a woman forced by tragedy into a man's role. Plunged into near destitution by her husband's early death, Christine rejected the usual choices for a respectable widow: entering a convent or taking another husband. Instead, she took a masculine path towards a literary career, wielding her pen and intellect to earn a living. She made history for three reasons: she was the first professional female writer in Europe, one of the earliest French humanists and a proto-feminist who levelled unprecedented attacks on misogynistic thinking that had pervaded Western culture for centuries.

Christine was born in Venice around 1364 and moved to Paris four years later, after her father was named physician to the French king, Charles V. Like nearly all girls at the time, she was denied a formal education. Although her relatively progressive father encouraged her 'inclination to learning', her mother kept her 'busy with spinning and silly girlishness', and Christine had to settle for the academic 'crumbs I gathered from my father's table'. At the age of 15 she was married to a handsome young scholar whom she grew to love deeply, and she was devastated by his unexpected death in 1389. Money difficulties compounded her grief, and the 25-year-old Christine found herself near bankruptcy. She spent years in litigation, sitting in cold courtrooms, clutching her bag and papers while enduring 'stupid looks from some fat drunkard[s]' as she tried to collect from his estate. Creditors repossessed the family's valuables, and the bereft widow now had to provide for herself as well as her three children, mother and niece. 'When I saw the flood of tribulations rushing upon me,' she recalled later, 'I wanted to die rather than to live.'

As an older woman, however, Christine would describe this wrenching period as pivotal and declare that her 'duties common to married women and also frequent child-bearing' had precluded a life of the mind. It was her husband's death that freed her to write. At first she penned pain-filled poems about his passing, but she eventually turned to fashionable lyric verse, and before long she was earning both respect and income from wealthy patrons, a Renaissance artist's main source of support. Aspiring to more serious work, however, she launched an ambitious self-education programme: 'I closed my doors, that is, my senses, so that they would no longer wander around external things,' and focused on Latin, history, the sciences and literature – both Classical and contemporary.

Armed with both freedom and knowledge, she wrote prolifically; by 1405 she had produced fifteen long works and an impressive pile of short ones. What took her beyond the courtly social scene and into the ranks of the learned elite, however, was the controversy over the famous medieval allegory *The Romance of the Rose*, a chronicle of a man's quest to pluck an unopened bud (or, less coyly, to bed a maiden). France's literati had debated its artistic merit for years, but Christine was the first to denounce its misogyny, taking the unheard-of stance that it heaped unfair denigration on women. Drawing on her own life for material, she decried girls' exclusion from classrooms and condemned the social neglect of widows. Men throughout history had derided 'the fairer sex' as feeble-minded sex objects and scheming adulteresses, and she tartly marvelled at how women could possibly embo both. In *The Book of the City of Ladies* she imagined a fortress to protect women and hypothesized reasons for men's ill-will: her most pointed suggestion was that sour old men with impotent bodies disparage women to 'spoil for others the pleasure that they themselves cannot enjoy'.

Christine wrote deftly on other topics as well. Commissioned to pen a biography of Charles V shortly after his death, she used a personal, detailed approach – a style admired in Italy but new to France – that became standard during the Renaissance. Both civil strife and the Hundred Years' War with England rocked France during this period, and Christine responded with patriotic verse honouring fallen soldiers and, remarkably, a military treatise that would later be read by such men as England's Henry VII and one of Napoleon's generals. In her last known work she lauded Joan of Arc, who in 1429 led a series of successful assaults against the English that returned a French monarch to the throne. Just weeks after the battle Christine wrote, 'The realm [has been] elevated and restored by a woman – something a hundred thousand men could not have done ... Oh, what an honour to the female sex!'

When Christine died, she had written an astonishing thirty books. Many early copies survive today, suggesting her works were widely read and often reissued in her lifetime. Allusions to and translations of her writing continued to be published long after her death, and 16th-century records show that powerful European women – Elizabeth I, for one – owned tapestries of scenes from *City of Ladies*, a text that frequently appears in today's university curricula. Indeed, much of Christine's work is still in print today, for any woman who, like her, has 'abandoned all feminine tasks' and 'devoted her mind to study'.

Leonardo Bruni

'THE LIGHT OF HIS AGE'

c. 1369–1444

In the early years of the Renaissance no one played a more central role in bringing the so-called 'new learning' into the Florentine intellectual mainstream than Leonardo Bruni. At a time when Classical authors still carried a pagan taint in much of Christendom, Bruni's tireless effort in promoting Greek and Roman letters helped overcome the doubts of all but the most suspicious scholars. Like many early humanists, Bruni was an outsider with very modest beginnings. The son of a small-time grain merchant from Arezzo, he moved to Florence in 1396 to study law and was soon captivated by the teachings of the visiting Greek savant Manuel Chrysoloras. For a time he wavered between the law and the Classics, but in the end could not resist the lure of ancient learning. As he later recalled: 'with the coming of Chrysoloras I began to have doubts. Although abandoning the study of the law seemed reprehensible to me ... many times while young I said to myself, "How could you leave and desert Homer, Plato, Demosthenes and the other poets, philosophers, and orators ... when you can see and talk together with them and fill yourself with their wondrous study? How can you let pass this skill divinely offered to you?"'

Greek won out over the law. After all, Bruni noted, 'There are plenty of teachers of the Civil Law, so you will always be able to study that. But this is the one and only teacher of Greek, and, if he should disappear, there would then be nobody from whom you could learn.' Although Bruni abandoned his legal studies, his skill in Classical letters still earned him the attention of generous and powerful friends of the sort a penniless scholar desperately needed. In particular, he won the support of Coluccio Salutati, chancellor of Florence, an old friend of Petrarch and a great promoter of Petrarchan humanism.

From Salutati, Bruni learned to appreciate a life that was 'active and civil' (*una vita attiva e civile*). Salutati had found this credo in Cicero's letters, and for Bruni it meant more than just an alternative to the medieval religious ideal of a contemplative life. He also saw the civil involvement that characterized Ciceronian Rome as a social model that would allow Florentines to bury their old factional antagonisms and to respond to challenges as a unified republican community. The city's successful resistance against the military aggression of Duke Giangaleazzo Visconti of Milan, in 1400–2 – which was couched as Florentine freedom against Milanese tyranny – provided a ringing justification for the application of Classical virtues to contemporary problems.

After the death of Salutati in 1406, Bruni left Florence for a spell as papal secretary. Attached to the courts of a succession of popes and anti-popes in the last days of the Catholic Schism, Bruni spent the next decade in Rome and Constance, but in 1415 he returned to his adopted Florence, where he spent the rest of his life. In 1427 he was appointed to Salutati's old post of chancellor, or chief secretary of the Republic, and he never gave up his passion for writing and the Classics. Starting as early as 1405, he produced a long series of fresh Latin translations of some of Plato's most important *Dialogues*, and Aristotle's *Economics* and *Politics*, as well as key works by Demosthenes and Plutarch. In Cicero and the other great Classical essayists, Bruni found exquisite examples of Latin prose and rhetoric. Mastering these works and understanding their subtleties was, for him, not only 'the foundation of all true learning' and the means 'by which fine taste is exhibited', but also the cornerstone of social interaction. Such finely crafted persuasive powers, Bruni believed, should lie at the heart of civil discourse.

Bruni characterized his work, which ranged from histories and biographies to practical treatises and moral letters, with the Classical term *studia humanitatis*, 'the studies of humanity' or, more simply, 'the humanities'. Although seeking a high moral tone in his writings, Bruni was at heart a secular thinker, focusing on societies and individuals rather than faith or revelation. To the conservative clerics who condemned Classical authors as dangerously pagan, he responded that 'The noblest intellects of Greece and Rome have treated of morals. What they have left us of Continence, Temperance, Modesty, Justice, Courage, [and] Greatness of Soul demands your sincere respect.'

In his last years Bruni completed what many consider his masterpiece, the *Historiae florentini populi* ('History of the Florentine People'), which ran to twelve volumes. After he finished the first volume, in 1415, the city's rulers granted him honorary citizenship. After completing the ninth, he was awarded a lifetime tax exemption. Bruni modelled his *Historiae* on such Classical masters as Caesar and, especially, Livy, in the belief that 'the careful study of the past enlarges our foresight in contemporary affairs ... From history, also, we draw our store of examples of moral precepts.'

∝

Jan Hus

BOHEMIA'S PROTO-PROTESTANT PRIEST

c. 1370—1415

Jan Hus, a Bohemian priest and professor, preached ideas that shaped the Lutheran movement — a full century before Martin Luther himself denounced the Catholic Church. Hus drew thousands to his sermons in Prague, where he railed against clerical corruption and protested against foreign control of Czech affairs. Despite wide popular support, however, he was ultimately executed for heresy, his death triggering decades of war against Czech nationals and waves of papal crusades against Hussite factions that carried on his teachings.

Born around 1370 in the kingdom of Bohemia, an area now comprising the present-day Czech Republic and parts of modern Germany and Poland, Hus attended the University of Prague, where he earned degrees in theology and divinity. Ordained as a priest in 1400, he was named rector of the university's cavernous Bethlehem Chapel, which was popular among commoners for being one of just two Prague churches with services in Czech rather than in Latin. Hus's native tongue was cumbersome in its written form, however, and after years of composing sermons in Latin but delivering them in Czech, he streamlined its alphabet, adding diacritical marks that trimmed a tangle of consonants and clarified confusing vowels. Modern Czech still reflects his innovations, as do other Slavic languages that use the Roman rather than the Cyrillic alphabet.

In the early 15th century a conservative German minority dominated churches, government and academia in Prague, which provoked progressive Czechs and increased tension that had been simmering since the Germans conquered Slavic lands in 967. Hus championed Czech nationalism and scolded his brethren for being 'more wretched than dogs', creatures that fight when threatened, while 'we let the Germans oppress us ... and occupy all the offices without complaint'. By 1406 the previously orthodox Hus had embraced the reformist tenets of the English theologian John Wycliffe. Denounced in 1382 as a heretic, Wycliffe, like Hus, believed the clergy had abandoned many core Christian values – emphases on scripture and apostolic poverty, for example. To thwart Prague's growing reform movement, Church leaders forbade Wycliffe's works to be taught, preached or even read, and in March 1410 copies were gathered from the community and burned outside the archbishop's palace.

Hus ignored the ban, however, and incurred still more ecclesiastical wrath by denouncing papal fundraising strategies such as selling indulgences, which promised greater divine mercy – usually a shorter term in purgatory – in exchange for money. In response the pope excommunicated Hus and threatened to deny sacraments to all of Prague unless he relinquished his ministry and left town. Taking refuge in the countryside, the priest remained out of sight but not silent: from exile Hus wrote *De ecclesia* ('On the Church'), his most famous work. Drawing on Wycliffe, Hus exhorted clergymen to dismiss temporal things as mere 'dung', and to emulate Jesus by 'laying aside pomp, avarice, and luxury'. He noted that the Bible neither contains the word 'pope' nor states that salvation requires a pontiff. Christ, not the pope, was the head of the Church, he maintained, for papal power was a human invention rather than a divine decree. Beliefs to the contrary were merely 'follies of the Unlearned'.

Hus's doctrinal attacks coincided with the Western Schism, a rift that was already destabilizing the Church. In 1378 two rival popes – one in Rome, the other in Avignon – had claimed legitimacy. An attempt in 1409 to heal the split produced yet a third pontiff, this time in Pisa, whom the Bohemians recognized as head of the Church. Each pope forged political allegiances that pitted kings and countries against one another, creating conflicts that rocked Europe. In 1414 thousands of clerical and secular leaders gathered in Germany at the Council of Constance to deal with the Schism and to address heretical threats. Seeing a chance to clear his name, Hus set off for Constance after two years of exile, armed with a safe conduct pass from Sigismund, the seemingly supportive Holy Roman Emperor.

But Hus was arrested shortly after arriving, and, after a committee reviewed his writings, he was accused of seeking to 'decry and overthrow the spiritual estate' and formally charged with heresy. Hus could avoid execution by retracting his claims, and he agreed to do so – if scripture proved him wrong. Refusing to admit guilt during eight months in prison, Hus exhausted the Council's patience and was declared guilty of heresy.

On the morning of 6 July 1415 seven bishops dressed him in – and then ceremoniously stripped him of – his priestly vestments. On his head they placed a paper crown decorated with demons and the epithet *heresiarch* ('leader of heretics'). He was chained to a stake, and with kindling stacked up to his chin he refused one last chance to recant. Once the fires were lit, an eyewitness reported, he was dead before his friends could say three Paternosters, and his ashes were dumped in the Rhine to prevent their being collected as martyr's relics.

Hus was more dangerous in death than in life: the execution pushed his movement from reform to revolt, and rising tension over the next six years sparked the Hussite Wars, which lasted until 1436. Today Hus is still considered a hero in the Czech Republic, where 6 July is celebrated as Jan Hus Day, a national holiday.

⚘

Pier Paolo Vergerio the Elder

SERVING FREE MEN

1370–1444

Even in its earliest years, the spirit of Renaissance that flourished in Italy started spreading beyond the Alps. It was carried to northern Europe by itinerant Italian humanists, many of them emigrating in search of paying positions with foreign courts. Among these wandering scholars was Pier Paolo Vergerio, who after nearly fifty years on the road eventually emerged as humanism's leading advocate in the Holy Roman Empire and especially in Hungary.

Vergerio was born on Italy's margins in Capodistria (Koper in modern-day Slovenia). The son of minor local nobility and a Venetian subject, he was a precocious youth who enrolled in the University of Padua at fifteen. A few years later, he joined up with the scholarly circle surrounding Florentine chancellor Colucci Salutati, but at eighteen he moved on to Bologna, to take a post at the university, teaching logic while studying physics and medicine. A few years later, he was back in Padua, enjoying the patronage of the city's ruler, Francesco Carrara, and enrolled in the law faculty.

Like many proto-humanists, Vergerio's fascination with classical letters led him to imitate the ancient masters with some compositions of his own. The most famous of these, which he wrote while still in Bologna, was the play *Paulus*. A comedy modelled on works by the Roman playwright Terrence, *Paulus* explored the temptations and dangers that a student faced in a university town run riot with wine and women. Such distractions Vergerio presumably experienced himself, in the taverns and brothels of Padua and Bologna.

Vergerio's student days ended in 1397, when war broke out between Padua and the Venetian Republic. Nominally still a subject of Venice, Vergerio left Padua in a hurry, setting off for Bologna. When the plague struck there in 1398, he fled again, wandering around northern Italy before ending up in Florence, around 1399. During a fruitful stay there, Vergerio took lessons in Greek from the visiting Manuel Chrysolaras and met Leonardo Bruni. The city's vibrant culture of civic humanism influenced him deeply, and when he left in 1405, he had picked up a practiced insight in applying classical thought to contemporary topics and problems. His intellectual activity remained prodigious, and in 1405, again back at the University of Padua, he was awarded concurrent doctorates in canon and civil law, the arts, and medicine.

In those same years, Vergerio also produced the book that would be his enduring legacy, *De ingenuis moribus et liberalibus studiis adulescentiae* (*On the Noble Character and Liberal Studies of Youth*). In it, he organized the emerging principles of humanism into a genuine educational program. Based, not surprisingly, on classical models, his program shifted learning from the rote memorization and formal debate characteristic of Medieval pedagogy, to encompass history, poetry, and morals. Vergerio especially encouraged training in rhetoric, for he saw the ability to persuade and lead one's fellow citizens as an essential attribute of a free men, or *liberi*. His programme of *arti liberi* – the 'liberal arts' necessary for such free men – also mixed study with periods of relaxation, discussion, and exercise. His methods for shaping patriotic and well-rounded citizens would dominate elite education in Western Europe until well into the twentieth century.

Despite the immediate success of *De ingenuis moribus*, Vergerio still could not find a permanent job, a common problem for practitioners of the emerging field of humanism. Heading south after 1405, he found employment as papal secretary for the anti-pope John XXIII, a position that in 1415 sent him to the Council of Constance. While there, he caught the attention of the Emperor Sigismund (1368–1437), who took him into the imperial court and away from Italy for good.

After several years of travelling with the Emperor around Germany, Vergerio ended up in Sigismund's Hungarian capital of Buda. There he met up again with several Hungarian students, old friends from his Padua years. For the next decade, Vergerio was active within both this intellectual circle and Sigismund's court, where he was named *Referendarius*, or imperial chancellor. Keeping up his humanist studies, he translated for Sigismund the Greek historian Arrian's *Anabasis Alexandri*, telling of Alexander the Great's campaigns in Asia. He also headed the imperial delegation that debated against the remaining Hussites in Prague, in 1420.

Later in his life, Vergerio apparently fell out of favor with both Sigismund and most of his Hungarian and Italian friends in Buda. Undiscouraged, he moved on to the cathedral town of Varad, where he spent his last years forging connections with and influencing a new generation of Hungarian and Polish humanists, including several who had an essential role in educating Hungary's future king, Matthias Corvinus, who was born in 1443.

ଔ

Filippo Brunelleschi

REALIZING THE IMPOSSIBLE CATHEDRAL

1377–1446

W hen Filippo Brunelleschi was born, the building that would make him famous had been under construction for eighty years. By the time he reached adulthood, Florence's Santa Maria del Fiore – then the world's largest cathedral – stood nearly complete. There was one glaring exception: a 43-metre (141-foot) hole where a massive dome was supposed to stand. The cathedral's medieval architects had designed an unbuildable building, simply trusting that some future engineer would work out the details for the largest dome in history. The solution came from Brunelleschi, a Florentine goldsmith whose creative vision not only solved the problem, but also changed the look of Renaissance architecture, painting and sculpture.

As a child, Brunelleschi lived with his prosperous family in a house just west of the cathedral site, and young Pippo, as everyone called him, would have regularly walked past the construction workers and their elaborate hoisting machines. At the age of 15 he was apprenticed to a local goldsmith's workshop, where he excelled at mathematical calculations and worked precious metals into everything from gold-leafed manuscript illuminations and elaborate reliquaries to imposing gilded tombs.

Brunelleschi became a master goldsmith in 1398, when famine and decades of plague had weakened Florence and a powerful Milanese army was advancing on the city. In a move to boost patriotism and to appeal to an apparently vengeful God, civic leaders announced a contest challenging artists to design new bronze doors for the baptistery, the oldest building in the city and the heart of the Florentine community. Although he was a finalist, Brunelleschi did not win the prize, and the disappointment is said to have driven him to Rome. There he and his friend Donatello studied surviving examples of Classical sculpture, sketched buildings and measured the proportions of ancient structures.

Thanks to this research, Brunelleschi grasped spatial concepts well enough to be deemed an expert in perspective by the humanist Domenico da Prato, and some time between 1413 and 1425 he changed the world of art for ever by working out the principles of one-point perspective. Lost to the world since antiquity, it was a mathematical system that allowed artists to create realistic three-dimensional scenes on two-dimensional surfaces. Before Brunelleschi's breakthrough, paintings of Florentine cityscapes had always been slightly jumbled, with the structures placed in conflicting angles as though viewed from different vantage points. In a Renaissance version of special effects, he stunned colleagues with an experimental painting of the octagonal baptistery in perfect perspective – an optical illusion of reality. Brunelleschi passed the knowledge on to his friends Masaccio and Donatello, who were the first artists to put the principles to artistic use, and to Leon Battista Alberti, who was the first to write about them.

Throughout his thirties and early forties Brunelleschi worked on assignments that led to major commissions in 1419: two important chapels, the Basilica of San Lorenzo and, finally, an orphanage for the city of Florence. His vision for that building, the Ospedale degli Innocenti, marks a turning point in Western design. Using elements of Classical architecture, he created a ground-floor loggia with an arcade of Corinthian columns separated by perfectly proportioned rounded arches. The Ospedale became a hallmark of Renaissance Italian architecture and inspired centuries of imitations.

Yet it was his proposal for the cathedral dome that established Brunelleschi's reputation as an engineering genius. The original plans had called for the cupola to float over the church crossing with no visible support: Tuscans dismissed the flying buttresses of Gothic cathedrals as ugly and old-fashioned. Again a contest was organized, and, working in code to prevent anyone from filching his ideas, Brunelleschi devised a self-supporting dome that, like the Pantheon in Rome, created a soaring, open space without columns, beams or arches inside, or exoskeletal buttressing outside. He proposed an outer shell stiffened with eight external vertical ribs over a more substantial inner shell that added strength and support. Built into the walls of each shell were horizontal sandstone hoops, larger at the bottom and narrowing towards the top, to counterbalance inward force. Borrowing from the ancient Romans, he specified an inner course of brickwork laid in a modified herringbone pattern, with several horizontal rows of brick interrupted here and there by a vertical strip that made the layer self-supporting. Near the base of the octagon's sides he placed massive, rough-hewn wooden beams, which, when linked at their ends with enormous iron clasps, formed a slightly elastic chain that flexed with the huge structure's inevitable shifts.

The building materials were so heavy – the dome required dozens of stone slabs weighing several tons each   that construction teams needed custom-made hoisting devices, which Brunelleschi also invented. Workers had raised and laid more than four million bricks to build the cupola by the time the cathedral was consecrated in 1436. That year he completed plans for one of his last commissions, the Augustinian church of Santo Spirito. Like San Lorenzo, it features balanced symmetry and a spare, serene interior in muted greys. Altogether, Brunelleschi's masterpieces helped set the Renaissance on its course, making his city a model for later architects. When he died in 1446, the city of Florence gave Brunelleschi its highest honour, burying him in Santa Maria del Fiore. With the passing of time, the grave of this famous Florentine was lost to memory until it was uncovered during restorations begun in 1972.

CR

St Bernardino of Siena

THE PEOPLE'S PREACHER

1380–1444

As a boy, Bernardino Albizzeschi never worried about his vocation –
only which religious order to join. Settling on the highly disciplined
Observant Franciscans, he was ordained a priest in 1404 and entered into
seclusion at a hermitage near Siena. A vision in 1417 convinced him to
abandon his books and cell, however, and to follow his true calling – as a
preacher. 'God', he later said, 'has given the instrument of the tongue only
to Man – noble instrument! You come to hear the preacher, and for two or
three hours he delights you! God didn't give us a more beautiful instrument,
a more blessed organ.' So convinced was he of his own rhetorical powers that
Bernardino told his followers that they could skip the Mass at the beginning
of his services as long as they stayed for the sermon.

Before long, Bernardino worked out the rhetorical style that would
make him the most celebrated preacher of the early Renaissance. Although
images of him painted from life show a frail and toothless old man, he was
vigorous in the pulpit – 'strong as a lion', he boasted, and able to preach for
hours. Coming to a new city, he would give long sermons on each of the
forty days of Lent, to such great crowds that he had to move outdoors to
the largest public square. Planning ahead, he took his own portable pulpit.

Bernardino's preaching skills clearly come through in many sermons
that were faithfully recorded on the spot by devoted followers who took
down every word and gesture in shorthand. He carefully crafted his message,
with each morning's sermon building on the theme of the week, and the
whole advancing to a broad conclusion. The path to this climax could be

leisurely, however, for he often digressed from his detailed discussions – of usury, heresy, vanity, witchcraft, prostitution, adultery, homosexuality or other popular sins – to spin anecdotes and to gibe at his audience: 'Have you understood me? Yes? I'm not talking in French!?' He punctuated his attacks on vice with highly choreographed and extremely popular faith healings and 'bonfires of the vanities'.

Bernardino's greater goal, however, and the reason he was usually invited in the first place, was to establish concord in cities often riven by faction. The communes of central Italy in particular were hotbeds of violence and vendetta, stirred up by individuals, clans and entire cities squabbling over honour, power and revenge. Consequently, Bernardino regularly decried 'the father [who is] the enemy of the son, the son of the father; a brother against brother, friend against friend, companion against companion'. As the cycle progressed, he would abandon his earlier joviality to decry the horrors of factionalism, which disrupted trade, spread poverty and allowed soldiers to loot and rape. He reminded his audience that, 'Like Jerusalem, [your] city is ripe for punishment', and thundered, 'I say to all of you: do not open your hands to works of blood! Do not open them, but rather pardon! pardon! pardon! Oh! To whom do I speak?' – and then, pointing to individuals – 'To this one and that one and this one … each one love his neighbour. And who is this neighbour? We are all neighbours, each one to the other!'

At this high point Bernardino would whip out the painted wooden *tavoletta*, or board, that he had designed. It carried the initials of the Holy Name, IHS, or *Iesus Hominum Salvator* ('Jesus, Saviour of Mankind'), within a golden sun on a blue background. On seeing it, men and women fell on their knees, shrieking and embracing each other, in cathartic brotherhood and a near hysteria of guilt and repentance. At the end of the cycle towns-people were often so moved that they threw away their factional or clan colours and took up the IHS symbol instead. Over the ensuing weeks town councils sometimes passed legislation, known as *Statutae Sancti Bernardini*, to set his sermons into law. Clan and vendetta were outlawed, and deviant behaviour – from luxurious dress and inappropriate games to sodomy and usury – would be 'punished by fire or fines'.

After Bernardino died in 1444, he was credited with a host of miracles and canonized just six years later. Yet the impact of his preaching was mixed in the long run. The *Statutae Sancti Bernardini*, so enthusiastically enacted, were ignored within a decade, according to later missionaries. Likewise, the factional discord against which Bernardino had preached so fervently remained strong. When the Sienese asked the citizens of L'Aquila – where he had died while on his final mission – to return the body of their native son, the Aquilesi, apparently unaware of the irony, refused with a torrent of abuse and threats.

Ը

Donatello

PASSION IN STONE AND BRONZE

1386/87–1466

In many ways Donatello was the first artist of the Renaissance. He was responsible for the revival of the Classical statue, a form of sculpture that had disappeared from Western art during the early days of Christianity. The first Christians saw free-standing statues as pagan idols, and artists who followed the new religion worked mostly in mosaic and paint. Any carvings were limited to relief panels and small statuettes, and the art of chiselling large figures was lost for a thousand years. In the Middle Ages larger Christian figures began to appear, but mainly as decorations on buildings or tombs rather than as independent pieces of art. During the 14th century, however, Gothic sculptors began liberating human forms from columns and cathedral doorways, and the new reverence for antiquity fuelled a demand for statues carved in the round. No sculptor recreated the Classical form with complete success, however, until Donatello at the dawn of the 15th century.

Donatello, whose name is a diminutive of Donato, was born in Florence in 1386 or 1387. His early life is murky, but two details are certain. At about 15 he was arrested for bloodying a German boy with a stick, and a few years later he began training with the eminent sculptor Lorenzo Ghiberti. At the time Ghiberti was working on the famous bronze doors of Florence's baptistery, having won a competition for the commission. Such contests abounded as the city's humanist leaders, eager to cast Florence as a new Rome, sought art for public spaces in the Classical style.

Both Donatello and Ghiberti landed commissions for the church of Orsanmichele, which included fourteen large external niches for substantial statues. The men finished the projects around the same time, but the results almost seem to be from different eras. Ghiberti's *St John the Baptist*, completed in 1416, is a stylized, late Gothic figure: his robes lie in decorative horizontal swags, for example, which bear little relationship to the human form beneath. Although Donatello finished his *St Mark* three years earlier, it seems more modern, with clothing hanging from the waist in realistic vertical folds and sleeves that bunch and gather about the arms. For the first time since the Classical era, sculpted fabric reveals rather than masks the body's underlying structure.

Even more important, however, was that Donatello had mastered the lost principle of *contrapposto*, or weight shift. First grasped by the Greeks 2,000 years earlier, this concept recognized that standing upright was an ongoing balancing act; to create a realistic figure, sculptors had to convey that sense of tension. Donatello's *St Mark* puts his weight on one leg while the other knee relaxes forward into his robes, a lifelike depiction of a man pausing to think before shifting his weight to the other side. The marble statue amazed the Florentines. It broke so radically with the past that many today consider it the first piece of Renaissance art.

Donatello acquired his Classical expertise at first hand. As a teenager he was said to have studied the Roman ruins with his friend Filippo Brunelleschi, the modern pioneer of perspective, and he spent time in Rome again during the 1430s. Following Brunelleschi's innovations, Donatello created a realistic relief sculpture with his *Feast of Herod* (1425), a bronze panel depicting a horrific biblical beheading. Along with *The Trinity*, a fresco painted by his friend Masaccio at around the same time, it is the earliest known work of art since Classical times to use the rules of perspective.

In addition to the *Herod*, Donatello was responsible for other innovations in bronze – a difficult medium, especially on a large scale. In the late 1420s Cosimo de' Medici commissioned a bronze *David* for his palace courtyard, and Donatello depicted the Old Testament hero wearing only a laurel-wreathed helmet, shin armour and a serene expression – the first free-standing nude statue since antiquity. And while living in Padua between 1443 and 1453, he created an unprecedented life-size crucifix for the basilica and resurrected the Classical equestrian statue – a revered form in ancient Rome – with his monumental *Gattamelata*, which honoured a recently deceased *condottiere*, or mercenary soldier, for Venice.

Donatello worked as eloquently in wood as in marble and bronze. His *Mary Magdalene*, carved from white poplar, is a harrowing image of the repentant prostitute. Once thought to be a late work from the mid-1450s, the sculpture is now believed by many art historians to date from the 1430s. She is emaciated from years of fasting, her eyes hollow and gaunt. Even in her original state – gilded and painted in lifelike colours – she was a moving example of ascetic piety. Donatello captures her emotional state with new realism, yet another departure from medieval sculpture. Serenity, worry, joy and anger register convincingly on the faces of the figures he created during nearly sixty years of productivity.

Towards the end of his life requests from patrons dwindled, but Cosimo continued to give Donatello commissions. The wealthy patron held him in such high esteem, in fact, that he arranged for the sculptor to be buried beside him. Donatello died three years after Cosimo, whose will was carried out: the sculptor was laid to rest in the Medici family crypt in the basilica of San Lorenzo.

ℭ
Cosimo de' Medici

'FATHER OF THE FATHERLAND'

1389–1464

Neither artist nor humanist, Cosimo de' Medici instead supplied the money so appreciated by both. Cosimo's unique skills not only as a financier but also as a politician and patron (all much the same thing in the 15th century) gave him a pivotal role in bringing Florence to the forefront of the early Renaissance. Relative newcomers, Cosimo's branch of the Medici clan began to emerge from obscurity only in 1397, when his father, Giovanni, founded a bank in Florence, with a branch in Rome. Thanks to his shrewd choice of managers and substantial capitalization, Giovanni was soon able to expand – to Venice in 1402, then elsewhere in Italy and, by 1435, over the Alps to Geneva, Bruges, Avignon and London.

Trained from childhood in the family business of bookkeeping, managing deposits, transferring funds and making loans, Cosimo and his younger brother Lorenzo had by the mid-1410s largely taken over the bank. They grew rich through issuing letters of credit – medieval travellers' cheques – and making high-prestige loans to those European princes who borrowed insatiably to outfit their armies and adorn their courts. With wealth came growing political clout in the Florentine Republic, which increasingly employed Cosimo as its representative to the papacy. He further solidified his political credentials and broadened his horizons in the 1420s with diplomatic trips to Switzerland, France and Germany, where he taught himself the local languages; he was also conversant in Latin and Arabic.

Although Cosimo kept a low profile and avoided flaunting his wealth, some thought he was dangerously ambitious. Seeking a scapegoat for its failed fiscal policies, the regime arrested and sent him into exile in 1433, hoping to balance the budget by confiscating the Medici fortune. Cosimo had foreseen this, however, and, having already transferred his assets to Venice, he went there to live in comfortable banishment, carrying on business almost as usual. Recognizing they had blundered in sending off their wealthiest and most prominent citizen, the Florentines soon changed their tune and invited him back.

At a time when Italian princes ruled with ostentation and often with terror, Cosimo eased his way into power, exiling his staunchest enemies but leaving Florence's political system intact. With remarkable nonchalance he walked around the city as he always had – without guards or fear: tales abounded of his casual encounters and gossip with ordinary citizens. In reality, Cosimo ran things in the spirit of a Mafia don – behind the scenes, from his imposing family mansion, while eager supporters held government offices and carried out his policies. He relished foreign affairs and boldly redrew the political map of Italy, brokering a new balance of power through the Peace of Lodi in 1454. His greatest coup was in 1439, in making Florence the venue for the Church council called to reunify Catholic and Orthodox Christianity. Having pope, emperor, patriarch and their retinues lodged together at the convent of Santa Maria Novella and meeting in Cosimo's own palace was a diplomatic and cultural triumph on a scale no Florentine had ever imagined. Even as the event solidified Florence's reputation, it also secured Cosimo's political grip.

Yet Cosimo's lasting fame has been more tied to his patronage of the arts. Even before his exile, he was investing around 15,000 florins a year on such projects as the Dominican convent of San Marco, the church and sacristy of San Lorenzo, and the chapel and church of the Franciscans at Santa Croce. He also spent lavishly on his own lodgings – besides the grand Palazzo Medici in the city, he built several handsome country villas. In the fine arts, Cosimo was more interested in sculpture than painting. He patronized Donatello for decades, advancing the sculptor funds to buy marble and commissioning his bronze *David*, which originally stood in the courtyard of the Palazzo Medici.

Lorenzo de' Medici once estimated that his grandfather Cosimo had, in a lifetime of patronage, spent 'the incredible sum' of over 600,000 florins divided 'among buildings, alms and taxes, let alone other expenses'. Cosimo himself looked back on his life and recalled how 'For fifty years I have done nothing but earn money and spend money, and I have realized that it is much sweeter to spend it than to earn it.' His fellow Florentines apparently agreed, since shortly after his death they resurrected and bestowed on him the ancient Roman title of *Pater Patriae* – 'Father of the Fatherland'. They were not aware, of course, that Cosimo's return in 1434 presaged a 300-year Medici dominance in Florence – one that would see their ancient republic overthrown and a rule as autocratic as any in Italy ushered in.

CR

Jan van Eyck

CAPTURING THE WORLD IN DETAIL

before 1395–1441

The cut of a ruby, a dog's wet nose, stubble on an unshaven chin – the lifelike details in Jan van Eyck's art amazed viewers accustomed to stylized Gothic art. Born in Flanders, van Eyck pioneered the Early Netherlandish School, whose members strived for extreme naturalism, even when portraying the supernatural. Northern art's realism evolved parallel to, but independent of, realism in Italy. Van Eyck's contemporary Masaccio, for example, brought one-point perspective and consistent light and shadow to the soft-edged figures of his frescoes, while Flemish artists focused on microscopic detail and light's transforming effect on surfaces. For van Eyck, the approach was more than an aesthetic preference: he translated a medieval view – that each item in the natural world reflected the mind of God – into the hyper-realism that characterized Renaissance art in northern Europe.

The early 15th century was a heady time for artists in both Tuscany and the Low Countries. Like Florence, the major cities of Flanders were important centres of banking; both Antwerp and Bruges brimmed with well-off patrons seeking luxurious textiles, elegant paintings and elaborate prayer books. Among van Eyck's earliest surviving works are pages from such a volume, tiny illustrations that suggest a training as a miniaturist. In 1422 he began work in The Hague as a painter for John of Bavaria, and in 1425 he was named court artist and *valet de chambre* to Philip the Good, the powerful duke of Burgundy, in Lille. In this prestigious position van Eyck's duties extended beyond the painter's studio, and in an unusual patron–artist arrangement Philip dispatched him abroad on several diplomatic missions.

In the early 1430s van Eyck moved with his wife and two children to a handsome stone house in Bruges, where Philip maintained his official residence, and there he completed the monumental *Ghent Altarpiece* (1432), one of the largest retables of the 15th century. Standing 3.5 metres (11 ½ feet) tall and opening some 4.5 metres (15 feet) wide, the imposing panels unfold to reveal sumptuous scenes of the fall and redemption of humankind. Van Eyck's attention to tiny particulars demanded great skill and a steady hand, but it also required paint silken enough to make a line the width of a single hair. Most 14th-century artists used egg tempera – raw egg yolk mixed with ground pigment – which dried quickly but tended to crack and flake over time. Decades ahead of the Italians, van Eyck and other northerners turned to oil paints, which transferred smoothly from brush to surface and allowed artists to work longer before a painting dried. The results were translucent, glowing colours and a lacquer-like finish impossible with tempera or the fresco technique.

Van Eyck also differed from the Italians in his approach to human forms. The Classical ideals then redefining art below the Alps had not yet reached northern Europe; without the ancient Romans for guidance, van Eyck relied strictly on his own vision. And he seemed to see everything: he gave the same painstaking clarity to each item, whether in the foreground or background, his eyes working as both microscope and telescope, as one modern art historian has put it. Although far from superficial, he was primarily concerned with surfaces, and his portraits are relief maps of facial planes and contours, copied from life rather than reconstructed according to Classical rules. His presumed self-portrait, *Man in a Red Turban* (1433), is a faithful rendering of outward appearance, all the way down to the sitter's bloodshot eyes and wrinkled skin – clearly not antiquity's notion of ideal beauty.

For van Eyck the sublime existed in life's prosaic elements. His *Arnolfini Portrait* (1434) seems to be a straightforward secular painting of Giovanni Arnolfini, an Italian financier, and a woman who may be his new wife or his betrothed. No cherubs hover above, no saints gesture toward the couple, but the everyday items in the room resonate with the sacred nature of matrimony. The small bedpost finial is a carving of St Margaret, patron saint of childbirth; the little dog represents fidelity; the convex mirror, like the eye of God, sees all. Miniature scenes from the Passion of Christ surround the mirror, which reflects not two but four figures – in a doorway facing the couple stand two mysterious men. The inscription above the mirror, 'Jan van Eyck was here', implies that one of them is the artist himself.

After his death in 1441, van Eyck-like portraits became popular in Italy, where painters studied his oil techniques and emulated his naturalistic candour. His fame spread southwards against the tide of cultural change streaming out of Italy, his northern influence finding its way into the works of Sandro Botticelli and others. To van Eyck himself, however, his exacting accuracy was more than a regional style – it was a form of worship, a tribute to his maker, whether through a glorious image of the Virgin Mary or the meticulous rendering of a muddy wooden shoe.

∞

Masaccio

PUTTING PAINTING IN PERSPECTIVE

1401–1428

Before the 15th century, faces in European art tended to be inscrutable, even expressionless. The settings – if paintings featured them at all – seemed flat, with edges and corners canted at impossible angles. When Masaccio moved to Florence in around 1418, the art world still followed this tradition, which had largely been forged by the painter Giotto nearly a century earlier. Masaccio brought a new naturalism to art, replacing the Middle Ages' more generic, idealized images with expressive characters set in spaces with a sense of depth – in fact, he was the first known painter since Classical times to employ mathematically correct lines of perspective in his work.

Born Tommaso di Ser Giovanni di Mone Cassai, he became known as Masaccio, meaning 'big, sloppy Tom'. According to the 16th-century historian Giorgio Vasari, the painter acquired the nickname because he did not care 'about worldly affairs … not even about how he dressed himself', devoting himself 'only to the details of art'. Where he learned those details is unclear, but his habit of outlining figures in red – a practice of manuscript illuminators – suggests training other than traditional fresco painting. Whatever his background, he was established in Florence as a painter by 1418 and reached the rank of master in 1422.

Even Masaccio's earliest work shows an eye towards innovation: he was already experimenting with perspective in 1422, for example, when he painted his *Madonna and the Saints* triptych for the church of San Giovenale, near Florence. He probably learned to construct a single vanishing point and to simulate three-dimensional space from his friend Filippo Brunelleschi, the architect and inventor who established the principles of artistic perspective. The drama and naturalism in Masaccio's subsequent art, on the other hand, echo the work of another friend – the sculptor Donatello, who was casting bronze relief scenes at just this time. Adapting Brunelleschi's advances to his own medium, Masaccio imbued his paintings with new depth – both visual and emotional.

These influences came together in two major works Masaccio painted in Florence. One was a large, multi-panelled fresco depicting the life of St Peter in the Brancacci Chapel of the church of Santa Maria del Carmine. Masaccio worked on the commission with the older and better-known artist Masolino da Panicale, who had begun the project around 1424. Painted some time around 1427, Masaccio's dynamic sections stand out next to the more static, traditional work of Masolino. With his paintings for the Brancacci Chapel, Masaccio was the first Western artist to show multiple scenes from a single point of view and to create the illusion of a three-dimensional stage: he established atmospheric perspective with realistically hazy backgrounds and showed shadows consistent with a single source of light, yielding forms that seem to move out of the picture plane and towards the viewer.

In medieval art unfathomable faces floated in rarefied spaces; in the Brancacci frescoes, however, Masaccio located his little narratives in the human world. *The Expulsion of Adam and Eve* is a small section with a harrowing image of the grief-stricken couple. Most other panels feature identifiable Florentine cityscapes and people with recognizable faces. Some figures were portraits of Brancacci family members, while one segment included Masaccio himself with three colleagues, suggesting that artists were no longer mere artisans but had become intellectual participants in their civic world.

Working on his own around the same time, Masaccio brilliantly demonstrated Brunelleschi's laws of perspective in the *Trinity*, a fresco on the nave wall of the church of Santa Maria Novella. The earliest known painting in perfect perspective, it is a striking *trompe-l'oeil* fresco of a recessed chapel with a coffered, barrel-vaulted ceiling – the style of Roman triumphal arches. Setting his vanishing point at the viewer's eye level, he constructed a pyramidal 'Throne of Mercy', with God the Father at the top offering the faithful his crucified Son, who is flanked by the Virgin and St John. Outside the niche, two mortals – the painting's patrons – kneel reverently. Both symmetrically rational and iconically mystical, the *Trinity* remains the first, and possibly one of the best, attempts at finding a balance between humanism and religion.

This ground-breaking painter – arguably the first of the Renaissance – never earned enough money to support himself: Masaccio could not afford the full membership fee for the Painters' Guild, and in 1425 a sausage-maker filed a complaint against him for unpaid debts. Shortly after finishing the *Trinity*, Masaccio died at the age of 27 of unknown causes, poor and hounded by creditors. But in his brief six-year career he managed to redefine painting in Italy with a small but pivotal body of work – pieces studied closely by artists from Botticelli and Michelangelo to Salvador Dalí.

2. Europeans at Peace

1450–1475

The Renaissance got under way slowly, but the pace of change quickened in the 1450s, thanks to a series of pivotal events – some related and some not – that followed each other with dizzying rapidity. In just a few years long-standing assumptions were challenged, toppled from their familiar positions like the pieces on a suddenly tumbling chessboard. It would take the next two generations – a time of unexpected prosperity and comparative peace – before everything could be set up again, and a new game, more complex and with different rules, could commence.

The transformation began in May 1453, when, after a siege of less than eight weeks, the Ottoman Turks captured Constantinople. In its last years the 1,100-year-old Byzantine Empire had shrunk into a micro-state, so its final collapse came as no great surprise to Europeans, although the event was still a psychological shock. The fall of this city – which was rapidly rebuilt as Istanbul, capital of the Turks – not only cost Christian Europe its greatest foothold in the East, but also crushed the crusading fantasies that had unified and defined the medieval worldview. Yet as one door closed, another opened. Many of the Greeks who fled their ancient empire came bearing Classical manuscripts of incalculable value, a treasure trove of learning in the form of works by early Church fathers, Classical dramatists, and Hellenist philosophers and poets, many of whom had previously been known in the West only by reputation, if at all. In the Italian cities where many of these refugees landed, the knowledge and love of Classical Greek had only just been rekindled, and this new infusion helped turn what had been a modest scholarly pursuit into a grand intellectual movement – one that soon swept beyond the Alps to challenge scholastic redoubts in Paris, Oxford and the Low Countries.

Just two months after Constantinople fell, English monarchs effectively abandoned their ancient dynastic claims to the throne of France. After generations of sporadic fighting and massive expense, the Hundred Years' War was over, and in the process two distinct nations were disentangled. In defeat, the English promptly turned on themselves, with a home-grown squabble – the War of the Roses – that kept them away from the continent for over a generation. By contrast, the victorious French were buoyed with a national self-confidence on a par with that of the Turks. Under a succession of able, or at least ambitious, rulers they extended their national boundaries while probing the resistance of Italy and the Low Countries for possible conquest by arms or through marriage.

Finding their divided and quarrelsome homeland attracting unwanted attention from both the Turks and the French, the more astute Italian rulers ended their constant internal struggles. In the northern Italian town of Lodi, on 9 April 1454, Florence, Milan and Naples signed a peace treaty that would later be extended to the other major powers in Italy: Venice and the Papal States. Recognizing both existing boundaries and the current balance of power, the Peace of Lodi was an admission that no one Italian state could conquer the others and that, in consequence, Italy – unlike France, England or Spain – would remain politically fragmented. Instead, in an attempt to resist outside predators while remaining independent of one another, the major Italian powers joined in what would be known as the Italic League. Their compromise, somewhat surprisingly, brought two generations of relative peace and prosperity to Italy, allowing creativity to flourish and eventually move northwards.

This spread was hurried along by the emergence, that same year, of the printing press. Johann Gutenberg, a goldsmith living in Mainz, Germany, had developed the concept of printing with movable type the previous decade. Although the source of Gutenberg's lasting fame was his finely crafted 42-line Bible, finished in 1455, he had made an arguably more significant breakthrough a year earlier, when he took on a strictly commercial job

– printing indulgence certificates for the local archbishopric. It was through such mundane work – rather than through a showpiece like his Bible – that Gutenberg revealed printing's real possibilities as a tool of mass communication. Within a decade or two presses were established all over Germany and northern Italy, driving down the cost of written material and radically expanding the reach of ideas both old and new. Literacy rates grew rapidly at the same time as languages themselves began to be standardized, further stimulating national awareness in Germany, France, England and Spain. The first great information revolution was under way.

Even as Europe's political and cultural landscape shifted, there were other, equally far-reaching changes abroad. In two papal bulls, *Dum diversas* (1452) and *Romanus pontifex* (1455), Pope Nicholas V allowed Christians to enslave pagans – in particular, Black Africans – and to annex their lands, as was customary during wars against Muslims. Although intended to encourage the exploration of western Africa, these pronouncements also removed the lingering moral qualms that had impeded both the expansion of Europeans throughout the world and their taking up the slave trade. As if to seal the Faustian bargain, in 1456 the Venetian explorer Alvise Cadamosto chanced upon the Cape Verde Islands, which would prove a key stepping stone in Europe's discovery of the world.

Europeans who lived through the flurry of changes of the mid-1450s discovered themselves in a more open world. They found that movement had become easier. Latin, the universal language of the Middle Ages, may have been giving way to a jumble of mutually incomprehensible vernaculars, but a fresh set of universals – art, architecture, economics, science and the new warfare – were forging connections across national boundaries. For a few decades much of the continent teemed with new ideas and yet seemed in balance, as men and women took stock of the new world around them.

Flavio Biondo

RE-IMAGINING THE GLORY THAT WAS ROME

1392–1463

Born in the papal city of Forlì, the historian and archaeologist Flavio Biondo received a thorough humanist training in the Classics before finding permanent employment as a secretary in the papal Curia in 1433. Upon arriving Biondo found a Rome quite unlike the *caput mundi* of antiquity, the 'Head of the World'. Over the course of the Middle Ages, Romans had shifted their city's physical and social centre of gravity, as those few who remained relocated to the lowlands between the Capitoline Hill and the Vatican. In the process they had deserted what had been the heart of the ancient city, centred on the Forum, the Colosseum, the Baths of Diocletian and the Esquiline and Caelian Hills. All this – the tumbled down temples, the crumbling villas and the catacombs stretching out to the old imperial walls – was left to the cattle drovers and shepherds.

With the end of the Avignon papacy in the 1420s, Rome came back to life as new wealth, along with hordes of clerics and courtiers, poured into town. Yet large swaths inside the city's old imperial walls remained desolate, full of ruins whose function was long forgotten, masses of marble fragments poking through the detritus left behind by collapsed buildings and the flooding Tiber. The 15th-century Romans called the Forum, once the centre of the Classical world, the *campo vaccino*, because for them it was quite literally that, a cattle field.

For Flavio Biondo, however, the ruins of Rome were less dismal than fascinating. He prized them both aesthetically and for what they could tell him about antiquity – information other humanists were seeking in written texts.

Biondo learned to read both ruins and texts, searching through the Latin Classics and studying the physical remains of forgotten monuments for their inscriptions, carvings and building materials.

During these years of careful collecting and analysis, Biondo produced a succession of books that hugely expanded Classical studies while virtually inventing the science of archaeology. His masterpiece in this new field was *De Roma instaurata* ('Rome renewed'), written in 1444–46. Here Biondo offered the first ever topographical description of ancient Rome, identifying hundreds of otherwise anonymous temples and civic buildings, suggesting their functions and situating them on a grid centred on the Capitoline Hill. For good measure, he also included the city's Christian monuments, especially those built on top of – or inside – earlier Classical structures.

With *De Roma instaurata* Biondo not only produced a remarkably precise guide to Rome but also resurrected the entire Classical world in all its cultural complexity. More than simply a work of history and archaeology, *De Roma instaurata* also appealed to its readers politically, challenging them to build Rome anew, equal in its glories to the ancient city. In his subsequent *De Roma triumphante* ('Rome triumphant'), finished in 1459, Biondo developed these themes further, offering Roman society, imperial and pagan, as a model for the papacy to follow in reforming its government and reorganizing its army.

Despite the immense popularity of Biondo's books (they were published as early as 1481) and his own spirited defence of the city's surviving monuments, the destruction of Rome's Classical heritage actually accelerated during his lifetime. The building boom set off by the returning papacy led builders to loot ruins for their reusable stone and so that their marble could be burnt for making mortar. Even as the Curial humanists took foreign visitors on tours of the Forum, the very monuments they were showing off were being dismantled to build new palaces for the cardinals and bankers flocking to the city. For decades the Colosseum itself was operated as a vast, man-made stone quarry. Classical buildings not converted into stone or quicklime were levelled anyway by a series of humanist popes intent on driving wide roadways through the medieval city – all part of their grand ambitions, ironically, of returning Rome to the splendours of its imperial past.

∞

Luca della Robbia

ART REBORN IN ANOTHER FORM

1399/1400–1482

Legend has it that young Luca di Simone della Robbia was so enthusiastic about his training that he put his feet in a box of wood shavings to keep them warm as he worked all night. He was originally apprenticed to a goldsmith – the education of many 15th-century sculptors – but by the age of 15 he was already studying the new style of dynamic figure sculpture in the Florentine *bottega* of Nanni di Banco. When Nanni died in 1421, Luca moved to the workshop of Donatello, a sculptor renowned for emphasizing drama in his work. In 1432 he enrolled in the stonecutters' guild and began carving his *Cantoria* (singing gallery). Along this marble screen, which enclosed the organ in Florence's cathedral, Luca carved a series of dancing, drumming and singing cherubs. The work is as appealing today as it was over 500 years ago, for the freshness, individuality and classical grace of the boys. More than just a procession of musical children, it is multimedia: the young figures sing and play in synchrony to the lines of Psalm 150, engraved along the marble band under the appropriate scenes: 'Praise [the Lord] with the sounding of the trumpet; Praise Him with the harp and lyre; Praise Him with tambourine and dancing; Praise Him with the strings and flute; Praise Him with the clash of cymbals.'

After working nearly a decade on the *Cantoria* and on other projects, Luca was said to have 'calculated how much time he had spent in finishing them and how little he had earned from them'. He apparently also realized that his style of figure sculpture – detailed, individualized and graceful – was less visually impressive when, like the *Cantoria*, it was installed at a height of 10 or 20 metres (30 or 65 feet) from the ground. And so, according to Giorgio Vasari a century later, 'he made up his mind to abandon marble and bronze and to see if he might gain more from other methods.'

It took nearly a decade for Luca to discover such methods, which combined the intimacy of painting with the durability and monumentality of marble. His technique of enamelling terracotta produced a lustrous, marble-like finish that caught the attention of the cathedral administrators. They hired him to produce an example, and he made them a lunette to go over the bronze sacristy doors that he was designing. Enamelled terracotta was by no means unknown in the 15th century, but Luca was the first to use it for high-relief compositions of architectural size. He kept his techniques and materials a secret, but we know that it was a tricky and delicate process, involving precision work and firings at a very high temperature. Stylistically, Luca's terracotta work, like his sculptures, avoided the complex geometries and crowded perspectives favoured by Donatello and Lorenzo Ghiberti, relying instead on elegantly simple arrangements of (usually white) figures against a solid coloured background. The sacristy lunette, in its Classical composition and emotional clarity, rivalled the best efforts of contemporary Florentine painters and was an artistic sensation. Soon the orders were pouring in.

In 1446 Luca persuaded his brothers to give up sculpting and join him in his new ceramics workshop on the sparsely settled north-west edge of Florence. The location meant that a fire escaping the kilns could not engulf the dense city, but it also happened that Piero, the son of Cosimo de' Medici and an early enthusiast for Luca's work, lived nearby. Encouraging him to experiment more with colours, Piero also convinced Luca to branch out from lunettes and roundels to more extensive vaulting and pavements, some of which still adorn the Palazzo Medici, just down the road from where Luca's *bottega* stood.

Vasari said that, through his invention, Luca and his brothers 'all earned a great deal more than they had ever earned from their chisels', in terms of reputation as much as wealth. They garnered commissions to adorn churches and palaces all over Tuscany and as far afield as France and Spain. Since

Luca's ceramic figures, unlike paintings or even most forms of sculpture, were almost impervious to the weather, they were also much in demand for outdoor display. In 1450 Luca's young nephew Andrea joined the family business and was soon making it still more productive by using stamps to create decorative leaves, flowers and fruits with almost industrial efficiency. Although widely imitated, Andrea, followed by his son Giovanni, kept up Luca's reputation for artistic excellence well into the 16th century. Only after the third generation did the workshop finally sink into relative mediocrity, becoming just another of Florence's many artisan *botteghe* – churning out sentimental copies of the remarkable compositions that had once made Luca della Robbia famous throughout Italy as both an artist and a technological innovator.

CR

Nicholas of Cusa

GOD AND MAN IN A (NEARLY) INFINITE UNIVERSE

1401–1464

Born to a well-to-do merchant in Kues, on the River Mosel in western Germany, young Nicholas Krebs supposedly fled the shipping business after his father beat him over the head with an oar for not paying attention. Travelling to the Netherlands, he studied first with the Brethren of the Common Life, followed by a period at the University at Heidelberg and then Padua, where in 1423 he received a doctorate in canon law. Nicholas began teaching at the University of Cologne in 1425, but his time as a professor was brief: within a few years he had won a position as secretary to the archbishop of Trier and begun doing legal work, first in Rome and then at the Council of Basel. Although initially he strongly supported the power of Church councils over that of the papacy, by the mid-1430s he had so completely taken up the cause of Pope Eugenius IV that he gained the (somewhat ironic) honorific of 'the Hercules of all the Eugenians'. As a reward, Eugenius named Nicholas papal legate on a number of missions, beginning in 1437 with a journey to Constantinople. There he had the delicate assignment of persuading the last wavering Greek clerics to come to Italy and discuss reuniting the Christian Church to present a common front against rising Ottoman power.

Appointed bishop and cardinal in 1449, Nicholas Krebs began calling himself Nicholas of Kues – Latinized as Nicholas Cusano or Nicholas of Cusa. Although he spent much of the next two decades travelling on Church business, Nicholas found the time to reflect and write extensively about subjects that intrigued him. Some of this writing was political as much as religious, reflecting his concern with reconciling branches of Christianity, whether Greek–Roman, Papal–Conciliar or German–Italian. Other questions were more purely theological – the impossibility for finite humans to achieve a conceptual understanding of an infinite God, for example. Men could overcome this barrier to comprehension, he wrote, by abandoning their dependence on conceptual intelligence. Instead, they could intuit God through coming to know what they do not know. Nicholas called this apparently self-contradictory process of learning *docta ignorantia* ('learned ignorance') and illustrated it through the geometric metaphor of the circle, with God as the centre and the circumference, both deeply within the material world and transcending it. Although knowing God conceptually was impossible, one could still, Nicholas wrote, try to learn the extent of one's own ignorance; in the process one might grow closer to God, as a polygon with an increasing number of sides grows closer to, but never equals, the circle in which it is inscribed.

The fascination that Nicholas held for geometry, numerology and astrology was manifest in much of his other work, where he considered the implications of a God who was both 'right here' and 'up there'. Because the deity, not the finite Earth, lay at the centre of the universe, Nicholas rejected Ptolemy's geocentric system and embraced the more radical notion of the plurality of worlds. It maintained that the Earth and the Sun were just two of the very large (although not infinite – only God was boundless) number of heavenly bodies. Along with geocentricism, Nicholas also dismissed the notion of circular planetary orbits and spherical planets as too perfect for a physical, impermanent universe, jettisoning in the process the Aristotelian premise of pure heavens in contrast to a corrupt Earth.

Nicholas of Cusa was one of the great thinkers of the early Renaissance, virtually alone among scholars from north of the Alps in his enthusiasm for humanist learning and Latin letters. In the course of his endless travels he unearthed a number of lost Classical works, copies of which he made available to his Italian counterparts in Florence and Rome. He even dabbled a little in observational science, writing short treatises on concave lenses, the properties of the mineral beryl and the appropriate shape of spoons.

Nevertheless, although many of his theories proved surprisingly prescient and broke ground for the later work of Copernicus, Bruno and especially Kepler, Nicholas's research remained firmly tied to a scholastic model based on theory and logic rather than experimentation. As such, he challenged medieval cosmology strictly on its own, Aristotelian terms, arguing within the pure, Neoplatonic world of number and form rather than through direct observation or trial and error. Although Nicholas's interests would play a vital role in both scientific and Reformation thought, his vision remained thoroughly circumscribed by an infinite God rather than by mortal men. He died while on a very medieval mission, recruiting Christian forces in central Italy for Pius II's crusade against the Turks.

∞

Francesco Sforza

THE SELF-MADE DUKE

1401–1466

I n Italian 'sforza' means 'extraordinary strength'. For Francesco Sforza it was a nickname, a *nom de guerre* inherited from his father, Muzio Attendolo – said to be so strong he could straighten horseshoes bare-handed. Muzio came from well-off nobility in the Italian Romagna, but he left the family estates, together with several brothers and cousins, to form a company of soldiers for hire. In the late 14th century these *condottieri* – men who held a military *condotto*, or 'contract', to fight on behalf of a patron – were regular features of the Italian landscape. They found work with all the petty principalities and free republics that needed some muscle to coerce their neighbours or defend themselves. Such soldiering provided work for thousands of under-employed men who found that fighting paid better than farming. A successful *condottiere* could also expect to be rewarded by his employer with a lordship of his own.

Francesco was born into the thick of this world, the favourite of Muzio's seven illegitimate sons. At 18 he was accompanying his father into combat, both for and against the papacy, Milan, Naples, Perugia and Ferrara, changing sides to go where the pay was better. In 1423 Muzio drowned while fording a river, and Francesco, although he was just 22, took over his father's mercenary band. He soon found the perfect employer. Filippo Maria Visconti, duke of Milan, was eager to regain family lands lost after his father's death in 1402. More of a politician and schemer than a soldier, Filippo Maria needed someone like Sforza, a strict and reliable disciplinarian who was not afraid (as many *condottieri* were) to risk a battle. Francesco usually won on the field, although his strong personality regularly got him into fights with his employer, who would retaliate by banishing him to garrisons in remote corners of the duchy.

Sforza consequently decided to establish his own lordship, as insurance against Filippo Maria's whims. Recognizing Rome's weak hold over its lands north of the Apennines, he conquered the city of Fermo and established himself over a wide swath of adjoining territory. Desperate to get back his favourite *condottiere*, Filippo Maria made Sforza a tempting offer – the hand of his (illegitimate) daughter and only heir, Bianca Maria Visconti. It took Sforza a year to annul his previous marriage, but in 1432 the betrothal was concluded. At this point, however, the two men had another falling out, leaving Sforza free to work for Milan's enemies, Florence and Venice. Only in 1441 did duke and commander patch up their differences and hold the wedding.

In 1447 Filippo Maria died, leaving no male heir. In the resulting power vacuum some Milanese patricians set up an aristocratic 'Ambrosian Republic', named after the city's patron, St Ambrose. At first, Sforza and his troops served the new regime, foiling Venetian attempts to pilfer Milan's subject cities. Before long he changed sides, however, and ended up blockading the city for nearly a year. Pushed to starvation, the ordinary Milanese finally forced their rulers to offer Sforza the city and its crown. In March 1450, together with Bianca Maria, Francesco Sforza entered Milan and claimed his prize.

Among the vainglorious, homicidal and self-aggrandizing Italian rulers who were his contemporaries (and descendants), Duke Francesco Sforza Visconti – as he henceforth called himself – stood out as both calm and rational. He won over the Milanese by setting up an equitable and efficient system of taxation that allowed him to fund a civic hospital and a navigation canal connecting the city to the River Adda. He also rebuilt and strengthened the old Visconti castle in Milan, thereafter known as the Castello Sforzesco – a none too subtle reminder that the Sforzas had come to stay.

With his soldier's straightforwardness, Sforza also succeeded in imposing some stability on the eternal chaos of Italian politics. He pioneered the use of diplomats, both to spy out his rivals' intentions and to smooth over disagreements. He and Cosimo de' Medici, the de facto ruler of Florence, formed a reliable partnership despite their states' ancient enmity; in 1454 this friendship was extended to the Kingdom of Naples, then to Venice and the Papal States. Amenable to giving away crumbs of territory or abandoning divisive positions in order to win over an old rival, Sforza was able to convince each in turn to sign Europe's first general non-aggression pact, known as the Peace of Lodi, which recognized and guaranteed the balance of power on the peninsula. For the rest of Sforza's life Milan was able to enjoy peace. He even loaned his best *condottieri* to the Venetians – his ancient enemy.

CR

Leon Battista Alberti

THE ORIGINAL RENAISSANCE MAN

1404–1472

Throughout his life Leon Battista Alberti liked to brag. He wrote how, with his feet tied together, he could jump over a standing man's head, how he 'could in the great cathedral [of Florence] throw a coin far up to ring against the vault' and how he would 'amuse himself by taming wild horses and climbing mountains'. It was rather boyish behaviour for an architect, linguist, cryptographer and the author of dozens of treatises, plays and poems, but in Alberti genius always mingled uneasily with his abiding need for attention.

Perhaps, as the bastard son of a Florentine noble in exile, Alberti felt stigmatized by his familial and civic illegitimacy. Although his father saw to it that he got the best education that ample resources could buy, the young Alberti was bereft when the old man died in 1421: contemptuous relatives withdrew his university funding and banished him from a city his family had honourably served since the 13th century. The burden of this double bastardy was lifted from Alberti only in 1428, when he received his degree in canon law and the authorities in Florence rescinded his exile. This was about the time that Alberti began calling himself *Leone*, or 'Lion'.

Alberti had cause for a lion's pride. At the age of 20 he was able to write a pastiche Latin comedy that so resembled the Classical works of Lepidus that many humanists thought it was a lost play. In the 1430s he produced the classic *I Libri della famiglia* ('The books of the family'), on the proper aims of conjugal life. Such secular, sociological studies were controversial in the early 1400s, and Alberti lamented that he had overheard 'some of his [own] relatives openly ridiculing both the whole work and the author's futile enterprise along with it'. Perhaps in consequence, Alberti, like most early humanists, opted for the security of a Church career. In 1431, having taken clerical vows, he was rewarded by the pro-Florentine Pope Eugenius IV with a sinecure in the papal chancellery in Rome. Thereafter he was free to spend his days exploring whatever caught his fancy.

Alberti's interests were extremely broad – he has long been considered to epitomize the Universal, or Renaissance, Man – but his particular passion was for grounding the arts in humanist thought as a way to legitimize both endeavours. A close friend of Masaccio and Brunelleschi, he witnessed the painting revolution under way in Florence. No great artist himself, Alberti instead intellectualized the process in his seminal study *De pictura* ('On painting', 1435), in which he used his Classical training to explore painting in theoretical and functional terms. In painting's new sensitivity to naturalism, perspective and portraiture, he saw that art 'possesses a divine power, in that not only does it make the absent present ... but it also represents the dead to the living many centuries later'.

It was in architecture that Alberti best put his ideas into practice, however. Immediately upon coming to Rome, he began studying the ruins for the design principles that ancient Romans had followed. After putting what he had learned into the design of sites such as the Palazzo Rucellai in Florence and the Tempio Malatestiano in Rimini, Alberti combined personal experience with humanist theory to write *De re aedificatoria* ('On the art of building', 1452). Although Alberti modelled his study on *De architectura*, by the classical Roman author Vitruvius, he went much further, not only describing how existing structures had been built, but also providing structural, aesthetic and social guidelines for future buildings. The first book ever published on architecture (in 1485), *De re aedificatoria* went through dozens of editions, in Latin and various vernacular languages, and was still being used as a practical guide over two centuries later.

Alberti was continually exploring new subjects. He wrote treatises on plays, poetry, fiction, archaeology, city planning and mathematical games. A fascination with numbers led him late in life to write a study on cryptography, *De cifris* ('On ciphers'), in which he set out for the first time the encryption device known as the 'polyalphabetic substitution circle'. Nevertheless, during his last decades Alberti was primarily a celebrity architect. He worked for the Medici and their wealthy followers in Florence and then travelled to Mantua, Ferrara and Urbino to advise the local lords on their building needs. In 1459 Pope Pius II commissioned him to redesign the entire town of Paenza using Vitruvian principles. The marvellous little city that Alberti created was the first truly humanist and Renaissance civic space to be realized in post-Classical Europe – a fitting culmination to the variegated career of Europe's first Renaissance man.

CR

Pope Pius II

HUMANIST, POET AND POPE

1405–1464

Quicksilver in wit and remarkably gifted in persuading others of his sincerity, Aeneas Piccolomini progressed almost effortlessly from humble beginnings to the pinnacles of power. The eldest son of a politically disgraced Sienese noble, Aeneas grew up working in the family fields and learned to read only thanks to a friendly priest. After enrolling in the University of Siena, he eagerly, if somewhat ineptly, followed the humanist curriculum, spending more of his time drinking than studying the Classics. He admitted to being highly impressionable: when Saint Bernardino came to preach against sin, Aeneas was moved to give up his dissolute life, but he took it up again as soon as the friar left. In 1432, while still engaged in legal studies, he attached himself to a passing bishop travelling to the Council of Basel and at a stroke abandoned the law for a new position as the man's ecclesiastical secretary.

After his first patron ran out of funds, Piccolomini found a succession of clerical masters at Basel, each a bit more prestigious than the last. He was sent on diplomatic missions around France and Germany, and went secretly to Scotland in an (unsuccessful) attempt to persuade the king to invade England. He became increasingly involved in German high Church politics, even while avoiding the priesthood because it required vows of celibacy. Eventually Piccolomini was taken on as courtier and secretary to the German emperor Frederick III, and thanks to the torrent of poetry, plays, satires, erotica, romances and Boccaccio-esque novellas he churned out, in 1442 he was named the court poet laureate.

It was as Frederick's go-between and advocate to Rome that Piccolomini gradually warmed to the Church hierarchy and to Pope Eugenius IV in particular. In 1445, when he was in Rome, he decided he was tired of licentious living and thought he might join the priesthood and 'forsake Venus for Bacchus' (priests were notorious for drinking). The rewards were immediate. Within a year Eugenius appointed Piccolomini bishop of Trieste, and in 1450 he was named bishop in his home diocese of Siena. Having further ingratiated himself with Frederick by overseeing the emperor's coronation trip to Rome in 1452, he had the necessary imperial support to be made a cardinal in late 1456. Barely a year later, after a hotly contested conclave, Piccolomini was elected pope.

In selecting his pontifical title, Piccolomini opted for Pius. It was, he said, to honour the poet Virgil, who had often used the accolade 'pious Aeneas' in his epic about Piccolomini's namesake. This first gesture towards the literature of antiquity was almost Pius's last, however, to the distress of humanists who journeyed to Rome hoping for his patronage. With the papacy he largely gave up writing, except for producing, late in life, the *Commentarii rerum memorabilium* ('Commentaries'). The only papal autobiography known to exist, the *Commentarii* provide a unique and surprisingly frank look both at Pius's own chequered youth and at the inner workings of the early Renaissance papacy.

Instead, Pius poured his humanist energies, at considerable effort and expense, into rebuilding his native village of Corsignano, which he renamed after himself: Pienza. Calling on architects such as Leon Battista Alberti and persuading his cardinals to erect buildings of their own, Pius created what was the first, and arguably most complete, Renaissance planned city, the inspiration for later visionaries such as Federico da Montefeltro, creator of Urbino. With a central square defined by its miniature cathedral, city hall and the Palazzo Piccolomini, Pienza was (and still is) a model example of enlightened urban design, a jewel of humanist rationalism in the backwaters of Tuscany – and a grand vindication for the family that was once exiled there.

Ultimately, however, Pius II, once so worldly and joyful by nature, was forced by events and by his own changing character to redirect his papacy.

The Ottoman conquest of Constantinople and subsequent expansion into the Balkans gave Pius his defining mission, and barely a year after assuming the papacy he proclaimed a crusade to retake the traditional capital of Eastern Christianity. It was not a success. Although he summoned the princes of Christendom to Mantua for a planning conference – and went there himself in a triumphal procession – few turned up, and only the Hungarians, who were directly threatened by the Turks, offered troops or funds. Complaining bitterly about the mercenary Venetians and the self-absorbed French, Pius finally took up the cross personally in mid-1464, hoping to shame others into action. Although already feeble, he marched to Ancona, where he found virtually no forces to lead and where he died while waiting for troops to arrive – poet turned crusader, the leader of a failed Christian military response to Islam.

∝

Lorenzo Valla

CONTENTIOUS FOR PLEASURE AND FOR PROFIT

c. 1406–1457

Among the dozens of young scholars jostling for attention and patronage during the early Renaissance, Lorenzo Valla stood out as both brilliant and bellicose. He pointedly attacked 'certain great writers already approved by long usage', professing to care not at all that they might 'rage against me, and if opportunity is afforded will … eagerly and quickly drag me to punishment!' So be it, he said, for in this heroic age of humanism 'to give one's life in defence of truth and justice is the path of the highest virtue, the highest honour, the highest reward!'

Coming from northern Italy, Valla received a stellar humanist education in Rome and Florence, learning his Latin from Leonardo Bruni and his Greek from Giovanni Aurispa, both the foremost experts of the day. While still at school, he was already writing in his signature polemical style: in one early essay (now lost) he proclaimed that the Roman rhetorician Marcus Fabius Quintilian was a much better Latin stylist than Cicero – whom Bruni particularly revered. Picking such intellectual fights seems to have helped Valla win the chair of eloquence at the University of Pavia in 1431. While there, he wrote *De voluptate* ('On pleasure'), extolling Epicurus and the enjoyment of natural human appetites. It was the first humanist defence of those Classical values that were obviously at odds with a thousand years of Christian teachings, which had taken stoicism from ancient philosophy and ignored most of the rest.

Having offended his more devout readers, Valla then attacked the inferior Latin of the great 14th-century Italian jurist Bartolo da Sassoferrato, which resulted in his ejection from the faculty at Pavia. After three years as a wandering scholar, Valla finally caught the eye of King Alfonso I of Naples, who in 1435 offered him a position as royal secretary. For the next twelve years Valla translated Greek Classics into Latin and entertained Alfonso in caustic disputations with other humanists at court. He also wrote some of the most original – and cantankerous – works of the humanist golden age, attacking the core of medieval philosophy on the grounds that earlier scholars' sloppy Latin had led to faulty argumentation and a mis-understanding of Aristotle. To set things right, in 1441 Valla produced *De elegantiis linguae latinae* ('On the refinements of the Latin language'), the first Latin grammar since ancient times and the first ever to create a stylistic and linguistic canon for the language systematically based on its greatest writers. First published in 1471 and reprinted more than fifty times in the next half-century, *De elegantiis* was hailed for cleansing medieval Latin of its neologisms and 'barbarisms'. Only later did the grammar's role in freezing Latin into a rarefied language for scholars and dilettantes, dooming it as a vibrant living tongue, become equally apparent.

Valla especially enjoyed using his philological skills and caustic wit to expose medieval forgeries, attacking cows that could be quite literally sacred. His most famous coup was *De falso credita et ementita Constantini donatione declamatio* ('Discourse on the forgery of the alleged Donation of Constantine'), from 1440. In it Valla attacked the papacy's primary justifi-cation for temporal power – the document recording the gift, or donation, made by Constantine the Great to Pope Sylvester I in the early 4th century. On leaving for Byzantium, according to the Donation, Constantine thanked Sylvester for baptizing him and for curing him of leprosy by giving him the western half of his empire. Valla cleverly revealed the falseness of the Donation in rhetorical and historic terms, but most significantly he demol-ished it as a linguistic anachronism that contained many Latin words and expressions of much later origin (the document has since been dated to around AD 750).

Valla went on to demonstrate that the Apostles' Creed was not written by the twelve Apostles, as legend had it, and he ridiculed the Latin of the

Vulgate as a clumsy translation of the original Greek. His brazenness was risky, and several times he was accused of heresy, escaping execution only through the timely intervention of Alfonso or a nimble escape to Barcelona. The newly elected humanist Pope Nicholas V still rewarded Valla, heretic or not, with a post he had long coveted, that of apostolic secretary. Valla promptly deserted his patron Alfonso and went to Rome to enjoy his peaceful sinecure, though he was still testy enough to attack the writings of St Thomas Aquinas before a gathering of Dominican friars not long before he died. Valla's philippics could no longer put him in danger, but sixty years later, when republished by the likes of Erasmus and Luther, they proved extremely uncomfortable for the Church.

✺

Maso di Bartolommeo

SUPPORTER OF THE ARTS

1406–1456

A stone cutter and bronze caster from southern Tuscany, Maso di Bartolommeo was not so much a great Renaissance artist as a competent and reliable one. Rarely hired to produce masterpieces, Maso was instead called upon for support work. He produced the marble steps, pedestals, fireplaces, and coats of arms; the bronze figurines, gates, bells, and candelabra that supported and embellished the altarpieces and statuary of his more famous contemporaries, such as Donatello, Michelozzo dei Micholozzi, and Luca della Robbia.

Nevertheless, Maso gained a special place in Renaissance art history, thanks to a lucky fluke – his account books survived. Other Italian artists kept accounts, but very few that are so informative and from so early in the Renaissance have come down to us intact. In these two little booklets, each measuring just four by eleven inches, Maso recorded the day-to-day workings of his business for roughly the last seven years of his life. In a precocious form of double-entry bookkeeping, he recorded his expenses for raw materials, wages, and essentials such as rent, firewood, and clothing. Against these outgoings, he entered his various commissions, along with payments received.

His accounts make it clear that Maso was not just a hired hand. He contracted directly with the same patrons who hired Donatello and Brunelleschi – such notables as Cosimo de' Medici, his son Piero, and many other luminaries of the Medici circle. Some came to Maso with private commissions, while others represented the guilds of bankers or textile merchants that essentially ran the city and paid for its most important churches and public buildings. Networking through these illustrious Florentines, Maso reached clients further afield – dukes like Federico da Montefeltro of Urbino and Sigismondo Malatesta of Rimini stopped by his shop, or *bottega*, in the center of Florence. When the visiting Astorre Manfredi, lord of Faenza, spotted Maso's copy of Petrarch's song collection, *il Chanzoniere*, on a *bottega* work-bench, the artist offered to lend it, noting how 'Lord Astorre said he wanted it, to have it copied [for himself].' He pointedly recorded the transaction as a credit in his account book.

If not a great artist himself, Maso at least got great art made, by organizing the labor of ordinary workers and craftsmen. His special contribution lay in linking up Florence's elites with its scruffier classes – carters, stone masons, and scrap metal peddlers. During the early Renaissance there were hundreds of entrepreneur-contractors like him, part businessmen and part craftsmen, each the master of a range of technical skills and each at the center of his own network of masters, apprentices, laborers, and clients. Though men like Maso won no lasting fame, their energy was the driving force behind the artistic revolution that flowered in cities like *Quattrocento* Florence.

Not all of Maso's energies went into the decorative arts. While still apprenticed to Donatello he had learned the fine art of bell casting, and when he set off on his own, he translated these skills from producing symbols of peace and community into a newfangled implement of warfare – the bronze cannon. For over a century, large cannon had been made of iron bands welded together, but Maso perfected a much safer, more dependable weapon, by casting two massive tubes of bronze that were then screwed together. Soon he was producing enormous *bombarde*, weighing over six tons and capable of hurling two-foot stone cannon balls that weighed up to 300 pounds.

Always the craftsman, Maso charged by the pound for what he cast. Since bells and fancy bronze work were highly decorated, they cost more per pound than cannon, but according to his accounts the modest-sized cannon called a *cerbottana* was still so heavy that it was more expensive than a free-standing bronze statue or a fair-sized altarpiece. Such a cost ratio might give some customers reason to pause. Lords like Federico da Montefeltro, who supported their duchies through their income as mercenary captains, might ask themselves – should their bronze budget go towards decorating their palaces or outfitting their armies?

The armaments business, though lucrative, was also sporadic. Once Florence signed the Peace of Lodi in April 1454, local demand for cannon temporarily dried up. Maso was soon forced to lay off most of his workforce and close his *bottega*. Hearing that the Republic of Ragusa (modern day Dubrovnik, in Croatia) was paying top ducat for cannon to place in its new fortifications, Maso decided to try his luck across the Adriatic. The venture apparently failed, however, since just a few months later he was back in Florence. Soon thereafter, in mid-1456, Maso died, leaving behind his account books that stated, on their final lines, that the state of Florence, still owed him for six months' past work.

Alessandra Strozzi

A MOTHER'S DREAMS AND MARITAL SCHEMES

1407—1471

In Renaissance Florence marriage was a process of mergers and acquisitions rather than courtship and love, especially for the wealthy elite.
Alessandra Macinghi Strozzi, matriarch of an old, distinguished family,
captured this nuptial intrigue in letters to her two oldest sons, Filippo and
Lorenzo. Both were exiled by the rival Medici clan, and with letters her only
means of communication Alessandra wrote often, sending long, gossipy
notes in colloquial Italian. This highly personal correspondence gives a rare
glimpse into the private life of a 15th-century woman.

Alessandra was married at 14 but widowed at 28, when her husband,
Matteo, and three of their children died of the plague during the family's
exile on the Adriatic coast. In political disgrace and financial disarray, she
and her five surviving children returned to Florence, where she handled
the family correspondence, a task that normally fell to husbands. As adults,
Filippo and Lorenzo were banished to Naples in 1458, and Alessandra began
sending them family updates and political news – the latter often in code.
And although she could read and write Italian fluently, her awkward prose
and odd spellings reflect the limited education of most noble women.

While lacking elegance, her writing brims with details of daily life.
She discusses constipation and the Lenten diet, her dispute with a pork
butcher, the price of almonds and, in a note to her youngest son, some new
linen underpants 'made up the way you like them'. She employed motherly
guilt when Filippo failed to keep up his correspondence, writing that he
could not have completely forgotten her, for a son naturally remembers

his mother, 'particularly one who didn't desert him when he needed her'. He was very busy, she knew, and if no letter arrived, she would simply ask around to see if he'd found time to write to someone else – if so, at least she would know he wasn't dead.

Her children's marriage prospects preoccupied her for many years. Writing to Filippo in 1447, she announced that his sister Caterina was to marry Marco Parenti, a wealthy silk merchant. Alessandra would have preferred a son-in-law with a better pedigree, but to place her daughter in a nobler family required 1,500 florins, a ruinous sum for the cash-strapped Strozzi family. Parenti seemed a bargain at 1,000 florins, and anyway it was unwise to wait, for Caterina was now 16, an age by which most of her peers had already married. Parenti treated his bride well, giving her a lovely gown of crimson silk velvet, a peacock-feather and pearl garland, and a pearl-draped head-dress. 'When she goes out, she'll have more than 400 florins on her back', the proud mother effervesced.

Alessandra was anxious for Filippo and Lorenzo to wed, not only to boost the beleaguered Strozzi name, but also because older widows expected to live out their lives with their sons' families. The exasperated mother spent years nudging the men towards various girls, but neither shared her sense of urgency. In Naples they worked long hours building the family's banking business but, while they postponed taking wives, they did not forsake women. Each enjoyed mistresses, which troubled Alessandra only because a lover delayed legitimate grandchildren. She joked with Filippo that one woman, a slave named Marina, treated him so well that it was no wonder he repeatedly put off marriage. Lorenzo's liaisons produced two illegitimate children, which she found equally unremarkable. '[You and Filippo will] both be unmarried for so long that you'll have a dozen of them,' she commented drily.

Taking a wife, however, was a serious business, and beauty, or a lack thereof, could make or break a deal. Assessing the candidates frankly, Alessandra noted one girl's promising credentials, but it was rumoured that she was clumsy. Another had a long face but good skin – even though it wasn't pale. Because well-born girls rarely left their homes, gathering intelligence was tricky. Alessandra spied repeatedly on one candidate's house to see if she sat chatting at the window – behaviour that could mean flightiness or even loose morals. After learning which church another girl attended, Alessandra sneaked into services there for a surreptitious peek. She followed another possible bride after Mass and later reported that 'it seemed to me from looking at her face and how she walks, that she isn't lazy' and 'is not soiled merchandise.'

When their exile ended in 1466, Lorenzo remained in Naples to manage the business, but to Alessandra's delight Filippo returned home, now nearly 40. He married a 16-year-old beauty named Fiametta, whom Alessandra approvingly compared to 'good meat with lots of flavour'. A grandson, Alfonso, was born nine months later and became the focus of Alessandra's remaining years. When Filippo was away, she sent him news of the boy, quoting his baby talk, noting his first steps. He toddled behind her around the house, she wrote, like a chick following a mother hen. And when he was fifteen months old, she pronounced him so advanced that she was teaching him to read. In her last surviving letter, a note to Filippo in 1470, she confirmed that Alfonso was well and added, almost as an afterthought, 'so are the rest of us'. Having declared since 1447 that her death was imminent, she passed away in 1471, her family at her side.

CR

Isotta Nogarola

YOUNG HUMANIST TURNED HOLY WOMAN

1418–1466

As a mere teenager in Verona, Isotta Nogarola was already a fully fledged scholar; by the time she was 20, she was well established as Italy's first female humanist. Being an articulate, learned woman, however, had its hazards. Writing under a pseudonym in 1439, one critic acknowledged her eloquence but alleged that 'an eloquent woman is never chaste' and accused Isotta of wanton promiscuity. It was an affront to God, he declared, that an impure woman should 'dare to engage so deeply in the finest literary studies'. Her public writing subsequently dwindled, and she retreated for several years to a book-lined study in her mother's house. Having already mastered the grammar, rhetoric and literature of humanism, she turned to theology and redefined herself as a religious scholar.

Even among elite families such as the Nogarola, girls rarely pursued advanced studies, and the few who did required a male relative's permission. Yet it was Isotta's widowed mother, herself illiterate, who arranged Classical studies for her four daughters. Isotta and her sister Ginevra excelled in particular, but Ginevra's scholarship came to an abrupt halt when she married. Isotta forged on alone, gathering advice and comments from family associates, the only appropriate male correspondents for a young unmarried woman.

Isotta may have reached too far in 1436, however, when she sent an unsolicited letter to Guarino Veronese, her own tutor's teacher and a famous scholar of ancient Greek. He did not respond, and Isotta's humiliation deepened as local women gossiped about her boldness. When she finally found courage for a second note, it was both petulant and reproachful. She bemoaned that she was born female, for 'women are ridiculed by men', and chided him with Cicero's dictum that we must behave humbly to our inferiors. But, she pouted, 'I see that you are unmoved and disagree with his teaching.' This time Guarino replied to her letter immediately, encouraging her work but also warning her to toughen up and to cultivate a more resilient, 'manly soul'.

More than a means of exchanging news, letter-writing in the 15th century functioned much like modern-day academic journals, allowing humanists to spread ideas, debate issues and generally advance their own careers. Ambitious young scholars circulated their writings in volumes called 'letterbooks' – Isotta was one of very few women in Europe to do so. These books, as well as individual letters, were copied and forwarded throughout intellectual circles, allowing Isotta's name and fame to travel even while she remained at home in Verona.

This resulting celebrity, however, triggered the anonymous attack on her chastity in 1439 that seemed to drive her into hiding. Little is known about Isotta in the 1440s, but letters to her began noting her godliness, and at least one writer urged her to perpetual chastity. Perhaps agreeing with these sentiments – or perhaps recalling her sister's truncated career – Isotta never married, but neither did she join a convent, the usual path for spiritually minded women. The Nogarola family's wealth and open-mindedness allowed her the unusual option of living with her family as a single, adult woman and pursuing her work. Thus freed, she took up sacred texts, early Christian writings and Aristotelian philosophy.

Around 1450 Isotta re-emerged as a religious writer, having reclaimed a life of the mind in a less threatening role. She continued to work in the major humanist forms, but this time they were refracted through a theological prism. In her most famous work, the *Dialogue on Adam and Eve*, she debates with Ludovico Foscarini, governor of Verona and a personal friend, the question of whose sin in the Garden of Eden was greater. Written in 1451, the fictional dialogue was probably based on a real discussion between Isotta and Foscarini. The Ludovico character asserts that Eve's stupidity and pride led her to transgress God's law and coax Adam into sin, while 'Isotta' notes that God himself gave Eve a weaker will and limited intelligence. Adam, with his 'greater understanding and knowledge of truth', should have known better.

The dialogue captivated Verona, not only for its themes of sex and sin, but also because the protagonists were a prominent married man and a celebrated single woman. Foscarini, with two doctoral degrees and a formidable mind, found Isotta a kindred spirit, and the two exchanged an astonishing number of letters for a couple not married to each other. Just a single note from her to him survives – a formal one from their early relationship – but his many extant letters to her are intense and ardent, although always couched in terms of her chaste life and fine intellect. Like a lover, he soothed her when she felt neglected, assuring her that he cherished her deeply. And he railed irritably against a marriage proposal she received, reminding her that as a committed virgin she must reject the 'libidinous way of life' and remain an 'intact and uncorrupted ornament' of Christian life.

Although they loved each other deeply, there is no evidence of a physical relationship. Yet Foscarini's visits to Isotta's house and their frequent correspondence were enough to provoke suspicion, and the bishop of Verona insisted they stop meeting. Nevertheless, after her mother died in 1461, Isotta moved into the Foscarini household, where she continued to study and work until her death in 1466

CR

Federico da Montefeltro

THE ARTFUL DUKE

1422–1482

The illegitimate son of a minor duke in the poor hill country of eastern Italy, Federico da Montefeltro turned unpromising beginnings into a dazzling career. At the age of 22 he took over the duchy of Urbino and, using his vast income as a mercenary soldier – supposedly he never lost a battle – he converted his court into the model for Renaissance civility and art. In his own time he was called the 'Light of Italy', a model for all Italian princes. Federico went far on sheer talent, although he never forgot his modest origins. While still a young *condottiere*, or captain for hire, he had learned to back the winning side and to reward professional loyalty, regardless of personal feelings. As a ruler, he followed similar principles with other Italian princes and with his subjects, many of whom were also his soldiers. Unlike many other rulers, Federico could consequently walk the streets of his capital without an armed guard, poking his head into workshops, chatting with artisans and in general trusting to the love and respect of his citizens for his safety.

Recognizing that Urbino was too impoverished to support his ambitions, he continued to serve other cities as a mercenary even after he became its ruler. Although he willingly entered into the Italian peninsula's shifting diplomatic alignments, he sided only with those who paid him to fight, never in a political alliance. Successful and innovative as a soldier – he was reportedly the first to use cannon on the battlefield – he brought his ample earnings home, eliminating the need for the heavy taxes that princes typically imposed.

In almost forty years as ruler, Federico turned his city into a sort of humanist theme park, a court that was renowned for both civility and learning. On a prominent ridge of what had been a shabby little hill town, he grafted an enormous palace, a cathedral church and the largest library in Italy outside the Vatican. To fill them, he hired scholars, artists and copyists from all over Italy and beyond. At its peak, under Federico and his son and successor Guidobaldo, the court employed or housed nearly 500 men and women. Besides some 60 counts, courtiers and lesser gentlemen, this number included half-a-dozen secretaries, 22 pages, 38 grooms and waiters, 5 cooks, 31 footmen, 50 stablemen and 100 or more miscellaneous lackeys; nearly 100 others worked as craftsmen or musicians. In comparison with powerful cities such as Milan or Ferrara it was a small court, but it loomed extremely large in a provincial centre like Urbino: fully one-third of the town's adults worked directly for Federico, and most of the rest made their living taking care of his courtiers. Everyone else – peasants included – found at least seasonal employment in the ducal army.

Federico spent vast sums on his capital – 200,000 ducats on building his palace, 50,000 on its furnishings and 30,000 on the library, at a time when 2,500 ducats could buy a grand merchant's house in Milan or Mantua. His eagerness to spend gave his court a certain *nouveau riche* brashness. Although he had books copied by the hundreds for his library, there is no indication that he read – or could read – the dozens he bought in Greek and Hebrew. Federico's interests as a bibliophile lay more in the appearance of books than in what they said: he was especially proud of their bindings, vellum and illuminations. He reportedly despised the newfangled art of printing as mundane.

Much of Federico's extravagance was part of a campaign, carried out with almost military efficiency, to gain legitimacy for himself and his lineage. He hired a series of painters, including Piero della Francesca and the Spaniard Pedro Berruguete, to portray him variously as pious, dynastic, uxorious, scholarly and valorous – while making sure they never showed the right side of his face, for he had lost an eye during a tournament in 1450. He had not, after all, been either the first or the legitimate son, and there were enduring suspicions that he had somehow been behind the assassination of his elder brother. Not until 1474 did Pope Sixtus IV finally name him duke, rather than merely lord, of Urbino – and that was only after he had (expensively) married his daughter to the pope's nephew. The outsider *condottiere* finally achieved his dream, but only at the cost of tying his duchy to a more powerful dynasty. When the sickly Guidobaldo died without heir in 1508, Urbino reverted to the papacy, and with it went most of Federico's books, art works and furnishings. Only the grand and graceful palace remains, perched like an enormous crown on the modest forehead of Urbino.

CR

Lucrezia Tornabuoni

SIDE-STEPPING SOCIAL STRICTURES

1425–1482

During the 15th century Lucrezia Tornabuoni was the most influential woman in Italy's most powerful family. The wife of Piero de' Medici and the mother of Lorenzo the Magnificent, she advised both husband and son on Florentine politics and civic affairs, and commanded respect from nobles and populace alike. Although she held no official role, the needy and otherwise down-and-out looked to her for help while others asked her to resolve family disputes or parish squabbles. She was also a patron of the arts and an author in her own right, composing sacred poetry to be sung with well-known tunes and adapting Bible stories about defiant heroines into narrative poems.

Lucrezia's husband, Piero, assumed control of Florence in 1464 following the death of his father, Cosimo. Nicknamed *il gottoso* ('the gouty one'), the sickly Piero was an intensely private man who lacked his dynamic father's social skills. Lucrezia, on the other hand, charmed Florence with her grace and her warmth, and her diplomatic abilities helped compensate for her husband's many shortcomings. Pain drove Piero to bed for weeks at a time, forcing him to entrust several diplomatic missions to others, including, on occasion, Lucrezia. In 1467, for instance, he dispatched her to Rome to discuss Venetian aggression against Florence with the pope. However, not all Florentines approved of her prominence: at the time few women ventured into the male-dominated papal court, and deploying a female ambassador, groused one critic of the Medici, shamed her husband and reduced Florence to 'the vilest repute'.

When Piero died in 1469, the 20-year-old Lorenzo became the de facto leader of Florence, and he sought his mother's counsel until her death thirteen years later. Although she had no training in humanist studies, Lucrezia was both educated and well versed in the politics of Florence and beyond, with plenty of diplomatic experience. She had numerous well-placed contacts in government, and friends sent updates from abroad with news about foreign affairs: conflicts among other Italian city-states, for example, or Christendom's wars against the Turks.

Nearly 500 letters to Lucrezia survive, the majority of which request help of some sort. One correspondent asked her to sway the hiring process for a new chancellor at the University of Pisa, while another called on her to mediate in a family feud that had festered for twenty years. A nun sought action against soldiers who pilfered produce from the convent farm; a prisoner begged for clemency; destitute girls asked for dowry funds so that they could marry with honour. Other notes came with gifts: one banished merchant, hoping to end his exile, sent lengths of fine linen, while a grateful man from Pistoia offered thanks for her kindness and added, 'I am sending you several trout.'

Supplicants typically addressed Lucrezia in maternal terms such as 'Most Illustrious Mother', and praised her compassion, her mercy, and other qualities commonly ascribed to the Virgin. This virtuous public persona – a mother figure with holy undertones – helped deflect censure, for even charitable work did not justify women's presence in the public realm. Florence's pious archbishop went so far as to preach that women should leave home only for Mass and, to restrict further their opportunities for sin, that they should limit even those forays to major feast days.

While her community work was public, Lucrezia's writing was private, mostly verse for family and friends that blended popular culture with sacred themes. Of her eight *laudi* – religious lyrics for secular music – four are set to the popular 15th-century tune 'Welcome to May'. For her sacred stories she used the metrical forms of much-loved Italian writers such as Boccaccio and Petrarch, weaving drama into traditional Bible narratives that she embellished with her own details – passages about palace draperies, for example.

She focused on unorthodox, resourceful women such as Judith, the brave widow with a 'manly heart' who saved the Israelites by penetrating the enemy camp, charming the general and beheading him as he lay in a drunken stupor. In Lucrezia's retelling of the Book of Esther, the queen defies royal custom and risks death when she enters the king's court without permission to expose a plot against the Jews. Lucrezia chose to write about women who, like her, crossed boundaries for the good of their people. As though to prove Florence's fretful archbishop wrong, she used scripture to show that serving God sometimes required a woman to trespass into male territory.

⳨ Gentile Bellini

PORTRAITS OF FACES AND FAÇADES

1429?–1507

Gentile's father, the Venetian painter Jacopo Bellini, named his son after his own teacher, Gentile da Fabriano, an early Renaissance master whose work bridged the stylized elegance of International Gothic and the revolutionary naturalism of Florence. Gentile developed a personal style indebted to both traditions, while pioneering the new medium of oil on canvas, which he preferred to tempera on wooden panels or the more traditional fresco. By the time he set up his own *bottega* in the 1470s, Gentile was already famous – ennobled by the emperor Frederick III in 1469 and named Venice's official state painter in 1474.

Gentile earned his initial renown as a portrait painter. His earliest surviving painting was a full-length rendition of the Venetian Patriarch Lorenzo Giustiani (1445) – the oldest oil painting still to be found in the city. Many of Gentile's portraits have been lost, but the surviving few – of several Venetian doges, of Caterina Cornaro, queen of Cyprus, and of various aristocrats – demonstrate his grasp of this new and daringly secular field of painting. Although Florentine painters had for several decades been inserting portraits of their patrons into altarpieces, Gentile was the first to portray his clients completely on their own, as individuals worthy of immortality in their own right.

In the late 1470s Gentile and his brother Giovanni were hired to redecorate the Great Council Chamber in the Doge's Palace. Rather than using fresco, they put up vast canvases, depicting the creation myths of the Republic as civic epics involving huge crowds and dramatic events in recognizable sites such as St Mark's Square. Just as dramatic and realistic were Gentile's renderings of Venice's triumphs at sea, which moved his 16th-century biographer, Giorgio Vasari, to praise him as 'no less acquainted with naval warfare than with painting'.

In 1479 Gentile was plucked from the Doge's Palace (leaving Giovanni to finish the job) and dispatched by the Venetian government as an cultural envoy of sorts to the Ottoman court in Constantinople. Mehmet II, sultan of the Turks, had expressed an interest in Italian portraiture, and the Venetians hoped to charm their old antagonist by sending that art form's master practitioner. Gentile lived up to expectations, creating a series of likenesses that left the sultan 'wondering how a mortal man could possibly possess such divine talent as to express natural things so vividly'. So entranced was Mehmet by Gentile's skills that some Venetians began to fantasize that the Sultan, believing that Gentile 'had been assisted by some divine spirit', might be inspired to convert to Christianity.

It was not to be. Gentile returned to Venice in 1480, Mehmet died in 1481, and the two states were soon back waging holy war. Most of Gentile's work in Constantinople – drawings of various Ottoman functionaries, a self-portrait, sundry erotic works that the sultan had specifically requested – have been lost. Only a few sketches in pen, a colourful painting of a Turkish scribe and a heavily restored portrait of Mehmet remain to give the barest suggestion of the work Gentile created, and the stir he caused, while in Constantinople. Likewise, little has survived of Gentile's later output in Venice – the entire cycle he and Giovanni painted for the Great Council Chamber was destroyed in a catastrophic fire in 1577. His monumental vision, simultaneously civic and epic, must be extrapolated from the four large oils that he painted for two of Venice's *scuole grandi* – confraternities committed to providing social services – towards the end of his life. In paintings large enough to allow for meticulously detailed individuals and architecture, Gentile made the city itself his primary protagonist. In the process he single-handedly started the long tradition of Venetian *vedutisti*, or cityscape painters, that would culminate over two centuries later with Canaletto and Francesco Guardi.

Gentile ended his life on a very different project, however. In his *St Mark Preaching in Alexandria*, he poured his passion for detail into an Oriental fantasy of his own devising – an over-sized exotic cityscape more than 3 metres (10 feet) high and nearly 8 metres (26 feet) long, with camels, a giraffe and dozens of high-turbaned pashas. At the centre he grouped a dense mob of heavily veiled women, who provide an audience for St Mark and ballast for the composition. In other works he painted after returning from Constantinople, Gentile had included Oriental motifs – a glimpse of carpet or a porcelain bowl – but this was the first time he, or anyone else, had produced a vision of the East on such a grand scale. Although he and other Renaissance Italians never realized the Christian dream of converting or colonizing Muslim territories, Gentile's *Sermon of St Mark* at least manages to capture Christendom's intense fascination with the Islamic world.

∞

Mehmet II

CONQUEROR OF CONSTANTINOPLE

1432–1481

Even as relative peace settled over Europe in the mid-15th century, one danger still threatened – Mehmet II, sultan of the Ottoman Turks. Not only the minor Balkan kingdoms but also the Italians, who had long enjoyed and profited from their privileged proximity to the East, suddenly found themselves exposed to tens of thousands of battle-hardened troops, as well as to a new and hostile navy. Europeans looked to the East and trembled at what they saw, imagining not just a familiar religious foe, but rather the wrath of God incarnate. Satan himself, the humanist bishop Leonardo Dati warned, had introduced Mehmet to the world, proclaiming, 'He is mine. He is the one whom I desired with all my heart. This is the sharer of evil deeds to whom I will give ghastly sceptres of the world.'

Mehmet became the terror of Europe and earned his title of *el-Fātiḥ*, 'The Conqueror', when he was just 21 by taking Constantinople. His siege of the city in 1453 took only three weeks and went off with textbook efficiency. Mehmet used his vast army – estimated at over 100,000 men – to cut the city and its waterways off from all hope of relief. Then with his enormous, newly designed siege cannon, he battered a hole in Constantinople's massive walls. Having occupied this last vestige of the Classical world, Mehmet rapidly extended and consolidated Ottoman power elsewhere, and his progress seemed inexorable. Few towns or nations could withstand the assault and firepower of his great armies, and any foolhardy enough to resist were horribly punished – their men slaughtered, their women and children sold off into slavery. His janissary legions soon mopped up the last independent Greek kingdoms in Anatolia and the Peloponnese, then overran the Balkans up to the Danube and Belgrade, which barely withstood his ferocious siege in 1456.

Undeterred, Mehmet set about expanding his empire beyond its heartland. He sent armies to probe Friuli, not far from Venice; his navy expelled the Genoese from the Crimea; he besieged the Knights of St John in their fortress on the island of Rhodes; and in 1480 his forces seized Otranto, on the heel of Italy itself. The fear that Mehmet provoked was everywhere. Tales of his butchery abounded – it was said his troops had killed over half a million civilians. Theologians denounced his faith as false and devilish, and crusades were called against him.

Mehmet saw things rather differently. Although his conquest of Constantinople traumatized Christians, to him it was the preordained transfer of power from one empire to the next. After the conquest, even many of his Christian adversaries admitted, 'No one doubts that you are emperor of the Romans,' and much of his military adventurism was simply to reclaim those provinces lost during centuries of Byzantine mismanagement – Greece, Syria, and even Italy. Mehmet especially had to turn Constantinople – 'a city of ruins, poor, and largely uninhabited' – into a fitting imperial capital. Far from gloating satanically over the fall of Christendom's ancient heart, he expressed deep sadness as he toured the city's wretched neighbourhoods. Then he went to work. 'When the sultan had captured the city of Constantinople,' noted a chronicler, 'almost his very first care was to have the city repopulated.' He began by offering thousands of unoccupied houses and vacant sites, now his by right of conquest, to his imperial subjects, so they might resettle his capital. To gain the allegiance of conquered Greeks, he preserved their churches, empowered the Orthodox patriarch and gave them, as *dhimmî* – protected people of the Book – better trading rights than they had enjoyed under their own empire. Similar provisions were extended to subject Jews, Armenians and other non-Muslims; as one rabbi put it, 'Here in the land of the Turks, we have nothing to complain of.'

Christian Constantinople was reborn as Muslim Istanbul. Within a generation the population had more than doubled and civic life soon returned, as Mehmet had mosques, madrasas, caravanserais and marketplaces erected throughout his new capital. He founded learning centres that attracted professors and imams, calligraphers and librarians; his construction projects were a boon to architects, builders and tile-makers; and his own new residence, the Topkapi Palace, was a city in its own right, filled with courtiers, bureaucrats, gardeners, cooks, tailors and courtesans. Trade picked up, and at Mehmet's invitation Christian artists and scholars flocked to offer the latest in Renaissance thought and design. The city's ensuing reputation for religious tolerance and openness inspired Pope Pius II to write to Mehmet, promising to support him as the new Caesar of the Eastern Roman Empire if he would embrace Christianity, and threatening him with a new crusade if he would not. As it happened, Pius did declare his crusade, which promptly failed. The new Islamic empire of Mehmet the Conqueror, on the other hand, would endure for half a millennium.

CR

3. The Emerging Nations

1470–1495

I t can be argued that modern Europe was born with the rise of the unitary nation state, with its shared, or at least predominant, language and its centralized authority. The process of coalescing began in the final quarter of the 15th century. France, greatly strengthened by Charles VII's brilliant expulsion of the English, had grown significantly under his successors by the end of the Hundred Years' War. Charles's son Louis XI (1423–1483), also known as the 'Spider King' for his patient scheming, managed to accomplish one of his dynasty's oldest goals: that of extinguishing its cadet branch and sometime rivals the dukes of Burgundy. This he did less by plotting than by hiring enough Swiss mercenaries to defeat and kill Duke Charles the Bold in 1477. Louis's son Charles VIII (1470–1498) pushed French borders still further by acquiring the duchy of Brittany in 1488 – not by invasion, but by forcibly marrying the hapless 11-year-old orphan daughter of the duke.

Unity and power came more slowly to England, where the contending York and Lancastrian branches of the royal family were too similar in size to produce an easy or permanent winner. In 1455 the two sides had launched a lengthy civil war, in which an array of quasi-independent dukes and earls fought over feckless candidates for the throne, primarily as a means of promoting their own territorial and dynastic interests. Although the fighting mostly sputtered out in 1471, the issues of succession were not resolved until 1485, when Henry Tudor, a comparative outsider, won the crown in the Battle of Bosworth.

More divided than France or England, Spain was far more successful in forming a nation state, at least initially. After a centuries-long struggle between Christians and Muslims for control of the peninsula, by the mid-15th century Iberia had emerged as a patchwork of kingdoms – Navarre, Castile, Aragon, Portugal and Moorish Granada. Although not as highly fragmented as, for example, Italy, each of the various monarchies had its own traditions and orientation – towards France, Africa, trade or the military – which virtually guaranteed conflict. The potential for political stalemate diminished in 1469, however, with the marriage between Ferdinand II of Aragon (1452–1516) and Isabella I of Castile (1451–1504), which united the richest of the Iberian kingdoms with the most populous and militant under a combined crown. The geopolitical momentum generated by this match led in fairly short order to the conquest of Granada (1492), the absorption of Spanish Navarre (1515) and – for a time – even a union with Portugal (1580–1640). Although the Spanish unification that began with Ferdinand and Isabella was more sweeping and immediate than that of France or England, it did not, ultimately, produce the same unitary monarchy and nation state. Spain remained much as it had before their wedding – an uneasy union of quasi-kingdoms still jealous of their ancient privileges and traditions.

The unifying and centralizing efforts of these late 15th-century rulers greatly increased monarchical wealth, allowing sovereigns to establish permanent armies and set up extensive bureaucracies in their court capitals, in or near Paris, London and Madrid. Aware of his relatively weak claim to the English throne, Henry VII rapidly established royal authority throughout his kingdom. Within weeks of entering London, he had created a more powerful chancellor and resurrected the King's Council, a judicial, administrative and diplomatic body that had been almost completely moribund since the days of Henry VI. In France, Louis XI was largely successful at imposing royal authority on the kingdom's nobility, and his aggressive taxation policies made his kingdom the richest in Europe – until the largely unsuccessful military adventures of his son dissipated this legacy.

Spain, perhaps because it was more fragmented than its contemporaries, took a broader, more cultural approach to forming a unitary state. In particular, in 1478 Ferdinand and Isabella set up the Holy Office, or Inquisition, in Spain, with the intention of creating a uniform national faith on a peninsula where large minorities of non-Christians had given rise to blurred religious boundaries. The two monarchs then persuaded the papacy to give them administrative control over the Spanish Church, a move that both promoted a national religious uniformity and furthered royal power. The dominant role of Castile in the newly forged Spanish kingdom was signalled by the creation of a Castilian grammar in 1492 — the first grammar of a 'modern' language and a strong indicator of Spain's emerging cultural identity and international significance.

By no means was all of Europe moving towards the unitary state in these years, however. The destruction by France of the duchy of Burgundy, itself a patchwork of peoples, created a number of dynastic orphans, most significantly the Netherlands, which ended up, rather uncomfortably, in the hands of the Habsburgs. Germany also remained deeply fragmented, a conglomeration of free cities, principalities and feudal dependencies. The Habsburg family dominated the German 'nation', but their bases of power, in Austria and the Low Countries, left them literally peripheral to much of the German population and to Germany's princes.

The failure of Italy to produce a unitary state in these years was perhaps surprising, considering the political sophistication of Venice, Florence and Milan. Yet the Peace of Lodi, which had guaranteed a certain balance of power on the peninsula, also denied any one city state legitimate claims over the others. For forty years (and well beyond the lives of the signatories at Lodi) peace largely prevailed in Italy, where recourse was made more often to ambassadors than to arms. Yet the result, by the mid-1490s, was an Italy fixed in its fragmentation and consequently far less able to stand up to the new nation states now on its borders.

William Caxton

A prosperous London mercer, or textile merchant, William Caxton moved his business to the bustling city of Bruges around 1453. But along with the woollen cloth, saffron casks and ermine pelts that he shipped between the Low Countries and England, he also sold hand-copied manuscripts. Fluent in Dutch, French and German, Caxton was himself an avid reader and enjoyed fashionable continental literature, especially French courtly romances. 'To eschew sloth and idleness' during a lull in business one year he decided to try his hand at translation and began with the Burgundian best-seller *Recuyell of the Historyes of Troye*. His friend Margaret, Duchess of York – the sister of the English king Edward IV – enjoyed the genre too and, after offering to read the draft, corrected his grammar, offered suggestions and encouraged the project.

Caxton's other friends also urged him on: many of them could read English but lacked enough French to read the original book. A mercer rather than a scholar, Caxton went slowly and was exhausted at the end, writing that 'my pen is worn, mine hand weary and not steadfast, mine eyes dimmed with overmuch looking on the white paper.' A successful seller of books who had now produced one himself, he was fascinated by the new printing press, which had been running in Germany for nearly twenty years but had not yet reached the Low Countries or England. While in Germany during the early 1470s, he bought a press himself and set up a shop in Cologne. His friends were delighted when, in 1473, he finally produced copies of *Recuyell of the Historyes of Troye*. Word spread, demand soared and eager readers

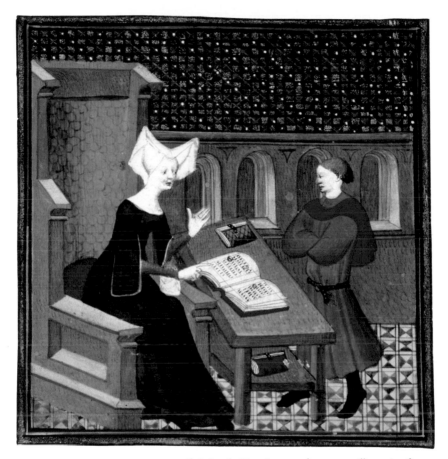

1 Christine de Pizan instructs her son: an illustration from the *Enseignemens moraux* ('Moral Teachings'), which she wrote for him around 1400. She denied that her sex was morally inferior, telling him that 'women can be good and sweet; / May it be your fortune such to meet.'

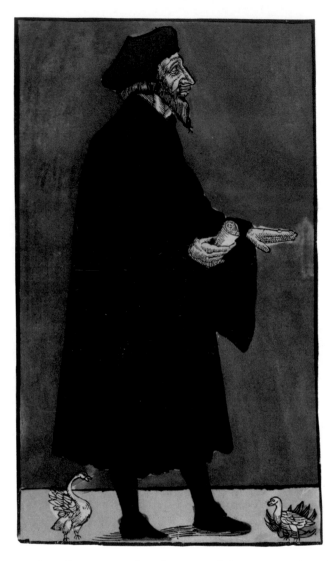

2 This 16th-century woodcut of Jan Hus includes a goose, Hus's symbol, and a swan, which represents Martin Luther. Hus protested against many of the same Church practices that drove Luther and his followers from Catholicism.

3 Opposite: St Bernardino from a fresco by Sano di Pietro (1450). Bernardino holds a model of Siena in which faith (the striped cathedral) and civil society (the Palazzo Pubblico) are protected by the city's stout walls.

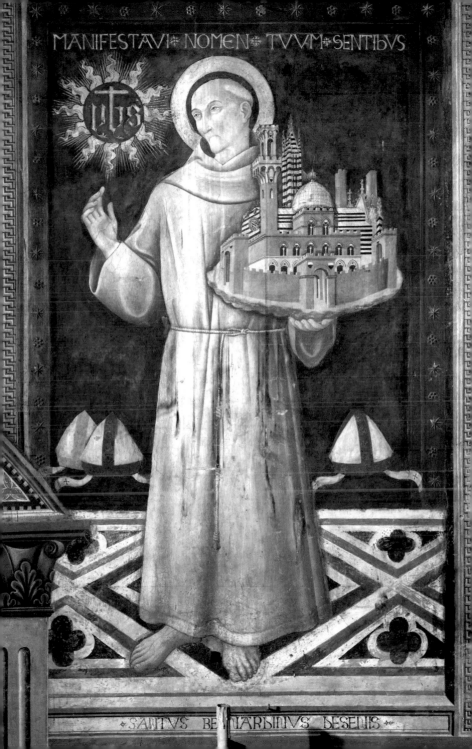

MANIFESTAVI · NOMEN · TVVM · SENTIBVS

IHS

· SANTVS · BERNARDINVS · DESENIS ·

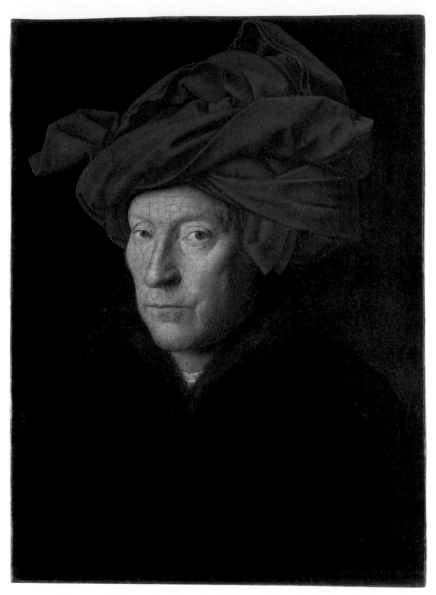

4 Van Eyck's *Portrait of a Man* (1433) may be of the artist himself, which would place it among Europe's first self-portraits to be created as independent works of art.

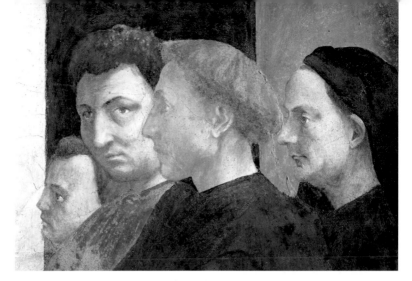

5 At the right-hand edge of the *Raising of the Son of Theophilus*, Masaccio slipped in portraits of himself and three friends: from left, we see Masolino, Masaccio himself, Leon Battista Alberti and Filippo Brunelleschi.

6 Detail of a Crucifixion by the Master of the Life of the Virgin (*c.* 1480). Nicholas of Cusa, kneeling before the crucified Christ, is identified by his crest: a crayfish (his family name, Krebs, means 'crab').

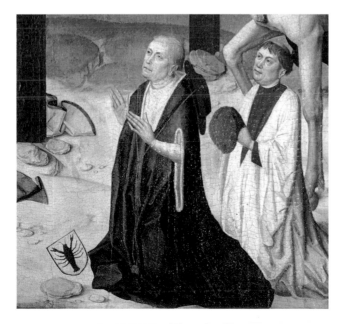

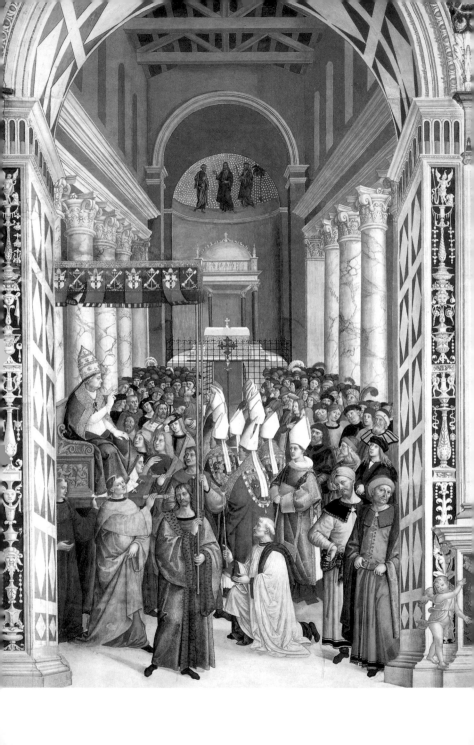

7 Opposite:
Pinturicchio's fresco
(1502–8) in the
Piccolomini Library of
Siena Cathedral captures
the climax of the papal
election process: Pius II,
newly crowned with
the tiara of St Peter, is
brought by litter into
San Giovanni Laterano.

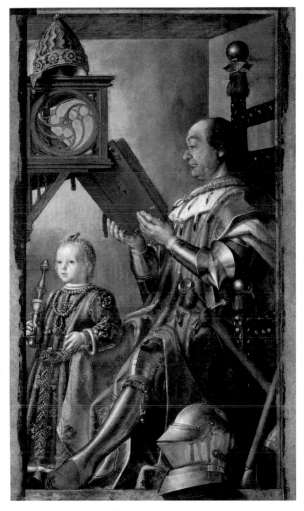

8 Federico da Montefeltro in his study, a painting by Pedro
Berruguete (1470s). Federico wears battle gear, ducal ermine,
and the Order of the Garter, awarded to him by Edward IV
of England.

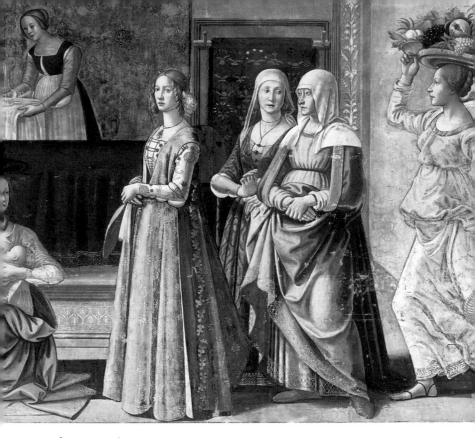

9 Above: Lucrezia Tornabuoni, second from right, in a detail from Domenico Ghirlandaio's *Birth of St John the Baptist* (1486–90), in Santa Maria Novella, Florence.

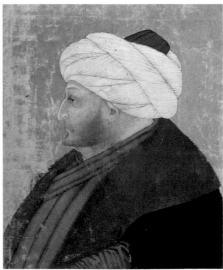

10 Mehmet II, by an anonymous Ottoman artist (*c.* 1480). Showing the sultan in his old age, this work was a product of the short-lived Turkish infatuation for Venetian- and Western-style art, brought on by Bellini's visit to Istanbul in 1479–80.

snapped up copies as quickly as he could print them. It was the first book ever published in English, and Caxton realized that there was a profitable niche to be filled.

While some people during that era were literate, very few understood Latin, the language of nearly every book in Europe. A sizeable swath of people in England could read only English – including courtiers as well as merchants and other members of the middle class. They too wanted the latest adventures from the continent, but hand-copied English versions were difficult to come by and prohibitively expensive. Seeing an opportunity, Caxton moved back to London in 1476 and opened a shop near Westminster Abbey – England's first printing business. Distinguished publishers on the continent already supplied England with scholarly and religious texts, but the market for titles in English was now wide open.

Caxton also continued to translate, and was much concerned with making his texts readable. There were many English dialects at this time, and people living 100 miles apart might be unintelligible to each other. Caxton tells of a merchant friend who, while travelling, stopped at a farmhouse for food: 'He asked after eggs, and the good wife answered that she could speak no French. And the merchant was angry, for he also could speak no French.' The stories he translated presented other problems. Caxton, who translated texts word-for-word rather than by sense, often ran into foreign terms without English equivalents and slipped them in unaltered. When his friends complained about his 'over curious terms', he resolved to cut back on the 'fair and strange' words of continental languages and celebrate the 'old and homely' expressions of his native English.

Of the nearly 100 titles Caxton published over his fifteen-year publishing career, the great majority were in English: a number were by popular English writers such as John Lydgate and Geoffrey Chaucer, whose *Canterbury Tales* Caxton called 'sugared eloquence'. Twenty-two were Caxton's own translations, many of which were foreign chivalric adventures that he wanted to share with English readers. To lure buyers to these unfamiliar works he loaded prologues with glowing comments from prominent readers; sometimes he boosted a book's glamour factor by declaring it essential reading for 'princes, lords, barons, knights' and, at the end of the list, 'all the common people'. Unfortunate readers without titles could at least own the same books as the aristocracy.

With his careful attention to public tastes Caxton prospered while many other early publishers went bankrupt. When he brought the printing press to England, it did not rock society with instant change – the pamphlet wars of religion were twenty years away – but he did give a great many more people something to read.

GIFT RECEIPT

Barnes & Noble Booksellers #2904
47 East Chicago Ave. Suite #132
Naperville, IL 60540
630-579-0200

STR:2904 REG:002 TRN:6946 CSHR:Kayla M

Rick Steves Florence & Tuscany
9781631216657   T1
(1 @ VR.HH)   VR.HH G
Lives of the Renaissance
9780500295069   T1
(1 @ RZ.HT)   RZ.HT G

Thanks for shopping at
Barnes & Noble

051.04C   08/20/2019 08:53PM

CUSTOMER COPY

With a sales receipt or Barnes & Noble.com packing slip, a full refund in the original form of payment will be issued from any Barnes & Noble Booksellers store for returns of undamaged NOOKs, new and unread books, and unopened and undamaged music CDs, DVDs, vinyl records, toys/games and audio books made within 14 days of purchase from a Barnes & Noble Booksellers store or Barnes & Noble.com with the below exceptions:

A store credit for the purchase price will be issued (i) for purchases made by check less than 7 days prior to the date of return, (ii) when a gift receipt is presented within 60 days of purchase, (iii) for textbooks, (iv) when the original tender is PayPal, or (v) for products purchased at Barnes & Noble College bookstores that are listed for sale in the Barnes & Noble Booksellers inventory management system.

Opened music CDs, DVDs, vinyl records, audio books may not be returned, and can be exchanged only for the same title and only if defective. NOOKs purchased from other retailers or sellers are returnable only to the retailer or seller from which they are purchased, pursuant to such retailer's or seller's return policy. Magazines, newspapers, eBooks, digital downloads, and used books are not returnable or exchangeable. Defective NOOKs may be exchanged at the store in accordance with the applicable warranty.

Returns or exchanges will not be permitted (i) after 14 days or without receipt or (ii) for product not carried by Barnes & Noble or Barnes & Noble.com.

Policy on receipt may appear in two sections.

Return Policy

With a sales receipt or Barnes & Noble.com packing slip, a full refund in the original form of payment will be issued from any Barnes & Noble Booksellers store for returns of

❦

Heinrich Kramer

THE INQUISITION'S WITCH-HUNTER

c. 1430–1505

To most people in the 15th century sorcery was real, engrained in their culture by pre-Christian folk traditions. The educated elite, however, were less influenced by popular culture and were guided instead by a 10th-century canon that declared the belief superstitious and heretical. The few theologians who did take witchcraft seriously tended not to see it as a threat to Christianity. Alarmed by such nonchalance, in 1487 the heretic hunter Heinrich Kramer wrote an encyclopaedic witch-hunting manual called the *Malleus maleficarum* ('The hammer of female witches'). In it he argued that black magic, or *maleficia*, caused most of the world's evils – everything from hailstorms and leprosy to male impotence. The book was an immediate, influential success, changing the Church's conception of evil and crystallizing the once nebulous notion of the witch.

Kramer, a German from Alsace, was a member of the Dominican order. When Pope Gregory IX founded the Inquisition in 1232, he gave these men the task of sniffing out heretics; ferocious guardians of orthodoxy, they were nicknamed 'Domini canes', or the 'Dogs of God'. Kramer's ardour for orthodoxy pleased his superiors in faraway Rome, but he rankled fellow friars, who found him arrogant and volatile, and at least one spat became an all-out brawl. Accused of embezzling Dominican funds, Kramer was barred from financial responsibilities within the order. In a sermon in 1474 he lambasted the Holy Roman Empire for encroaching on papal authority, and personally insulted Emperor Frederick III. He was subsequently given a prison sentence, but instead of spending time in gaol Kramer was promoted:

the Dominicans' master-general waived the punishment and named him to a post with the Inquisition.

Kramer showed a knack for winnowing out witches and was promoted again, becoming southern Germany's head inquisitor. But on reaching the region's towns he met with resistance from courts, the traditional sites of *maleficia* trials. At the local level, witchcraft had always been seen as a way to commit a crime rather than as a crime in itself – destroying a neighbour's orchard with a spell was no different from setting it on fire with a torch. Town officials so often balked at his zealotry that the infuriated Kramer turned to Pope Innocent VIII, who officially declared witchcraft heretical and thereby confirmed the jurisdiction of Inquisitors. Now with explicit control over witch prosecutions, Kramer bore down on Innsbruck, believing the town was plagued with love spells cast by bitter single women. But during one hearing in 1485, authorities grew uneasy when he brusquely interrogated a suspect about her sexual habits, and they ultimately dismissed the case because of procedural errors. Innsbruck's bishop, calling the friar 'childish', ordered him from the region.

The humiliated Kramer withdrew to Cologne and, to refute his critics, began his *Malleus*, a tightly organized treatise arguing that witches were both real and pervasive. According to Kramer, the Devil lured far more women than men into witchcraft. Women's weaker minds were more susceptible to evil; their weaker bodies made them crave the power of magic. Most damning, however, was the fact that they were 'more given to fleshly lusts than a man' – a trait Kramer discussed at length. Insatiable feminine desire drove a woman to 'carnal filthiness' with the devil's incubi, especially if she were too old or too homely for a human lover's regular attention.

Witches tended to target crops, draft animals and human health, particularly reproductive functions. For example, a man's penis might suddenly disappear – a common problem, according to the *Malleus*. Witches collected twenty to thirty male members at a time and hid them in bird's nests, Kramer explained, where the severed organs 'move about in order to eat oats and fodder'. In the guide to prosecutions he helpfully included templates for interrogations as well as torture instructions. If a red-hot iron failed to produce a confession, should one lie to a witch about her eventual execution? Kramer was cagey on the question but suggested that a woman might be more likely to confess, and thereby save her soul, if she were not held back by fear of death. Whether or not she admitted her guilt, an accused woman usually faced execution, with burning the mandatory method: confession might spare her soul, but her evil body must be purged from the earth by a bonfire's purifying flames.

Kramer surpassed other witch-hunting Inquisitors in both passion and success. In the early days of the witch craze – the 14th and 15th centuries – around 900 Europeans were tried for witchcraft; Kramer personally claimed to have convicted more than 200 suspects. Nevertheless, the Dominicans ultimately condemned him and his tactics, and in 1500 he was sent to Bohemia to convert heretical Hussites and to prosecute the Waldensians, a pacifist sect deemed too friendly to witchcraft (they opposed all capital punishment, even for convicted witches). When he died there in 1505, Kramer's *Malleus* had fixed the European definition of a witch, raised folk magic to the level of heresy, and fuelled a hysteria about witchcraft that escalated until 1600. With 30,000 copies circulating around Europe, the book framed discussion of *maleficia* for the next 200 years. An estimated 45,000 people perished in executions between 1500 and 1700, many of them at the hands of *Malleus*-wielding prosecutors. Catholics and Protestants agreed on few matters, but witch-hunters of both persuasions turned to Kramer's infamous manual.

CR

Francisco Jiménez de Cisneros

THE GRAND INQUISITOR

1436–1517

In Spain's dual kingdom, created by the marriage of Ferdinand and Isabella in 1469, there was in essence a third monarch: Francisco Jiménez de Cisneros. Helping Ferdinand overcome the innate conflicts between Aragon and Castile – each with its own history, cultural outlook and traditions – won Cisneros acclaim as a co-founder of the new Spanish nation and empire. The spiritual guidance he provided for Isabella likewise allowed him to set the religious tone – a mixture of passion and intolerance – that would dominate and distinguish Spain for centuries to come.

Born in a poor village north of Madrid, Cisneros studied law at the University of Salamanca before moving to Rome to serve on the Curial court. His skills pleased Pope Pius II, and he returned to Spain in 1465 with a papal letter ordering the archbishop of Toledo to grant him the first available benefice. Unfortunately, the archbishop was keen to promote one of his own followers; when Cisneros insisted on his rights, the story goes, the prelate had him thrown into prison until he surrendered his claim. For six years, Cisneros refused to yield, until the archbishop gave up and granted him the post, which he promptly traded for one in a more sympathetic diocese. Such dogged self-righteousness characterized Cisneros's life and career. Although successful as a cleric, at 48 he suddenly joined the Franciscans, replacing his birth name of Gonzalo with Francisco. Troubled by a deep sense of his own unworthiness and commitment to the ancient, ascetic traditions of Spanish Christianity, Cisneros spent the rest of his life committed to fasting, hair shirts, self-flagellation and sleeping on the naked earth.

Hearing of his ascetic reputation, Queen Isabella appointed Cisneros as her confessor and primary counsellor in 1492. Although he was already in his late fifties by this time, Cisneros's ecclesiastical career was only beginning: in 1495 Isabella had him elevated to archbishop of Toledo, which made him the primate of Spain and chancellor of Castile. Characteristically, however, when he was offered the position, Cisneros is supposed to have fled from Isabella's audience hall in shame. Only after six months of pleading from the queen and a direct order from the pope did he give in; and even so, he continued to reject the office's attendant pomp and luxury until the pope ordered him to live in the episcopal palace and put on the necessary robes. Although averse to the trappings of high office, Cisneros was certainly willing to wield the power that came with it, and soon he was aggressively imposing on Spain his almost messianic vision of a nation reborn in faith, combat and empire.

Cisneros began by reforming his own order. He cracked down so rigorously on Franciscan abuses – forbidding friars to leave their assigned parish, keep concubines or avoid preaching – that several hundred of them supposedly left Spain for North Africa and declared themselves Muslims. Meanwhile, deciding that the large *Mudéjar*, or Moorish, population that had remained in Granada after the conquest of 1492 represented a threat to the realm, Cisneros led an Inquisition team to the region to forcibly convert them and burn thousands of their holy books. When, predictably enough, the *Mudéjares* revolted, Ferdinand sent in the army, and once the uprising had been quelled Cisneros was able to proclaim that, as rebels, they had lost all title to their land, whether they converted or left. Thousands fled to North Africa, opening Granada to Spanish settlement.

After Isabella died in 1504, Cisneros essentially co-ruled with Ferdinand, who appointed him Grand Inquisitor of Castile and persuaded Pope Julius II to make him a cardinal. In 1509, although well over 70, Cisneros led an invasion of North Africa that culminated in the conquest of the Algerian city of Oran. The campaign was part of his longed-for crusade against the Moors that ultimately had to be abandoned after Ferdinand became entangled in fighting the French over Naples. Although Cisneros remained active in government – even serving as regent for a year after Ferdinand's death in 1516 – he became increasingly concerned with leaving what he considered a grander, more spiritual legacy. In 1499 he founded the University of Alcalá de Henares, largely as a means of rounding up the scholars for just such a monument: the Complutensian Polyglot Bible (Complutum was the ancient Roman name for Alcalá). Many of the Greek, Hebrew and Aramaic manuscripts used for the work came from Cisneros's private library, and he supervised much of the scholarship, which was completed in 1517, although it was not published until three years after his death.

Felix Fabri

PIOUS PILGRIM, WISECRACKING WANDERER

c. 1441–1502

A native of Zurich, Felix Fabri took religious vows and joined the Dominican order at the age of just 12. In 1468 he entered a monastery in the southern German city of Ulm. Yet the recluse's life of meditation and prayer did not altogether agree with Friar Felix, and by his late thirties he found himself obsessing about a pilgrimage to the Holy Land – so much so 'that whether I was asleep or awake I hardly ever had any other subject before my mind'. Escaping from his little corner of Germany was not easy. Not only did he have to get a special dispensation to leave his monastery, but, as Fabri admitted, he was also 'alarmed, and feared for my life, [for] I dreaded the sea, which I had never yet seen'.

Nevertheless, in April 1480 Friar Felix made the six-month journey to Jerusalem and back. This proved as frightening as he had imagined: over the Alps, and on the voyage from Venice to Jaffa and back, he narrowly escaped the plague, Turkish corsairs, shipwreck and violently quarrelsome companions, while putting up with 'stale bread, biscuit full of worms, tainted meat and abominable cookery'. Yet, despite the risks, 'we did not spend more than nine days in the Holy Land ... running round the holy places without understanding or feeling what they were.' Even before he got home, Friar Felix was already planning another pilgrimage, this time determined to do things properly.

So it was that in 1483–84 he signed on as 'chaplain and confessor' to four German knight-pilgrims, travelling with much greater comfort and safety – eventually beyond Palestine to St Catherine's Monastery in Sinai.

During this trip Friar Felix kept extensive notes on everything and everyone he encountered, 'frequently [writing] as I sat on an ass or a camel'. Once safely back in Ulm, he wrote out his observations, the *Evagatorium in Terræ Sanctæ, Arabiæ et Egypti peregrinationem* ('Wanderings on a pilgrimage in the Holy Land, Arabia and Egypt'), which he offered to those who stayed at home, 'so that they also, in mind, if not in body, might enjoy the pleasure of visiting the holy places'.

In this often rollicking account of life on the road Friar Felix produced, if not the first, certainly one of the most personal and exhaustive travel narratives of the Renaissance. Running to 1,500 manuscript pages, the *Evagatorium* details not just the holy sites that Fabri visited, but also how he and others experienced them. On visiting saints' relics, the pilgrims would pray, kiss the body 'several times' and then 'take jewels [which they brought for this purpose] and touch the relics of the holy place with them, that they may perchance derive some sanctity from the touch ... thus [the jewels] are returned to the friends of the pilgrims dearer and more valuable than before.' He also noted how he and other friars and priests bribed the Muslim guards of the Holy Sepulchre to let them spend the night inside the church, among the most sacred sites and relics of the Christian faith, but then fell to fighting among themselves over who would have the privilege of saying a personal Mass there.

Acutely conscious of national differences, Friar Felix dealt sharply and humorously with Venetian duplicity, French arrogance, Turkish thuggery, English thick-headedness and the drunkenness of practically everyone he met. He wrote of being assailed by hotel touts in Venice and of the general laughter when one of them fell off his gondola; of the pilgrims drinking so much sweet Cretan wine in Candia that they had to be carried back on board their ship; and of skulking across the plain of Judaea on mules by moonlight to avoid the ubiquitous Arab bandits. Through his accounts we learn the elaborate succession of sites that 15th-century pilgrims were to visit in Jerusalem, Bethlehem, Hebron, Jericho and the Dead Sea; the rituals associated with each place; and how often and how far the actual experience fell short of the ideal.

Unlike many pilgrims, Fabri seems to have made his journey to the Holy Land not in response to a vow or personal crisis, but for self-improvement. Presenting himself as 'dull-minded and slow of understanding', he saw his pilgrimage to the lands of the Prophets, the Nativity and the Passion as an educational experience, where even someone 'of some small learning will return learned to no small degree'. This Friar Felix certainly did, although, as the *Evagatorium* makes clear, his new sagacity never took away his wit, sharp eye or personal prejudices, even after he had left the road and returned to the quiet obscurity of his monastery in Ulm to finish his days.

CR

Antonio de Nebrija

THE INVENTOR OF SPANISH

c. 1441–1522

Consumed with their own quest for unification and empire, 15th-century Spaniards found little need for Classical humanist studies. Their universities, while venerable, were highly traditional, remaining firmly focused on the established disciplines of theology, medicine and law. That Spaniards ever became aware of Latin's other educational purposes or of its potential to open up new social and even moral vistas was largely thanks to the lifelong efforts of Antonio de Nebrija.

Antonio Martínez de Cala e Hinojosa (to give him his original name in full) was born in Lebrija, in Andalusia. Later, in a gesture that advertised his passion for Classical studies, he Latinized his name to Antonius Nebrissensis – using the Roman spelling of his place of birth – which is commonly rendered Antonio de Nebrija. Nebrija enrolled at the University of Salamanca aged just 15, but he was soon complaining about the state of Latin studies there, deploring the fact that Latin was taught through rote memorization of set pieces, with no concern for underlying structure or the aesthetics of the language. After taking his degree in rhetoric and grammar in 1461, Nebrija promptly decamped for Italy, where for the next ten years he studied not only Latin, but also Greek and Hebrew. He returned to Spain in 1470 without any prospect of a university position – not least because he had come back as a self-declared knight of humanism, 'to overthrow the [intellectual] barbarity that is spread far and wide all over Spain'. Instead he married, began what became a very large family and lived for a time in virtual poverty.

Nebrija attached himself to Bishop Fonseca, adviser to King Henry IV of Castile, and eventually won a professorship at Salamanca. He immediately revived his ambition of introducing the Spanish to the principles of Latin usage and grammar, and in 1481 he brought out *Introductiones Latinae* ('Latin Introductions'), a university-level textbook that enjoyed quick and lasting success (and was still in use in 19th-century Spain). By the mid-1490s he had greatly broadened his audience by translating his Latin grammar into Castilian and publishing Latin–Castilian and Castilian–Latin dictionaries. Queen Isabella, who had spent years struggling over the language, was supposedly among his readers.

Eventually Nebrija's passion for ancient languages led him into biblical studies, which interested him more than the Classical authors preferred by Italian humanists. The Inquisition frowned on investigating the Gospels through early Greek and Hebrew texts, however, and in 1505 the Holy Office seized Nebrija's notes as potentially heretical. Only the intervention and eventual support of Cardinal Jiménez de Cisneros, the Grand Inquisitor himself, allowed Nebrija to resume his scriptural studies; but suspicions of heresy, along with a certain intellectual arrogance on his part, so alienated him from colleagues in Salamanca that in 1513 he was denied the top chair in grammar there. Smarting from this rejection, Nebrija moved to the University of Alcalá de Henares, founded by Cisneros in 1499, to offer Spanish students both traditional scholasticism and the latest humanist approaches from Italy. Nebrija spent the rest of his life at Alcalá, mostly as one of several scholars working on the Complutensian Polyglot Bible, Cardinal Cisneros's grand project of a multilingual Bible in Vulgate Latin, Greek, Hebrew and Aramaic.

Meanwhile, Nebrija had another project – a grammar for vernacular Castilian. Leon Battista Alberti, among others, had talked about doing something similar with Italian, but Nebrija was the first to assert that a spoken language might have general grammatical rules that could, or even should, be laid out for study as Latin was. Initially, the concept baffled his contemporaries: Queen Isabella supposedly wondered, 'What do I want a work like this for, if I already know the language?' Nebrija responded by reminding the Queen of the power that even everyday language had, both in saving souls and in knitting together the newly created Spanish kingdom: 'Not only the enemies of our faith will feel the need to learn the language of Castile,' he wrote, 'but also the Basques and Navarres [of northern Spain].' Isabella must have been convinced, for she accepted a presentation copy of the *Gramática de la lengua castellana* on 18 August 1492. At the time Nebrija supposedly proclaimed, 'Your highness, the language is the instrument of the Empire' – prescient words, since just two weeks earlier Christopher Columbus had set sail heading west, and before long Nebrija's *Gramática* had turned Castilian into Spanish – the language that would unify not only his nation, but also much of the New World.

CR

Matthias Corvinus

HUNGARY'S HUMANIST KING

1443–1490

I n the 15th century, as Florence grew rich through banking and luxury
textiles, Hungary still languished as a mostly rural feudal kingdom. Its
largest city, Buda, had just 10,000 inhabitants at a time when Paris bustled
with nearly 300,000. Yet Hungary was one of the earliest areas beyond the
Alps to embrace the Renaissance, and its links with Italy grew stronger
when the great humanist king Matthias Corvinus began his 32-year reign.
The first ruler outside Italy educated in the humanist tradition, this learned,
charismatic leader both wrested power from Hungary's enemies abroad
and built a sophisticated court and magnificent library that were renowned
throughout Europe.

Matthias was the younger son of Jan Hunyadi, a minor nobleman and
major military hero. Hunyadi gained almost mythical status upon his death
in 1456, just weeks after routing Turkish invaders in a pivotal battle at
Belgrade. Threatened by the legendary Hunyadi name, Hungary's king
lured Jan's two boys to Buda, then executed the elder and imprisoned the
younger. The king died unexpectedly without an heir, however, forcing the
Hungarian Diet, or parliament, to choose a replacement. Foreigners had
ruled the country since 1301, and with a chance to crown a popular son of
Hungary they elected Matthias in 1458, elevating the boy from prison to
throne and filling citizens with nationalistic pride.

Schooled in the *studia humanitatis*, Matthias, like many young humanists,
adapted a Latinate surname – his derives from *corvus* ('crow'), a bird that
appears on the family crest. He ruled in a Machiavellian style, destabilizing

internal and external threats with dispatch. Parliament had hoped for a more malleable monarch – even seasoned rulers had previously truckled to them in exchange for funds. Matthias, however, circumvented this problem by raising his own capital. He streamlined government and taxed formerly exempt landowners, using the money to raise a force of well-paid merce-naries – the Black Army, which at its peak comprised 30,000 men, all under his personal command.

After their defeat by Jan Hunyadi in 1456, the Turks returned to conquer Serbia in 1458 and continued to advance north-west as Western Europe watched in alarm. They occupied Bosnia for several years, inching ever closer to the Adriatic, until King Matthias led his Black Army against them in 1464. He and his forces stopped the Turks in their tracks, prompt-ing celebrations throughout Europe in general and in Italy in particular. Italians viewed Hungary as Christendom's first line of defence against the infidel Muslims, believing, as Pope Calixtus III wrote, that Matthias had been sent by God to continue Jan Hunyadi's 'glorious struggle to stamp out Mohammedanism'.

To rout the enemy decisively, Corvinus needed far more troops, but other Christian states refused to contribute. The Black Army kept the Turks from penetrating Hungary, but Matthias had neither the war chest nor the will to continue a unilateral crusade on behalf of all Christians. To the chagrin of several consecutive popes, he settled for containing rather than conquering the Ottomans. In 1465 he signed a truce with them and focused instead on the kingdom's north-west borders. Over the following twenty years he added vast expanses of land, and in 1485 he conquered Vienna, which even the formidable Turks would fail to do – twice. That victory, mentioned in the Hungarian national anthem, remains a high point in the nation's history to this day.

But Matthias was as bookish as he was bellicose. He spoke six languages fluently; he was a passionate astrologer; and he read widely among histo-ries and Classical literature. An admirer of Italian style, he commissioned Classical sculptures and renovated Gothic buildings in the fashionable *all'antica* style. It was his wife, Beatrice, however, whom he married in 1476, who brought Italian customs to the kingdom. A colourful, strong-willed Neapolitan princess, Beatrice found Hungary unrefined – that is, insufficiently Italianate. As a remedy, she replaced the court's informal traditions with royal protocol, coaxed more Italians to court and transformed Hungarian dining with French and Italian cheeses, forks and ice cream.

Of all Matthias's achievements, however, it is the Corvinus library that remains most famous today. Matthias collected between 2,000 and 2,500 books, an astonishing number in the era before widespread printing; in comparison, his French counterpart, Charles VIII, owned about 130 volumes, and major universities held fewer than 1,000. The Hungarian king dismissed the printed book as fad and commissioned hundreds of manuscripts from the finest Florentine workmen. In fact, he vied with Lorenzo de' Medici for the best copyists and illuminators, and the two men's collections were similar in size and content. When Matthias died in 1490, Lorenzo wrote to his son that 'Matthias is dead; there will be a glut of copyists', and promptly hired the talented artisans who had lost their Hungarian commissions.

Like his predecessor, Matthias died without an heir, leaving only an illegitimate son born to an Austrian mistress. In his final years he had tried to secure the boy's succession, but parliament chose a foreign king, Vladislav of Bohemia, who failed to sustain the Black Army and lost Hungary's military gains. All future monarchs also hailed from outside the kingdom, making Matthias the last Hungarian king of Hungary.

❧

Lorenzo de' Medici

'THE MAGNIFICENT'

1449–1492

Lorenzo de' Medici was groomed from birth to rule Florence. Cosimo, his grandfather, could see that his own son, Piero 'the Gouty', lacked the health and spirit to lead the Republic for long, so he focused his attention and generosity on Lorenzo, the elder of Piero's two sons. The growing child was given the full humanist treatment – the broad education in Classical Latin and Greek that by the mid-15th century had become standard for scions of elite Italian families. Even before Piero died in 1469, Lorenzo was already living as a prince – going on diplomatic missions, collecting art, breeding horses and leading the philosophical discussions at Cosimo's Platonic Academy. He also showed genuine talent as a poet: his sensitivity in lyric and rustic verse brought Italian vernacular poetry back from the oblivion to which the humanists' infatuation with Latin letters had long consigned it. In 1469 Lorenzo married Clarice Orsini, a daughter of old Roman nobility, elevating his branch of the Medici into the Italian aristocracy. This skilful forging of nuptial strategies continued with his own offspring, whom he married to the children of dukes, the ancient Florentine nobility and, in the case of one daughter, to a pope's bastard. Only one son was left unmarried – he was destined to be a cardinal.

Skilled though he was in politics and diplomacy, Lorenzo was not so successful at running the family bank, whose funds he used to continue the patronage and bribery Cosimo had employed to cement the Medici hold on Florence. From the beginning Lorenzo was both crass and sloppy in his management of investments and debts. He gave his branch managers in Milan, Bruges and Rome far too little responsibility and mixed Medici money with the public purse, making bank loans to other princes without much collateral and letting his firm's financial needs dictate Florence's foreign policy. Florentine patricians who opposed him politically soon got their taxes raised.

Inevitably, some in Florence feared or envied Lorenzo's wealth and increasingly autocratic manner. In 1478 opposition came to a head. The Pazzi, another Florentine banking family, whom Lorenzo had manoeuvred out of a delectable tax monopoly, joined forces with Pope Sixtus IV, angry from losing a diplomatic gambit to the Medici, and decided to assassinate both him and his brother Giuliano. Their justification was the restoration of Florentine liberty, for which the hot-blooded Pazzi youths carrying out the deed attacked the brothers in the most public possible place – at Easter Mass in Florence's cathedral. Giuliano they stabbed to death, but Lorenzo managed to escape. The hoped-for public uprising against the Medici never materialized and, once Lorenzo had mobilized his allies, he took pitiless revenge on the entire Pazzi clan, along with such secret co-conspirators as the archbishop of Pisa, who was hanged from a window in Florence's Palazzo della Signoria.

With the Pazzi Conspiracy successfully crushed, Lorenzo took advantage of public fears and his fresh popularity to create a powerful security state that he could control through his own supporters. No longer simply a private citizen, he ruled Florence without serious opposition for the rest of his life. Able, with his adroit diplomacy, to control the balance of power on the peninsula, Lorenzo now felt free to indulge in his cultural passions and become a full-time patron of learning and the arts. Philosophers and poets such as Marsilio Ficino and Pico della Mirandola flocked to the city, looking for financial support or at least a good place for dinner and discussions. For painters and sculptors, Lorenzo established Europe's first academy of art – briefly home to the young Michelangelo – and although he himself commissioned few works from the likes of Ghirlandaio or Botticelli, he enjoyed serving as a broker, tying up his wealthy friends with the most fashionable artists.

Lorenzo spent lavishly on himself, driving his bank to the edge of bankruptcy less by patronizing living artists than by collecting – Greek and Latin books for his Laurentian Library and masses of antique statuary, jewels, coins and medals for his villas. Many praised his cultivated tastes for ushering in a new Florentine Golden Age, and it was not just the usual sycophants who called him *Il Magnifico* ('the Magnificent'). Yet Lorenzo built no foundation to extend or protect his cultured world. Two years after he died, his Golden Age crumbled in the face of an invading foreign army and the endless bickering of local rulers. With it also went the Medici, as Lorenzo's feckless son Piero ('the Unfortunate') was driven from the city by an upsurge of republicans who abruptly decided they were fed up with refined tastes and one-family rule.

CR

Luca Pacioli

Although he was a Franciscan friar, Luca Pacioli's interests ran less towards theology than towards science, mathematics and mysticism. As a youth he had been apprenticed to a painter – Piero della Francesca, one of the most talented and influential artists of the early Renaissance. Although Piero had the usual team of apprentices, some of whom later became famous, there is no sign that he actually taught Luca painting. Instead, the boy was schooled as befitted his special gifts and his master's own interests – in science, numbers, geometry and their application to the arts of proportion and perspective.

Pacioli left Piero in 1464 to spend a few years in Venice, where he studied mathematics and was supposedly exposed to the perspectival skills of Gentile and Giovanni Bellini. Then he travelled to Rome, where he became a pupil and friend of Leon Battista Alberti, papal secretary and the leading humanist scholar on painting and architecture. Here Pacioli continued his private study of mathematics and geometry, remaining in Rome until Alberti's death in 1472. He then joined the Franciscans, attracted by the order's preaching traditions but also interested in the opportunities it offered to teach; shortly afterwards, he was given the newly established chair of mathematics at the University of Perugia.

After several decades teaching mathematics at universities and privately, Pacioli put all his experience together in a grand volume published in Venice in 1494, called *Summa de arithmetica, geometria, proportioni et proportionalita*. Although the *Summa* contained little that was truly new, it lived up to its title in summarizing the state of mathematics in the late 15th century, a time when numerate scholarship did not yet fully differentiate between the applied and the theoretical. While the first, second and fifth sections of the *Summa* dealt with arithmetic, algebra and Euclidian geometry, the third provided tables of weights, measures and monetary exchange rates. In the fourth, on the other hand, Pacioli offered a guide to double-entry bookkeeping. It was the first time anyone had ever summarized how to manage debits and credits in this way, and it has earned Pacioli the accolade of 'Father of Accounting'.

The fame generated by his *Summa* soon garnered Pacioli an invitation from Ludovico Sforza, duke of Milan, to join a court filled 'with the most astute architects, and engineers, and finders of new things'. Chief among these was Leonardo da Vinci, with whom Pacioli got along famously; he later reminisced about those 'happy times when we were in the same service in the marvellous city of Milan'. Pacioli began tutoring Leonardo in arithmetic and geometry, and they kept up their friendship even after the French conquest of Milan in 1499 forced them to flee – first to Modena and then to Florence, where they kept in close contact until 1506.

His friendship with Leonardo liberated Pacioli from his somewhat pedestrian concerns with bookkeeping and arithmetic, and inspired grander speculations. In the late 1490s he worked on what was arguably his masterpiece, *De divina proportione* ('On the divine proportion'), in which he asserted that it was mathematics 'that constitutes the measure and test of all ... sciences and disciplines', since 'it was clear', Pacioli claimed, 'that all other sciences are only opinion, and only these [mathematical truths] can be called certainties.' The eternal and essentially irrational nature of such geometric forms as the circle and square, the five Platonic solids and the so-called Golden Ratio were for Pacioli evidence of their divine origin, as was their role in making perspective, architecture, musical harmonies and the human form aesthetically pleasing. Leonardo illustrated *De divina proportione* with etchings of complex polyhedra, whose sides and vertices Pacioli claimed had a symbolic and material place in every science from theology to astronomy to military arts. In return, Pacioli is said to have helped Leonardo with the theology of the *Last Supper*.

While writing *De divina proportione*, Pacioli began his last study, *De viribus quantitatis* ('On the power of numbers'). The work was never published, but like his other books it was a summary – this time a collection of mathematical puzzles, magic tricks and proverbs. Besides a series of logic and number games involving stacks of coins, baskets of eggs or men in a lifeboat, Pacioli showed how to do card tricks, eat fire, juggle and make an egg walk across a table. For Pacioli there was nothing absurd about jumping from the eternal verities of proportion to brainteasers and conjuring tricks: mathematical puzzles, with their very long pedigrees, directly connected his time to the age of Euclid and Pythagoras. With them the verities of numbers were revealed in human exchange, much in the same way as the *Fables* of Aesop revealed moral truths. Besides, as Pacioli noted, when the *savant* managed to pull off one of these tricks, 'to the uneducated ... it will seem like a miracle.'

CR

Sandro Botticelli

FROM PAGAN SCENES TO APOCALYPTIC THEMES

1445–1510

The seventh of eight children, Alessandro Botticelli was born in 1445 to a Florentine tanner and his wife. The boy began training as a goldsmith but preferred painting, and around 1460 he joined the workshop of Fra Filippo Lippi, a highly regarded artist whose patrons included Cosimo de' Medici. Botticelli learned quickly, recreating the elder artist's puckish blond angels and translucent skin tones with ease. He also adapted Lippi's distinct method of outlining shapes – a hand, a jawline, the curve of a lip – in sharp black, creating crisply defined edges between fields of smooth, lustrous colour. Botticelli used a line of black paint as if he were drawing, which showcased his superb draughtsmanship, and he refined the technique throughout his life.

Having reached master status in the late 1460s, Botticelli established his own workshop in Florence, and in the 1470s began his long association with the Medici family. He created his most famous works for them along with some not so famous ones, such as a banner for Giuliano de' Medici to carry across the Piazza Santa Croce before a jousting tournament. Botticelli's *Adoration of the Magi* (1475) is a paean to the Medici men: Cosimo kneels before the Virgin as his sons Piero and Giovanni and grandsons Lorenzo and Giuliano look on handsomely. On the far right of the scene a fair-haired man – a self-portrait of Botticelli – looks out at the viewer.

Botticelli's most productive period was from about 1478 to 1490. The *Adoration of the Magi* drew the attention of Pope Sixtus IV, who was then completing a new building in the Vatican – the Sistine Chapel – and in 1481 he summoned Botticelli and other leading artists to Rome to fresco the interior. During his year in the Eternal City Botticelli painted *Scenes from the Life of Moses*, *The Temptation of Christ* and *The Punishment of Korah* on the chapel walls, and, in the upper niches, portraits of past popes. After completing the frescoes in 1482, Botticelli returned to Florence, where in addition to regular Medici commissions he did a brisk business with upper middle-class families seeking fashionable art for their homes. He created a number of pricey tondi (round paintings with labour-intensive circular frames), as well as *spalliere* (narrative scenes on panels that were set into wainscoting or on to chests or benches).

Botticelli's clients commissioned sacred works – such as altarpieces and Madonnas – as well as profane ones – scenes of anti-Medici conspirators being hanged, for example, which were displayed publicly to deter the family's remaining enemies. In the 1480s he finished his best-known works, *Primavera* and *The Birth of Venus*, both large paintings with mythological scenes, life-size figures and complex symbolic imagery. Commissioned by the Medici, they follow the Neoplatonic fashion of the day, although the settings seem oddly flat, and some figures – Venus herself, for instance – have unnaturally elongated arms and necks. An excellent draughtsman who understood the principles of perspective, Botticelli seemed to reject some of the new artistic ideas in favour of a more stylized approach that was all his own.

One of his most ambitious Medici commissions was a series of illuminations for a lavish manuscript copy of Dante's *Divine Comedy*, which he began in the early 1480s and worked on well into the 1490s. Botticelli's biographer Giorgio Vasari noted in his *Lives of the Artists* (1550) that the artist read and re-read Dante's text and spent so much time on the project that he neglected other commissions. The poem affected Botticelli profoundly and may have influenced his work, which took on a starker, more serious quality around 1490. Florence was undergoing a similar shift itself at this time, in thrall as it was to the fire-and-brimstone preacher Girolamo Savonarola, who considered art with Classical themes to be pagan heresy. Botticelli's brother was a devoted follower of Savonarola; the artist himself seems to have been a supporter, but how passionate he was is unclear. The preacher's apocalyptic vision certainly informed his later art, particularly the *Mystical Nativity* (1501). At the top, an error-ridden Greek inscription refers to the Book of Revelation, for example, while small demons cavort at the bottom of the painting – an unusual addition to a Nativity scene. Meanwhile, the angels dancing in a ring above the manger carry ribbons inscribed with lines from one of the preacher's allegorical writings.

Botticelli continued to paint during the last decade of his life, but his style remained static. Compared with innovations by other artists in Florence – especially Leonardo da Vinci and Michelangelo – Botticelli's work seemed increasingly old-fashioned. By the time he died, his popularity had already waned, and for centuries he was largely forgotten. In 1874 the English critic John Ruskin resurrected his art, praising it as 'beyond all other work in Italy' and giving rise to a cult of Botticelli that continues to this day.

☙

Josquin des Prez

RESTLESS CHOIRMASTER, STAR COMPOSER

c. 1450–1521

Although enormously significant in Renaissance music, Josquin des Prez remains a shadowy figure. Born in Picardy-Hainaut, in northern France, Josquin was orphaned young. Later he picked up the Flemish nickname van de Velde, 'of the Fields', rendered in French as des Prés or des Prez. Reportedly he sang in the cathedral choir in nearby Saint-Quentin, although church accounts of the time have long since been destroyed. He does not definitively appear in the historical record until 1477, when he turned up at the other end of France, in the ducal choir in Aix-en-Provence. For years he remained on the move, searching for lucrative positions as a singer–composer. He may have spent the early 1480s in Paris, Ferrara or even in Hungary, but in 1483 he was definitely in the choir of Duke Sforza of Milan. From there he passed into the service of the duke's brother Ascanio Sforza, bishop of Pavia, and when Ascanio was made a cardinal in 1484, Josquin accompanied him to Rome. Before long he had won a place in the papal choir. Very possibly this was when he, like generations of Vatican choristers, carved his name on the Sistine Chapel wall – the only example of his autograph known to exist.

Although the position was prestigious, Josquin did not remain as a Vatican chorister for long. By 1498 he was back working for Duke Sforza, and when Milan was conquered by the French in 1499, he may have returned to France. A few years later he returned to Italy, this time to work for Duke Ercole I d'Este of Ferrara. Although Ercole's court was one of the most musically active in Italy, Josquin stayed in his choir just a few years before an outbreak of the plague sent him fleeing back to France. Only then, at the age of about 50, did he finally settle down, finishing his life in Condé-sur-l'Escaut, not far from his birthplace.

Josquin's wanderings allowed him to forge a link between the two great musical schools then current. In his native Franco-Flemish tradition the emphasis on counterpoint created a dense, highly ornamented polyphony that aimed for transcendent serenity, often at the cost of rendering the text incomprehensible. The more lyrical and homophonic Italian style, which Josquin first encountered in Milan, followed the humanist approach, by contrast, in which text was primary and music played a supporting role. Although he remained true to his native style, Josquin learned enough about Italian harmonic energy and its clearly expressed lyrics to synthesize it successfully with the melodic inventiveness and tranquillity of the north. From this blend emerged the graceful High Renaissance polyphony that would become associated with his name.

Already widespread in Italy and France, Josquin's fame, especially as a composer of secular music, was assured in 1501, when Ottaviano Petrucci (1466–1539), a printer in Venice, included him in the first ever collection of musical scores printed with movable type. Petrucci called his work – an anthology of French part songs by Josquin and other (largely French and Flemish) composers – *Harmonice Musices Odhecaton* ('One hundred [songs] of harmonious music'). The *Odhecaton* revolutionized European musical culture. Previously, musical scores had been drawn by hand, or at best printed with clumsy, often incomplete woodcuts – singers might have to draw in their own staves. Petrucci's *Odhecaton* represented the first mass-produced musical text, costing a twentieth the price of older versions while also accurately rendering the increasingly popular Franco-Flemish polyphonic style. Singers or instrumentalists of the four-part songs dominating the book found their individual scores laid out, two on each side on facing pages, in a highly readable manner that made the music easy to learn and perform.

After his *Odhecaton* had introduced Josquin's name to a musical audience beyond court and cathedral, Petrucci published dozens more anthologies of songs, masses, motets and Italian-based *frottole* (precursors to the madrigal).

The inexpensive collections helped fuel a new, international style of music – the first in Europe since Gregorian chant six centuries earlier. At its core were Josquin's songs, based on his syncretic blend of northern and southern styles. More than willing to profit from the opportunities offered by this new technology, Josquin responded with a prodigious output of new vocal and instrumental texts, both sacred and secular. By the time of his death, at around 70, he had composed some 370 works. Many other pieces, not quite in Josquin's style, were also published by admiring contemporaries under his name, apparently hoping to cash in on the fame of the modern era's first international musical star.

❧

Aldus Manutius

PRINTER AND PURVEYOR OF POCKET BOOKS

1450?–1515

The information industry arrived in Venice with a bang, barely a decade after Gutenberg published his first Bible. Within five years the city had experienced a classic new-technology boom-to-bust. First the presses multiplied like mushrooms, churning out scores of humanist, Classical and religious works. Having exceeded market demand for an untested product, printer after printer then promptly went bankrupt. By 1473 a few consolidated publishing houses were picking up the pieces – playing it safe by focusing on religious works for cathedrals and monasteries, where demand, although limited, was at least steady.

Nevertheless, Venice was still Europe's leading publishing centre when Aldus Manutius arrived there in the late 1480s. Coming from the Papal States (he signed his name 'Aldus the Roman'), he had received the best in humanist education, boasting proficiency in Latin and Greek letters and good connections with top scholars and several princes. For a while his career was that of a typical humanist – teaching the Classics to aristocratic youths and writing Latin and Greek grammars to earn a little on the side. Aldus had greater dreams, however, and these eventually brought him to Venice.

Like many humanists after the fall of Constantinople, Aldus feared that the scattering of Greek scholars and their libraries could cause Greek literature itself to disappear for ever. Believing that he had responsibilities to the works he had been taught to love, Aldus took up the printing business to confront that risk – not as an artisan seeking a living, but as a scholar and a preservationist. His choice of Venice was an easy one: the city was not only pre-eminent in printing, but also home to thousands of Greek refugees. Some owned Classical volumes for Aldus to copy; others would work for him as grammarians, typesetters and proofreaders.

It took about six years for Aldus to secure enough long-term loans to get his press up and running. He also had to design and cast type fonts for Classical Greek, which, unlike Latin, still existed in multiple versions, some containing hundreds of individual letters, diacriticals, abbreviations and ligatures. After a few test runs of light poetry and grammars, he launched what would become his first triumph: a complete Aristotle (1495–98). Running to five folio volumes (measuring 31 × 21 cm, or 12¼ × 8¼ in.), the Aldine Aristotle, as it is called, offered readers the first ever standardized rendition of the Western world's greatest philosopher, in highly legible 'plain text' – Aristotle shorn of the commentaries and emendations that had encrusted his work over the centuries.

The Aldine Press then tackled the remaining Greek canon, including Homer, Thucydides, Herodotus, Sophocles, Euripides and Demosthenes – fifty-eight different volumes in all, including thirty works never published before. All were printed in plain text, without the traditional annotations that could both distract and comfort readers. This may explain why none of these works made Aldus rich, since only around 5 per cent of humanist scholars were skilled enough in Greek to read them without notes. Consequently, although Greek letters remained his core activity and personal passion, Aldus increasingly brought out Latin and Italian works of both Classical and contemporary authors. It was in designing these works – which actually generated a profit for the press – that Aldus revolutionized both printing and the entire world of literature.

One of these innovations was a completely new format. Working with his long-term punch cutter, or letter designer, Francesco Griffo, Aldus developed cursive script – what foreign book dealers soon called 'italic'. The typeface allowed more words on the page than traditional Roman or Gothic while remaining highly readable. Aldus premiered cursive in his edition of the works of Virgil (1501), which he printed in a radically reduced octavo format (8.5 × 15 cm, or 3½ × 6 in.). In his advertising broadsheets (also an Aldine innovation) he called his reduced-sized editions *libri portatiles*, and they were just that: 'portable books', no longer confined to libraries but available for anyone to slip into a pocket.

Aldus's other advances were no less significant. He was the first to systematize punctuation in its modern form; he also originated the practice of page numbering. Aldus fell short in just two areas. He was unable to assemble the scholars or the funds to publish the first Polyglot Bible – that honour would go to the Spanish – and he failed to set up his longed-for Greek 'New Academy' of like-minded Hellenist *savants*. His main legacy was his press. Under Aldus's son and grandson, the Aldine Press continued publishing until 1597, bringing out over 900 editions (many with print runs in the thousands) and realizing Aldus's dream of preserving the Classical canon so central to the humanist enterprise.

❦
Leonardo da Vinci
'THIS MAN WILL NEVER DO ANYTHING'
1452–1519

Throughout his life Leonardo da Vinci was hailed for his painting skills – his ability to reproduce natural phenomena such as rocks, vegetation and water while also capturing the dynamic grace of his human subjects. Yet his reputation was founded on very few examples – not even twelve completed works are assuredly his. Among these, however, are two of the most universally acclaimed works in the artistic canon, the *Last Supper* (1495–98) and the *Mona Lisa* (1503–19). Neither painting is now much to look at: the first has essentially self-destructed because of Leonardo's faulty technique; the second is surprisingly small and retains little of its original warmth of colour. But, secure in their cultural Parnassus, they have generated centuries of adoration and debate, making it difficult to realize how revolutionary both were in their day.

Leonardo's life can be broken down into three periods. The first began with his birth as the illegitimate son of a provincial Tuscan notary, lasting through his apprenticeship until his flowering as a young artist in Florence. Then, at around the age of 30 and with the encouragement of Lorenzo de' Medici, Leonardo moved to Milan, where he spent the bulk of his adulthood as court artist, set designer and engineer for Duke Ludovico Sforza. After the French conquered the city in 1499, Leonardo's life began its last, highly unsettled phase, as he wandered between various Italian cities – Modena, Florence, Rome and back to Milan again – before ending his life at Amboise, in the Loire Valley, as the pensioned guest and friend of the French king François I.

Roaming from place to place and from project to project, Leonardo was renowned for abandoning assignments. He continually signed contracts – with convents, confraternities, even governments – received advance money, laid out preliminary designs, began painting and then left for another commission or client. He was easily distracted: painting bored him, and he rarely progressed in a linear fashion. Watching him at work, Pope Leo X (who did not offer him a contract) supposedly complained, 'This man will never do anything. Here he is thinking about finishing the work before he even starts it!'

Although his contemporaries raved about Leonardo's artistic skills and insight into nature, when he set out to list his talents in 1481, he stressed above all his ability as a theatrical set designer and military engineer; only at the end did he mention that he could paint. During his years with Ludovico Sforza, he churned out endless plans to revolutionize Milanese fortifications, armaments and drainage, proposing entirely new approaches in such industries as metal founding, excavation and power generation. Few of these schemes ever materialized. At best, they ended up like his design for an equestrian statue of Ludovico's father, Francesco – partly realized, then abandoned and later destroyed by the Milanese, who had little interest in bankrolling a monument to the Sforzas' dynastic glory.

Almost by default, Leonardo's modern reputation largely rests on his notebooks. This vast hoard of private papers – some 8,000 folio sheets, many written on both sides, some barely hand size – was collected after his death. Freely mixing text and sketches, Leonardo used his notebooks to record observations, to work out ideas and sometimes simply to fantasize. He intended to publish some of his musings on artistic theory but never did so. To ward off the casual snooper, he wrote all his notes backwards.

Secretive as he was with his ideas, much of Leonardo's genius remained hidden from contemporaries – despite his occasional boasts or sly hints – and most of his ground-breaking insights into optics, astronomy, human anatomy, mechanics and flight had to be rediscovered or reinvented by later thinkers. Still, he did broadcast one overarching conviction – that deductive modes of medieval scholasticism had to be abandoned for direct and careful observation of nature: 'instead of [wasting time] defining the soul, which is a thing that cannot be seen, [it is] much better to study those things that can be known with experience, because only experience does not fail.'

Yet Leonardo also rejected humanism, which in his view, after a century of re-energizing Western thought, had followed scholasticism into worshipping authority. Inevitably, his insistence on direct, personal experience alienated him from the humanist academic establishment, and he reacted bitterly. Having mastered Latin only in his thirties and having never learned Greek, he complained that 'I well know how, since I am not well read, some pre-sumptuous types think they can denigrate me as a man without letters. Stupid people! ... They don't realize that my concerns are more things to be dealt with through experience than through the writings of others.' Ultimately, the genius of his age died with his best art unpainted and his best thoughts unread, leaving behind few followers but a great many unrealized dreams.

❧

King João II

'THE PERFECT PRINCE'

1455–1495

Known to his Spanish adversaries as 'el tirano' ('the tyrant'), King João II was called *O Principe Perfeito* ('the Perfect Prince') by his fellow Portuguese. It was a reference not to his good manners, but rather to the ruthless and amoral way he secured and held royal power, using the same techniques that Niccolò Machiavelli would famously outline in *The Prince*. Crowned in 1481, João found his treasury depleted by the African military adventures of his father, Alfonso V, and a nobility conspiring against him with neighbouring Spain. Biding his time to discover just who his enemies were, the new king then unleashed a judicial terror, abruptly arresting and executing the duke of Bragança, chief of the plotters, for conspiring with Queen Isabella of Spain. He rapidly dispatched scores of others, including the bishop of Évora, poisoned while in prison, and his own cousin, whom he personally stabbed to death. The survivors were forced in public to swear a new, highly detailed oath of allegiance to their king.

Having dealt with his nobility, João could grant greater commercial freedom to the merchants in cities that had long chafed under tight aristocratic control. Although convinced that Portugal's economic fortunes lay abroad, João was not inclined to pursue his father's programme of conquests in Morocco. Instead, he followed the lead of his great uncle, Prince Henry the Navigator, who had set Portugal on a course of exploration abroad. Under Henry's sponsorship, successive expeditions had already settled the Azores, Madeira and Cape Verde archipelagos off the West African coast. Explorers then pushed south, below Mauritania, and, if the African coast was too dangerous for settlements, Portuguese caravels could at least bypass the established trans-Sahara routes for the profitable trade in spices, gold and slaves.

By Prince Henry's death in 1460, the Portuguese were regularly venturing as far afield in Africa as the empire of Benin. Royal support for such policies largely ended under Alfonso V, however, and was resumed only when João began energetically sending out new expeditions early in his reign. In 1482 he established a new Portuguese fortress, trading centre and town at São Jorge da Mina (Elmina, in modern-day Ghana). From there his expeditions could range much further: Diogo Cão reached the mouth of the Congo in 1484, and Bartolomeu Dias passed the southern tip of Africa in 1488. Although spectacular for its time, Dias's journey was actually just half of a two-pronged experiment devised by João and his 'council of scholars'. That same year João sent expeditions to explore both the Red Sea and the Persian Gulf routes to India, exploring east Africa as far south as Mozambique in the process. This twin effort made it clear to the king that there was indeed a sea route to India, one that Portugal could fully control. As a sign of his optimism, he changed the name Dias had given to the southern tip of Africa from Cabo das Tormentas ('Cape of Storms') to Cabo da Boa Esperança ('Cape of Good Hope').

While João's aggressive imperial programme greatly enriched his small country, it also reignited a series of colonial disputes with Spain, which had its own exploration schemes (the two nations had been squabbling over the Canary Islands since the 1450s). That dispute was resolved by the Treaty of Alcáçovas (1479), which gave the Canaries to Spain but promised everything south of there to the Portuguese. João's brief monopoly came to a sudden end in March 1493, however, when Christopher Columbus, sailing for Spain, stopped off in Lisbon with stories of newly discovered lands in the west – islands, he claimed, off the Asian coast. João immediately denounced Columbus as an intruder into Portuguese waters and threatened the Spanish with war. King Ferdinand of Spain doubted that those western seas held anything worth fighting for, but he still quickly sent the news to the (Spanish) pope, Alexander VI, who obligingly granted the Spanish all lands located more than 100 leagues (555 kilometres) west of the Azores and Cape Verde Islands. João was enraged, but during negotiations he managed to keep his anger under control, at least in front of the Spanish and papal ambassadors. His restraint paid off: the resulting Treaty of Tordesillas (7 June 1494) moved the boundary line 1,500 kilometres further west. Ten years later it was revealed that this new arrangement had given the Portuguese claim to a large slice of Brazil. Some suspect that, thanks to earlier, secret expeditions, João already knew that a New World lay beyond this line, but he never admitted it. Instead, for the remaining year of his life, he plunged into planning Portugal's breakthrough voyage to India, finally accomplished by Vasco da Gama in 1498.

CR

Antonio Rinaldeschi

GAMBLER AND BLASPHEMER

died 1501

Almost the only thing known about Antonio Rinaldeschi is that he was very unpleasant. He was born into minor Tuscan nobility, and his father, Giovanni, had enough property to make a will – in which he called Antonio an 'unworthy heir', possibly because the young man beat him. After Giovanni died in 1500, Antonio fought with his stepmother and half-sisters over the inheritance. After settling in court, he mostly frittered away his share, drinking and gambling. Some claimed he was demented by the ravages of syphilis.

On 11 July 1501 Rinaldeschi's intemperance took him over the edge. Playing dice in Florence, at the Fig Tree tavern, he lost his money, his cloak and his temper. While leaving his companions, he cursed the Virgin Mary; like many gamblers of his day, he identified her with Lady Luck. Not far away, he went further, picking up a handful of donkey dung from the street and throwing it at a fresco of the Virgin painted above the doorway of the church of Santa Maria degli Alberighi. Although apparently no one saw him, Antonio panicked at his own impiety and rushed off to hide in a villa outside town.

Discovering the sacrilege, the police asked around and soon heard about Rinaldeschi's cursing the Virgin at the Fig Tree. By 21 July they had tracked their man down to a suburban convent, where, at the moment of arrest, he all but admitted his guilt by trying to kill himself with a dagger. Bleeding but not seriously wounded, Rinaldeschi was taken to the city prison, the Bargello, where he was accused of gambling, blasphemy and attempted suicide. He confessed, to the judges and to a priest, and was hanged that night from a window of the Bargello.

Although Rinaldeschi's crimes were not usually capital offences, these were nervous times in Florence. A few years earlier the Medici had been driven out and the millenarian preacher Girolamo Savonarola executed. The comparative stability of the 15th century had vanished, as members of the pro-Medici elite, Savonarola's stubborn faithful, and radical republicans all jostled for power. Meanwhile foreign and Italian armies threatened Florentine liberty: just two months before Rinaldeschi's mishap the unscrupulous Cesare Borgia had camped his army under the city walls until given a huge bribe to leave. At such times who would risk divine wrath by overlooking such blasphemous deeds?

Yet Rinaldeschi's misbehaviour awoke popular piety as much as public fear. Although most of the dung thrown at the painting fell off, a small glob remained attached, 'seeming to almost be a dry [plaster] rosette' near the Virgin's head. Someone noticed how this resembled a diadem or crown, and soon a crowd had gathered before the church, excited that the Virgin had seemingly turned this insult into glory. They lit candles before the image; the archbishop came to have a look. After Rinaldeschi's execution the image was cleaned, but some trace of the 'crown' remained; it was said to possess healing powers, and the sick and crippled were soon hanging ex-votos on the wall. An act of sacrilege had generated a cult, and within a month the city authorities began demolishing the houses adjoining the church in order to build a shrine. By the 1520s the entire original piazza before the church had been enclosed, with the defiled painting moved to a position over the high altar.

Memory of this affair had largely fizzled out by the early 18th century. It would have disappeared altogether were it not for a painting commemorating the event by a minor Florentine artist in 1502. Composed in nine cartoon-like sub-panels, the work resembles a Renaissance predella, the small-scale, narrative painting commonly placed under an altarpiece. In minute and vivid detail it tells the full story of Rinaldeschi's rage, blasphemy, capture, trial and execution.

There is more to this work than crime and punishment. Although contemporary with Michelangelo's *David* and Leonardo's *Mona Lisa*, the panel was inspired by a very different spirit, one owing less to the Florentine humanism of Lorenzo de' Medici than to Savonarola's sermons of sin, redemption and salvation. The little devil fluttering around Rinaldeschi's head while urging him on in the first three panels is driven away in the fourth and replaced by an angel in the sixth and eighth, as the sinner chooses submission to the law and the Church. In the final panel Rinaldeschi, fully penitent, commits himself to God, as two angels successfully wrestle his soul away from his demons. Depraved by dice and dung in the early scenes, Antonio Rinaldeschi's misspent life ends with him abandoning sinful things and surrendering his pride for salvation. The panel was a sermon in paint, directed, during these tumultuous years, at the entire Florentine social order.

ℭℜ

4. Sudden Shocks

1490–1515

M any Europeans viewed the approach of the year 1500 with foreboding. They were not just troubled by the usual apocalyptic fears: it was more that their hard-won sense of stability and continuity, acquired over the previous two generations, seemed to be rapidly vanishing. Especially in Spain, the home of Europe's newest and most dynamic monarchy, changes were coming thick and fast. On 2 January 1492 the fortress palace of the Alhambra, the last Muslim stronghold in Spain, was surrendered to King Ferdinand II and Queen Isabella. So ended a 780-year crusade to retake the peninsula from Islam, although the spirit of Christian triumphalism that had animated the Spanish *Reconquista* continued to energize Spaniards well into the next century.

Ferdinand and Isabella wished, above all, to make Christianity universal in Spain, and so they set out to unravel a centuries-old social fabric woven of Christians, Moors and Jews. On 31 March 1492 the monarchs issued the Edict of Alhambra, demanding that, on pain of death, all Jews in the newly enlarged kingdom either convert to Christianity or depart. Only around 60,000 chose baptism, while between three and ten times that number (the exact figure is unknown) elected to emigrate. At a stroke the Spanish monarchy had purged the peninsula of both a 1,500-year-old social presence and a large part of its entrepreneurial and financial class. At the same time public unease about the religious reliability of the hundreds of thousands of newly baptized *conversos* created a climate of suspicion in the new nation. The recently formed Inquisition rushed to fill the new void in the Spanish social contract.

Barely two weeks after this edict, Ferdinand and Isabella agreed to fund the Genoese navigator Christopher Columbus in his scheme to reach Asia by sailing west. After Columbus came back in 1493, it took most Europeans – elites, scholars and ordinary men and women – nearly a generation to realize what he had accomplished. However, the Portuguese king, João II, was quick to accuse Spain of making an unfair claim on newly discovered lands and seas. The Treaty of Tordesillas (1494), by which Spain and Portugal settled their dispute and divided the world outside Europe between them, gained more attention among Europe's rulers than did Columbus's discoveries.

The year 1492 proved equally pivotal in Italy, for it marked the beginning of the rapid collapse of the peninsula's long-standing balance of power. On 9 April, Lorenzo de' Medici, the de facto ruler of his native Florence and a guiding force behind a long period of Italian peace, died at the age of only 43. Three months later came the death of Pope Innocent VIII, who was very much Lorenzo's creature and his relative by marriage. These sudden changes in the political landscapes of Spain and Italy reverberated widely throughout the European social order.

Spain's expulsion of the Jews had an immediate impact: a demographic tidal wave first hit neighbouring Portugal (where, for a few years, the Jewish refugees made up 10 per cent of the population) but soon reached further afield. This new diaspora rekindled the fraught questions of Jewish rights and identity in places where they had lain dormant for centuries. The arrival of Jewish immigrants in Antwerp and Amsterdam inspired attempts at assimilation but also sparked public violence. The Sephardic population around Venice grew so rapidly that in 1516 the Venetian Senate voted to invite the Jews into the city to settle in an enclosed compound they called the Ghetto. By far the most open-handed, however, was the Ottoman Sultan Bayezid II (c. 1448–1512), who so admired the Spanish Jews for their mercantile savvy that he sent his fleet to Granada to ferry them to the Levant. Declaring that King Ferdinand had 'beggared his own country and enriched mine', Bayezid established thriving Jewish communities in Thessaloniki, Sarajevo and Istanbul. In the last of these, they set up the first Levantine printing press as early as 1493, along with other Western novelties.

In four voyages, Columbus never produced concrete evidence that a route to Asia lay to the west, but his efforts spawned imitators in northern Europe, which lay closer to the lands he had found. As early as 1496, England's Henry VII, annoyed by the presumptuous Treaty of Tordesillas, began to organize his own voyages, commissioning the Venetian explorer John Cabot to seek the fabled Northwest Passage on England's behalf. After Cabot's modest and ultimately unsuccessful attempts came a steady stream of English and French fishermen, who were soon uncovering vast and extremely profitable new fishing grounds around the 'New Found Land' that he had discovered.

The power vacuum left in Italy by Lorenzo's death in 1492 – and by that of Don Ferrante, king of Naples, two years later – lured first the French and then the Spanish to try their luck at snapping up whatever Italian statelets might be available. For the next sixty years the two sides fought a series of highly destructive campaigns for control of the peninsula. Even the papacy fell into Spanish hands for a while, when Cardinal Rodrigo Borgia purchased for himself the throne of St Peter, in one of the most corrupt papal elections ever held. When Borgia, calling himself Pope Alexander VI, claimed his prize on 11 August 1492, Lorenzo's second son, Giovanni de' Medici – no idealist himself – supposedly exclaimed, 'Now we are in the power of a wolf, the most rapacious perhaps that this world has ever seen. And if we do not flee, he will inevitably devour us all.' In the event, Alexander and his children did their best to fulfil his prophecy.

❧

Christopher Columbus

'ADMIRAL OF THE OCEAN SEA'

1451–1506

C hristopher Columbus, the son of a weaver and part-time cheese vendor, was also a son of Genoa, and like many Genoese he went to sea for his living. In his youth he visited the Levant and reportedly sailed to Guinea, England, Ireland and possibly even Iceland. By the early 1470s he was in Lisbon, where his brother Bartolomeo had found work as a cartographer. Combining his practical navigational experience with Bartolomeo's geographical training, Columbus arrived at the defining conviction of his life – that it was possible to reach the spice-rich islands of the East by sailing west. For much of the next twenty years, often reduced to poverty, Columbus pleaded his cause to any who would give him a hearing – the kings of Spain and Portugal, the Genoese and Venetians, even the English. All of them turned him down.

Although many agreed that 'since Genoa was Genoa, there was never born a man so well equipped and expert in the art of navigation' as Columbus, few rulers of his day had the time, money or interest to invest in his scheme. Those who seriously studied their geography believed – quite rightly, as it happened – that he had grossly underestimated the size of the globe and exaggerated the length of Eurasia, reckoning that the shores of China were only a fifth of the distance from Europe that they actually were. At last, however, Columbus persuaded Ferdinand and Isabella of Spain to overrule their advisers and supply the necessary funds and ships for his projected voyage. Somewhat prematurely, they also appointed him Admiral of the Ocean Sea and Viceroy of the Indies.

Columbus and 120 men set out on 3 August 1492 with a carrack (the *Santa Maria*) and two caravels (the *Niña* and the *Pinta*). He sailed first to the Canary Islands and then, on 6 September, left the known world behind him, heading west. After only five weeks of steady winds, on 11 October one of his sailors scooped a fresh flower from the sea; the next day the ships made landfall on a small island somewhere in the modern-day Bahamas that Columbus named San Salvador. He then proceeded along the northern shore of Cuba – 'the most beautiful island the human eye has ever seen' – established a fort on Hispaniola and set sail for home, arriving back in Spain on 15 March 1493.

The expedition returned with a little gold, no spices, some tobacco, a few parrots and around ten natives whom Columbus had kidnapped. He had not found Japan or the Spice Islands, and he had lost his carrack, the *Santa Maria*, which sank off Hispaniola. Still, the Spanish were excited by this new direction to their imperial enterprise, and they embraced Columbus as a hero. He easily attracted 1,200 volunteers and seventeen ships for a return trip six months later. Like his first voyage, Columbus's second (1493–96), third (1498–1500) and fourth (1502–4) expeditions were characterized by a mixture of visionary plans, great discoveries, bungled opportunities and chronic misreadings of geography. Although he proved expert at crossing the North Atlantic by riding its elliptical, clockwise winds, he ignored the mounting evidence that he had not reached 'the Isles of India beyond the Ganges'. At the mouth of the River Orinoco, where it was obvious that so much fresh water could come only from the high mountains of a great continent, Columbus insisted that the continent was Asia and the mountains were in Paradise. Voyaging along the coast of Panama, he heard rumours from local people that a vast new sea lay just a few days' journey inland, but he was persuaded by a dream not to pursue the matter.

Besides his failings as a navigator, Columbus was also a terrible administrator. Regularly deserting his settlements to go exploring, and unable to maintain authority, he was by turns neglectful and harsh, brutalizing settlers until they mutinied and sent him back to Spain in chains. He was cruel to the natives he encountered, massacring some and coercing others into looking for gold or supplying food. Those who fled, he hunted down with dogs, and he horrified the queen by boasting that he could supply 'as many idolatrous slaves as your Majesties desire'.

Columbus ended his days broken, loitering on the fringes of the Spanish court, increasingly delusional about the many wrongs he thought had been done to him. In truth, the world had moved on from his great vision. Spanish settlers and fortune seekers flocked to the Caribbean, not as a way-station to the East but as a busy colony in its own right. It was left to Vasco da Gama, sailing in the other direction in 1498, to pioneer for Portugal the most practical sea route to the Indies. Three years later, on a Portuguese expedition to chart the coast of Brazil, another Italian, Amerigo Vespucci, made his own navigational calculations and concluded that Columbus had been wrong: this was indeed a new world.

☙ John Cabot

SAILOR FROM VENICE, EXPLORER FROM ENGLAND

c. 1451–1498

Having come to Venice as a boy and received citizenship there in 1475, John Cabot (born Giovanni Caboto) made his way as other Venetians had done for centuries – buying and selling goods in the Levant. His son Sebastiano later claimed that Cabot got as far as Mecca and marvelled at the spices and silks brought there by caravan. He asked where all these riches came from, but no one knew – only that they originated still further east. Some have speculated that at this point Cabot, well aware that religious conflict had closed the old Silk Road to Christians, began dreaming of another way to get at the source of all this wealth.

Cabot's commercial fantasies apparently exceeded his business skills, for in 1488 he went bankrupt and had to flee Venice to escape his creditors. After wandering a few years, he settled in Valencia, just as Christopher Columbus passed through on his triumphant tour of Spain in 1493. Hearing the story of the great man's first voyage, and convinced that Columbus had not sailed far enough to have actually reached China, Cabot petitioned the Spanish monarchs to fund a voyage along a more northerly route. As they already had an explorer, they turned him down.

Then Cabot tried his luck in England. He had reason to be optimistic. The English famously chafed under the Treaty of Tordesillas of 1494, which divided the globe between Spain and Portugal. Moreover, the sailors of Bristol were already experienced at exploring the northern and western Atlantic, as far as Iceland and beyond. Still, it took Cabot over a year to drum up the necessary financing from Italian bankers in London and Bristol merchants.

On 5 March 1496 Cabot's friends finally persuaded Henry VII to issue him a royal patent for a northern voyage, backing his intrusion into Spanish waters while giving him commercial monopoly rights over any wealth and lands 'of heathens and infidels' that he might discover. Although Henry's patent ordered the Bristol merchants to make five 'ships or vessels' available, they gave Cabot only one that would float. Moving perhaps too hastily, he set sail in the summer of 1496, only to have his crew rebel over the badly outfitted ship, wretched weather and unknown seas. After a few weeks he was back in Bristol.

A year later, in early May 1497, Cabot tried again, with a crew of eighteen men on the tiny *Matthew*, which weighed just 50 tons. After five weeks he 'discovered, 700 leagues off', what he claimed was 'the mainland of the country of the Great [Khan]'. After landing just once, to take on supplies, Cabot coasted south for a month or so and then returned to Bristol on 6 August. Compared with Columbus's first voyage, this was a speedy and superficial trip. Cabot did ceremonially claim this 'New Found Land', planting not just an English flag but a Venetian one as well, but he found no native peoples – just some leather snares and a bone needle, which he brought back as proof of human habitation. Nor was his landfall precisely known, although subsequent consensus has settled on either Cape Bonavista, in Newfoundland, or Cape Breton Island. What Cabot did bring back, however, was some very good news for the Bristol men: he had located the Grand Banks – a fisherman's dream, where cod gathered in such dense schools that they could be taken from the sea with wicker chests. He even called his new-found land Bacallaos, the 'Land of Cod'.

Cabot was lionized on his return. He had given England a nationalistic boost, a territorial claim of its own and riches more tangible than spices or gold. 'Great honours are done to him,' wrote a fellow Venetian: 'he goes dressed in silk and calls himself the Great Admiral.' Even the parsimonious Henry, who initially granted him a miserly £10 after the voyage, eventually funded one of Cabot's ships for the next journey. This was a much bigger affair – five ships and some three hundred men, including several London merchants and a contingent of friars. Cabot's little fleet set off in early

May 1498, but, with the exception of one ship that soon returned, it disappeared from history. Some contemporary letters and his son Sebastiano's reminiscences long afterwards suggest that a few of the explorers returned, but not Cabot himself. Perhaps he died on Bacallaos. When the Portuguese explorer Gaspar Corte-Real visited the area in 1501, the natives gave him what seem to have been the only remaining traces of the expedition – a broken Italian sword and some silver ear-rings of Venetian manufacture.

Girolamo Savonarola

FIRE IN FLORENCE

1452–1498

At the age of 20, when many of his peers were out hunting and carousing, Girolamo Savonarola sat inside, scribbling grim poems. In one, 'On the Ruin of the World', he laments that humanity is 'so pulled down by every vice/That it will never stand again.' His parents expected the sober young man to settle in his home town of Ferrara after graduating from the university there, and they were devastated when, in 1475, he stole away to join a monastery in Bologna. He wrote a tender letter to console his mother and father, but when they were still bereft months later, he was less patient. 'What are you crying about, you blind ones?' he wrote, insisting they celebrate the fact that Christ had chosen him as one of his militant knights.

In the spring of 1482 Savonarola was sent to Florence to teach logic at the Dominican convent of San Marco, where his duties also included community preaching. His unpolished delivery and odd northern accent repelled urbane Florentines, however, and when the humiliated friar was recalled to Bologna he worked to hone his speaking skills. Savonarola had impressed at least one man in Florence, though – the philosopher Giovanni Pico della Mirandola, who, with his friend Lorenzo de' Medici, brought Savonarola back to teach logic at San Marco. The tiny friar with an intense gaze and prominent nose returned in 1490, a far more polished, confident man than before.

Florence's century of success had created an upper class of wealthy, educated people with a taste for worldly goods. Savonarola thundered from the pulpit, castigating them for their tepid piety, greed and sensual pleasures, which Florence offered in abundance. He called to abolish the oligarchic government – an idea that comforted the poor and worried the rich – while clerics grew uneasy as he claimed that Christ spoke through him. As the friar's two to three-hour sermons grew increasingly apocalyptic, current events added to the city's anxiety: Lorenzo's recent death had destabilized Florence, France threatened to invade Italy, and looming ahead was the year 1500, which for many Christians heralded the end of times.

Savonarola's followers grew quickly in number and intensity: opponents dubbed them 'the wailers' for their habit of weeping during the friar's sermons. He enlisted children to report relatives' and neighbours' immoral behaviour, and during Carnival boys and girls were dressed in white and paraded through the streets to disrupt festive debauchery. They searched the city for playing cards, mirrors, pagan-themed art, wigs and titillating books – anything that smacked of impiety – and piled them in the main government square to be burned in Savonarola's massive Bonfires of the Vanities. Untold pieces of precious art perished; even Botticelli was said to have cast many of his own paintings into the flames.

Claiming to know the future, Savonarola predicted that the city's sins would soon bring God's wrath; when in 1494 Charles VIII of France arrived with an army, the friar fairly crowed with vindication. Wicked Florence needed punishing, he declared, and he warmly greeted the puzzled French monarch, essentially thanking him for the invasion. Charles left Florence unscathed, but the incident convinced even more people of the friar's special link to God. By the mid-1490s crowds of 15,000 were thronging to his sermons in Florence's massive cathedral, where he stirred up civic pride by proclaiming Florence a New Jerusalem that would beget a purer Catholic faith.

Having caught wind of events in Tuscany, Pope Alexander VI summoned the friar to Rome in 1495 to discuss his divine revelations and his plans to remake Christianity. Rightly suspicious, Savonarola refused to go, and thus began a battle between the little friar and the Holy See. For three years Savonarola ignored commands to cease preaching and stop casting himself as a conduit of God, and in the spring of 1497 Alexander finally excommunicated him. This dramatic step stunned the friar's supporters, and the city quaked with controversy over whom to back – the pope or the would-be prophet. When the Franciscans, who loathed Savonarola, challenged the Dominicans to a trial by fire, Florentines flocked to see whom God preferred. But a sudden drenching storm halted the contest, and the angry crowd, denied its spectacle, stormed San Marco. Savonarola and two assistants were taken prisoner and, after weeks of interrogation and torture, condemned as heretics. In May 1498 the three were hanged and burned in the same public square where Savonarola had staged his Bonfires of the Vanities. The next day San Marco was ritually cleansed to remove the taint of heresy; in the weeks to come, the whole city received a doctrinal scrubbing as authorities exiled Savonarola supporters and confiscated all copies of his writing.

ℛ
Jakob Fugger

FINANCIER OF CHURCH AND EMPIRE

1459–1525

Many of the Renaissance's wealthiest clans had humble beginnings, but few can have started quite as modestly as the Fuggers. The founder of the lineage, Johannes (or Hans) Fugger, was a small-town weaver who moved to Augsburg, the chief city of Bavaria, in 1367. Johannes soon branched out into importing textiles. One of his sons, Jakob the Elder, did well enough to win a place in Augsburg's merchants' guild, and Ulrich and Georg, two of Jakob's seven sons, excelled even further, winning a contract to outfit and clothe Emperor Frederick III of Habsburg, his son Maximilian I and their respective entourages for an imperial visit to Burgundy. To show his appreciation, Frederick knighted the Fugger brothers, gave them a coat of arms and allowed them to take up banking as well as commerce. Within a generation this would bear extraordinary fruit.

Jakob's youngest son, Jakob the Younger, was originally destined for the priesthood and not involved in such matters, but in 1473 Ulrich decided to send him to Venice to learn the latest business practices. Fascinated with double-entry bookkeeping (then little known in Bavaria), Jakob precociously used his accounting skills to test the profitability of the various Fugger enterprises, and as a reward Ulrich charged him with managing the family business in Innsbruck. Within a few years he was making substantial loans to the local head of the ruling Habsburg family, who in return handed over the management (and profits) of his rich Alpine silver mines to Jakob. By the 1490s Jakob was running most of the family's commerce, shipping raw cotton from Egypt through Venice and over the Alps to Augsburg, and adding other imported goods, such as silks and spices. He had ships built to carry such products directly to the Low Countries and Spain, and funnelled his profits into mining. He eventually gained control of much of the silver and copper (essential for bronze cannon) produced in Hungary, Bohemia and Silesia.

Building on his commercial networks, Fugger also ran an immense family bank, specializing in large loans to cash-strapped princes. Already expert in all matters of bookkeeping, letters of credit and bills of exchange, he established an exclusive messenger service that linked Fugger banks, warehouses and mines with the head office in Augsburg. Before long his couriers also circulated a business newsletter, a regular inter-office communication that kept branch managers abreast of intricate shifts in politics and economics and reliably one step ahead of the competition.

Fugger's financial might propelled the Habsburg family into dominance in the early 16th century. When Emperor Maximilian I died in 1519, there were several contenders for the elective throne. The seven prince-electors of the empire had promised initially to support Maximilian's grandson Charles of Habsburg, but as election day approached, a few princes grew evasive, having heard of the possibility of bigger bribes than Charles had offered from the French king, François I. The balance of power in Europe teetered precariously until Jakob Fugger stepped in. Having organized a banking cartel to amass a staggering 850,000 florins (nearly 3 metric tons of pure gold), Fugger bought the election for Charles without a hitch, especially since he had also effectively shut down Europe's credit markets to François's agents, who were unable to come up with a matching bribe.

Fugger also played a fundamental role in financing papal projects, most notably Pope Leo X's notorious scheme in 1517 to fund the rebuilding of St Peter's Basilica in Rome, by selling indulgences, or remissions from sin, to the German faithful. The slogan that followed the indulgence sellers around the empire was 'Once the coin in the coffer clings, a soul from Purgatory heavenward springs!' – but not until Fugger had collected all those gulden, pfennigs and groats and transferred their value by letter of credit to Rome, minus his personal cut of 50 per cent.

It was never clear how much Fugger was motivated by profit and how much by piety or patriotism. Devotedly Catholic, he built churches all over Augsburg, as well as charitable homes for the elderly, called the Fuggerei, which still exist. He was so involved with Imperial finances that by the time Jakob died, Charles was essentially treating the Fugger bank as his treasury. Yet Fugger's big business also created big enemies. Martin Luther condemned him personally for his role in papal financing, while François and many others blamed him for turning Charles V from an already powerful monarch to the head of a world-spanning state. Although Jakob Fugger won most of his financial battles, his opponents won the historical war when it came to tarnishing the Fugger name among later generations.

CR

Desiderius Erasmus

THE TEMPERATE REVOLUTIONARY

1466/67–1536

According to Desiderius Erasmus, scholastic theologians fretted over pointless questions. Instead of God sending Christ to earth as a man, for example, they asked whether he could have given him 'the nature of a woman, of the devil, of an ass, of a cucumber, of a piece of flint? How then would the cucumber have preached, performed miracles, and been nailed to the cross?' Erasmus was joking, mostly – scholastics really did debate the first three possibilities. Such pondering failed to stir the Christian heart, he believed, and empty ritual had distanced the faithful from their faith. Erasmus sought to reignite Christianity with the Gospels, an idea that had been stamped out during isolated attempts at reform in the 15th century. With the help of humanism and the printing press, however, he gave new momentum to the drive for reform, which attracted mainstream Catholics and proto-Protestants alike – for a while.

Born in Rotterdam, Erasmus was the second illegitimate son of a priest and a physician's daughter who, although unmarried, together secured a first-rate education for their children. After both parents died, however, guardians packed the boys off to a monastery; denied the university life he desired, Erasmus chafed under his order's restrictions. He took comfort in Classical literature, and by 1492, when he reluctantly agreed to be ordained as a priest, he was an accomplished Classical Latinist and an elegant writer. A good knowledge of Latin could open doors; for Erasmus, it parted the monastery gates. The bishop of Cambrai hired him for a temporary assignment, and, once free of his order's walls, Erasmus never returned.

In 1495 he enrolled at the prestigious Sorbonne, the University of Paris's theology college, but he found the level of Latin disappointing and the lectures tedious. To ease his boredom and grinding poverty he composed easy-to-use Latin guides and tutored wealthy students, one of whom – a young English lord – invited him to England in 1499. At Oxford University, Erasmus connected for the first time with a community of humanists. Seeking the most accurate texts possible, a handful were studying ancient Greek writings in the original rather than in Latin translation. The New Testament had also been composed in Greek, Erasmus knew, but for centuries it had been available only in Latin. Could the earliest Christian texts yield a purer version of scripture? In a decision that changed his life and that may have changed history, Erasmus decided to apply humanist methods to Christian writings. He resolved to learn Greek to get closer to the Word of God.

Erasmus abandoned the Sorbonne, which frowned on Greek studies, and taught himself the language while working as a private teacher. In 1506 one tutoring job took him to Italy, where he travelled for three years; his favourite city was Venice, where the publisher Aldus Manutius had gathered the West's greatest Greek scholars. In 1508 Erasmus left Italy for England, and on the way he began his best-known work, *The Praise of Folly*. A satire written to amuse Thomas More, whom he had met on his previous trip, the book ridicules mindless ritual in general and monks in particular. He mocks their desire to do 'everything by the book', tying their shoes a particular way, sleeping a prescribed number of hours, wearing cloaks in certain colours. Fixated on external trappings of faith, they 'make frightful scenes over a habit worn with the wrong girdle'. Monks believed God would reward them for living 'the life of a sponge, always fixed to the same spot'. Such deluded Christians prayed for 'anything except to be spared from stupidity', for, after all, 'It's so agreeable to know nothing.'

To strip away the man-made follies that encrusted Christianity, Erasmus prepared and published the first Greek New Testament in 1516. Alongside this text he included a new Latin version that he translated directly from the Greek, noting where early manuscripts differed from the Vulgate Bible, which was technically the only allowed version of scripture. He dedicated the volume to Pope Leo X, who welcomed the Dutchman's scholarship. More orthodox churchmen, however, worried that to accept Erasmus's Bible was to admit the Church had followed a flawed document for 1,200 years.

By 1520 Erasmus was a renowned scholar with ties to nearly every leading humanist on the continent. He was a cool moderate in increasingly heated religious debates, and at first both camps tried to claim him. When he repeatedly refused to take sides, however, Catholic extremists began pointing out parallels between him and a young German theologian, Martin Luther. The two did agree on several points: both endorsed vernacular Bibles, for example, and both dismissed the worship of relics, the cult of saints and the selling of indulgences. But Erasmus broke decisively with Luther in 1524 by condemning predestination, a crucial aspect of Lutheran doctrine. Luther, who had initially admired Erasmus, came to see him as too timid, too subtle. 'Erasmus is an eel,' he declared. 'Only Christ can grab him.'

Even after Luther denounced Erasmus, conservatives accused him of Lutheran leanings, and he spent many of his last years defending his Catholicism. He believed to the end that the religious rift could be healed, and in his final years published an optimistic little book titled *On Restoring Unity in the Church*. He was Europe's best-selling writer when he died in 1536, the author of 10 to 20 per cent of all the books circulating in Europe by one estimate. For a generation humanists carried on in his name, but they were ultimately eclipsed by extremists at either end. In 1559 Catholic leaders banned Erasmus's entire body of work, essentially bracketing him with the Protestant movement he never supported. In a letter of 1528 Erasmus had reported that Franciscan monks had accused him of 'laying the egg that Luther hatched'. It was a grand statement that 'should earn them a fine big bowl of porridge', he wrote, but 'the egg I laid was a hen's egg, and Luther has hatched a chick of a very, very different feather.'

CR

Niccolò Machiavelli

THE FIRST POLITICAL SCIENTIST

1469–1527

Within years of his death Niccolò Machiavelli's name had become synonymous with personal deviousness and political ruthlessness, which would have surprised those who knew him in life. A somewhat bland civil servant, playwright and philosopher, he wrote just one published book, whose pronounced aim was to 'oblige citizens to love one another, to decline faction, and to prefer the good of the public to any private enterprise'.

Machiavelli came from civic-minded stock, loyal Florentines who for over two centuries had devotedly supported the Republic – so much so that Niccolò's father, Bernardo, withdrew from civil affairs in protest at the ascendancy of the Medici family, preferring to raise his children in genteel poverty. As a result, Niccolò could never afford the Greek lessons that might have placed him among Florence's humanist elite, but his Latin was still good enough to spark a deep fascination for the Classical world.

He particularly embraced the literature of republican Rome, with its dictum that only participation in public affairs developed a man's true worth – his *virtù* – as a human and as a citizen. *Virtù* had been central to the civic humanism preached by Leonardo Bruni and Leon Battista Alberti but had become unfashionable under the Medici, when courtly eloquence and Neoplatonism prevailed. Once the Medici were ousted in 1494, however, Florence underwent a Republican revival, and Machiavelli's moment had come. Put in charge of home security and foreign correspondence, he was Florence's chief civil servant and roving ambassador for the next fourteen years. His work as the Republic's courier, diplomat and agent gave him a special perspective on how the politics of his day operated. He was not, as it happened, the best of diplomats – he was too impulsive, blunt and transparent for shrewd negotiations – but he did come to recognize the similarities between his own political experiences and those he found in the writings of Cicero and Livy. He marvelled at 'the wonderful examples which the history of ancient kingdoms and republics present to us', while moaning about 'the lack of a real knowledge of [this] history' among his fellow diplomats and bureaucrats.

Using Classical letters for contemporary political insight might have remained Machiavelli's private hobby had the Medici not retaken Florence in 1512. Although their return was only mildly vengeful by the standards of the time, they were not kind to Machiavelli. Arrested and tortured, he was then given the most demoralizing punishment of all: banishment to his modest farm just south of Florence, where he was ignored for nearly a decade. Stuck on the sidelines, Machiavelli again imagined himself in Classical terms – as the Roman patrician, fallen from favour and exiled to the country, who rediscovers himself in solitude through simple farm work, reading and writing. Taking his unwanted retirement as a blessing, he then set about composing essays that essentially created the discipline of political science.

The most enduring of his works were two books begun in his first year away from Florence. In *Discourses on the First Decade of Livy* (1513–16) Machiavelli examined the workings of republican governments; in *The Prince* (1513) he explored principalities. As in his life, he used examples from the Classical (and sometimes the biblical) world to explain contemporary political dynamics. In *The Prince* these brought him to the conclusion that would get him and his philosophy damned as 'Machiavellian': that a prince, while pursuing power, had to operate free of all moral restraints and be willing to lie, double-deal, threaten and sometimes murder to secure his state. In reality, *The Prince* was more descriptive than prescriptive, for Machiavelli personally preferred a mixed government, and he noted how, in both Classical and contemporary regimes, 'when there is combined under the same constitution a prince, a nobility and the power of the people, then these three powers will watch and keep each other reciprocally in check.'

The pain of Machiavelli's exile, which he felt so strongly at first, diminished as the Florentine authorities began letting him visit friends in the city. By reading and commenting on handwritten copies of his works, they kept his reputation alive and eventually persuaded Florence's ruler, Cardinal Giulio de' Medici, to partially forgive Machiavelli and to name him the city's historian, with a commission to write a *History of Florence*. Once again enjoying official, if peripheral, status in local government, Machiavelli still had to learn how to think like a good Renaissance courtier, telling the story of his native city without making too much of its republican past or denigrating the Medici. He apparently succeeded, for just before his death he finished a *History of Florence* that was sufficiently sanitized to be acceptable to his new patron, Giulio de' Medici, now Pope Clement VII.

CR

Tommaso Inghirami

HERO OF THE VATICAN, HEROINE OF THE STAGE

1470/71–1516

Remembered today largely as the subject of a portrait by Raphael, Tommaso Inghirami is shown sitting at his desk, a plain, middle-aged, somewhat pudgy man dressed in monkish robes and cap. Though unassuming in appearance, he seems to hover at the brink of the blessed: caught in the midst of his writing, he glances upwards into the light, apparently struck by a distant, perhaps divine, thought. As it happened, Inghirami worked at the Vatican and held several high offices there, but he was more adept at the Classics than at theology. During his lifetime he was especially well known for his performance skills, for he was one of the great stars of the Renaissance stage. In the painting that immortalized him he actually colluded with Raphael in a little stagecraft, striking a pose that not only set a spiritual tone, but also went some way to conceal the fact that he was severely cross-eyed.

Born into the minor nobility in the provincial Tuscan town of Volterra, Tommaso was orphaned before he reached 2 years old. A kindly uncle soon carried him off to Florence, however, and there he was taken under the wing of Lorenzo de' Medici, who saw to it that he had a full humanist education in rhetoric and the arts. As an acolyte of *Il Magnifico*, Tommaso soon showed his genius for Classical studies, and at the age of just 13 was sent to Rome, well equipped with introductions and connections to the papal court. Thoroughly trained in the Latin Classics, Inghirami gained rapid recognition for his recitation skills: by the time he was 20 he could improvise Latin verse for hours before spellbound audiences. Before long he began acting in the Classical plays that were all the rage among learned circles in the Vatican. So popular was his rendition of Phaedra, the heroine of Seneca's tragedy *Hippolytus*, that he took the Italian version, Fedra (or Fedro), as his stage name.

In a world where theatre was political as much as politics were theatrical, Inghirami advanced quickly on both fronts. His brilliant rhetorical disquisition before Emperor Maximilian I on the occasion of a papal diplomatic mission got him named an Imperial count palatinate. A succession of popes, from Alexander VI to Julius II to Leo X, all of whom despised one another, nevertheless agreed on their appreciation of Fedra, and all showered honours on him. Although he never took holy vows, Inghirami was still recognized with a number of important and well-paid Church offices, including secretary to the College of Cardinals and head of the Vatican library (now a position reserved for a cardinal). Learned and urbane, always well spoken and apparently pleasant to everyone he met, Inghirami represented the cultivated, if not especially pious, culmination of the Renaissance in Rome. Raphael recognized his special place in the pantheon of his cultured and sophisticated acquaintances, portraying him as Epicurus in his grand fresco *The School of Athens* (c. 1510–12).

More a performer than a scholar, Inghirami left behind little writing. He did, however, commission another portrait of himself, from an anonymous painter who caught him in very different circumstances from Raphael's graceful fantasies. The work is an ex-voto, offered by Inghirami to Christ, St Peter and St Paul for rescuing him from an early 16th-century road accident. Although lacking Raphael's refinement and compositional skills, the painting tells a dramatic story: how Fedra, riding along the Via Sacra near the Arch of Septimius Severus (the Colosseum is in the background), was thrown by his skittish mule beneath the wheels of a laden ox cart, where – by a miracle – he narrowly escaped being crushed to death. The burly carters, the solicitous colleagues and, above all, Inghirami's expression of terror combine in a scene as common to ordinary Renaissance life as it was alien to the stylized art of Raphael or the Classical dramas performed by Fedra himself.

This portrayal of a near tragedy has led some to speculate that the injuries sustained in this accident caused Inghirami's death in 1516, at the fairly young age of 45 (and four years before Raphael himself died). This seems unlikely, however, since the priestly robes Fedra is wearing date the painting – and thus the event – to some time before 1508.

Albrecht Dürer

THE RENAISSANCE COMES TO GERMANY

1471–1528

In Albrecht Dürer's opinion, his fellow German artists were stuck in a medieval rut. They needed instruction, he wrote, 'for they lack all real art theory, [and must] learn to better their work'. He therefore embarked on a mission to prise Germany's artists free of Gothic paradigms and to align them with the modern standards of 15th-century Italy. A gifted painter, draughtsman and writer who travelled extensively, Dürer became a cultural conduit between north and south, introducing his countrymen to a version of the Italian Renaissance that blended Classical ideas, the latest scientific theory and a northern flair for detailed naturalism.

Born in Nuremberg, Dürer completed his apprenticeship in 1490 and then set off on his four-year *Wanderjahr* ('wandering year'), visiting workshops in western Germany to polish his skills as a woodcutter. In Colmar he was inspired by the work of Martin Schongauer, a recently deceased engraver who combined the best elements of Germanic emotion and Netherlandish naturalism. Schongauer's manner influenced Dürer throughout his life, especially in the expressive faces of his later subjects.

Not long after marrying in 1494, and having only recently completed his extended *Wanderjahr*, Dürer left his Nuremberg home – much to the consternation of his new wife, Agnes – to embark on a painter's pilgrimage to Italy. During a year in Venice, he studied the mythological themes and Classical proportions of Italian art, and completed a number of delicate, detailed landscapes and nature studies in watercolour and pencil. At the time such work was considered a preliminary step towards finished pieces, but Dürer's refined pieces helped to promote the natural world from background filler to a valid artistic subject and to put the two media on a par with oil painting.

After returning to Nuremberg, Dürer established a workshop with a new business model that involved building up stock in advance rather than linking production to client orders. He focused on engravings and woodcuts, which, unlike traditional paintings and sculpture, were readily stored, affordably priced and easily shipped. In addition, his prints were astonishingly realistic: before Dürer, most woodcuts yielded relatively crude results, but his innovations produced crisp, nuanced images. Shrewdly chosen subjects compounded his success: scholars and humanists gravitated toward his Classical works; the less educated preferred religious scenes. Just before 1500, the year in which many Christians believed the world would end, Dürer's apocryphal prints from the Book of Revelation sold especially well, swelling his coffers and further spreading his fame.

Like the best Italian artists, Dürer rejected model books – the pictorial guides of stock images that traditional artists used. Medieval thinkers had believed that art derived from the perfect image of an object, not from its flawed, mundane reality; and German artists had customarily depicted a seated Madonna by consulting their model book instead of posing an actual woman on a real chair. Dürer's approach was a humanist's one: 'Art is rooted in Nature,' he declared, 'and whoever can pull it out, has it.'

He was a famous man by the time he returned to Italy in 1505; collectors coveted his prints of German landscapes and steep-roofed architecture, but Dürer was not wholly satisfied. In a letter from Venice he fretted that the Italians dismissed his paintings, and he turned to the city's great works, especially those by Gentile Bellini, for guidance. The old master's influence suffuses Dürer's *Feast of the Rose Garlands* (1506), which melded vivid Venetian hues with traditional Germanic views: botanical detail, Nuremberg in the distance and, disturbingly for the Italians, Emperor Maximilian I on equal ground with Pope Julius II. The painting earned 'much praise but little profit', he complained, but it silenced those who claimed he did not 'know how to handle colours'.

Back in Germany, Dürer was suddenly much in demand as a painter. While visiting Nuremberg in 1512, the emperor Maximilian I admired the artist's idealized painting of Charlemagne and requested several portraits of himself. Travelling in the Netherlands in 1520 and 1521, Dürer met Desiderius Erasmus and the emperor Charles V, who both commissioned portraits. A pioneer in conveying his sitters' personalities, Dürer seemed to hone his portraiture by repeatedly taking himself as his own subject, beginning with a striking silverpoint drawing done at the age of 13 and continuing in various media and states of dress throughout his life. One sketch has him stark naked, another in a sombre brown coat and distinctly Christ-like pose. Previous artists had tended to slip self-portraits into the periphery of group scenes, but Dürer treated his images as independent pieces of art, creating a new genre that reflected the heightened Renaissance sense of self-awareness.

Although his schooling had been limited, Dürer was both a skilled mathematician and a confident writer, a composer of bawdy poems, countless letters and volumes of journals. Between 1525 and his death in 1528 he recorded much of his acquired knowledge in treatises on proportion, perspective and military fortification. Ironically, in the decades after he died, his writings may have had a greater impact than his paintings, many of which were hidden away in private collections. His prints, however, continued to circulate widely and to exert a profound influence on printmakers – as they still do today.

CR

Nicolaus Copernicus

REVOLUTIONARY OF THE CELESTIAL SPHERES

1473–1543

orn in the Polish city of Toruń, Nicolaus Copernicus lived a life of
quiet, if substantial, accomplishments, which were to be thoroughly
overshadowed by the book that he published at the end of his life – a volume
he reportedly held only once, on the day he died. Orphaned young, Nicolaus
was taken in by his maternal uncle, who rose to power as prince–bishop of
Ermland (or Warmia, in north central Poland). Under his uncle's guidance
Copernicus studied first at the University of Kraków and then in Italy, graduating in canon law from Ferrara in 1503. He also studied medicine while
in Italy and, although he never received a degree, he practised unofficially
as a physician while serving as a cathedral canon and civic administrator at
Olsztyn, the capital of Warmia. While caring for patients, he also ferreted
out abandoned fiefs, managed the defences of Olsztyn when the city was
besieged, and worked out which statelets in the Holy Roman Empire had
the right to mint coins.

Copernicus's obvious abilities and good family connections put him on
the shortlist for at least one bishopric. He also delved deeply enough into
economics and coinage reform to come up with the theory behind 'Gresham's
Law' – the idea that debased currency tends to drive pure coinage out of circulation – over half a century before Sir Thomas Gresham himself. However,
his true, though private, passion was astronomy, which had fascinated him
since his student days. While at Ferrara, he had attended lectures on astronomical theory and had begun making his own observations. In Rome for
the jubilee of 1500, he witnessed a lunar eclipse, and once back in Poland he

set up an observatory in the castle of Olsztyn, where he recorded the movements of the sun on a chart that still survives on the castle's interior wall.

Copernicus knew about Ptolemy's complex geocentric theory of the planets, which was almost universally accepted in his time. He also studied those few Classical scholars who had held that the sun, rather than the earth, was at the centre of the universe, around which the heavenly bodies orbited. It took some calculating, but Copernicus eventually came up with such a heliocentric model, one that seemed to explain solar and planetary movements. In 1514 he wrote it up in a booklet called *Commentariolus* ('Little commentary'), which he passed around among his friends.

It took Copernicus until 1531 to work the simple model proposed in the *Commentariolus* into a complete theory about the motion of the earth and its relation to the sun. Word got out that someone on the edge of Europe was working on a new cosmology, and before long other scholars – and several bishops – wrote for clarification. Worried as much about his model's theological implications as about any theoretical difficulties, Copernicus dithered in responding. Finally, in 1539, the mathematician Georg Joachim Rheticus left his post at the University of Wittenberg and simply moved in with the now aged Copernicus, to persuade him to publish. Under Rheticus's encouragement and direction, the Copernican theory slowly emerged – a 'First Narration', then a chapter on trigonometry and finally, in 1543, the complete *De revolutionibus orbium coelestium* ('On the revolutions of the celestial spheres').

Beyond its astronomical import, Copernicanism had vast cosmological implications. It not only plucked humanity and the earth from the centre of God's universe, but also vastly increased the size of that universe. No longer a secure point under heaven, the earth, Copernicus said, moved in two ways at once, revolving around the sun while rotating on its axis. The grand sweep of the stars, the seasonal variations of the sun and the motions of the planets could all be explained by these twin motions of our own earth.

For a book that would spark a revolution well beyond its own title, *De revolutionibus* initially aroused little excitement. Part of the problem was that, when the book was published, a preface was added by a Lutheran theologian – which many readers assumed Copernicus had written – down-playing the work as merely a hypothetical model and not observed reality. Moreover, the theory had serious flaws – among them the assumption that planets orbited the sun in perfect circles – which initially rendered it less accurate than the patchwork Ptolemaic model it claimed to replace. Yet some, at least, quickly recognized the threat that Copernicus posed to both biblical literalism and Christian universalism. Within three years of its publication and its author's death, the Inquisition was already demanding that *De revolutionibus* be banned as heretical.

Isabella d'Este

Thanks to his skilful matrimonial politicking, Ercole I d'Este, Duke of Ferrara, found brilliant matches for his two legitimate daughters while they were still children. Beatrice, the younger, was paired off with Ludovico Sforza, soon to become duke of Milan. The consort of the most powerful man in Italy, she turned capricious, imperious and somewhat cruel, and, after a headlong pursuit of luxury and spectacle, she died at the age of only 21, while giving birth to her third son. Isabella, Ercole's elder daughter, was more cautious, or at least more clear-headed, and outlived both her husband and most of her contemporaries to become known later as the 'First Lady of the Renaissance'.

Married at 16 to Francesco II Gonzaga, marquis of Mantua, Isabella found herself running the most cultivated mid-size court in Italy, home since the late 1450s of the painter Andrea Mantegna, who blended technical expertise and humanist teachings. Isabella adapted the court values of nearby Urbino, presided over by Francesco's sister Elizabetta, and volubly championed by the arch-courtier Baldassare Castiglione. She and Francesco expanded their art patronage by establishing a Gonzaga chapel choir and by hiring composers, instrument makers and some mid-level humanist poets. For Isabella, poetry was never really finished until it had been set to music, and she had her composers come up with catchy tunes for courtiers' verses and set popular songs to more refined music, a form known as the *frottola*.

As marquise, Isabella's main duty was to produce heirs, and after a slow start she bore seven children in fifteen years. She also had to serve as de facto ruler of her little state during Francesco's frequent absences, mostly as general for – and, for a year, prisoner of – the Venetians. Her abiding interests, however, were collection, decoration and artistic patronage. On her relatively limited household budget she could never afford grand public works in the Medici or Sforza manner – a projected monument to Virgil came to nothing – but she could glorify her new family and herself in her *studiolo*, her private reading and reception room. Although she never mastered Latin, let alone Greek, Isabella was enthusiastic about the Classics, especially in their Neoplatonic guise, blending ancient aesthetics and Christian morality. Guided by her humanist advisers, she worked out elaborate metaphorical scenes for artists to realize on her *studiolo* walls. When the aged Mantegna proved too slow for the job, she recruited Perugino, Cosimo Tura and Lorenzo Costa.

While pursuing her decorative schemes, Isabella had to confront the emerging ethos of the artist as inspired creator rather than obedient craftsman. She once famously chided Perugino for letting his own pursuit of artistic excellence upstage the elaborate fable she wanted him to portray, and she continually shifted her patronage, looking for someone both talented and tractable. She found it almost impossible to lure the best artists to a modest court like Mantua, and despite her importuning through personal letters and agents, the likes of Raphael and Leonardo gave her only sketches for promised works that they never finished; from Giovanni Bellini she accepted a ready-made Madonna instead of the mythological scene she really wanted. Facing these difficulties, Isabella ended up buying works originally commissioned by others just to have examples from the great painters of her day. She consequently, and perhaps unwittingly, furthered the notion of artistic genius and diminished the dominance of aristocratic patrons. She also helped generate something quite new, however – a marketplace for second-hand art that would eventually redefine the roles of artist and patron.

Although she aspired to Lorenzo de' Medici's role as Italy's arbiter of art and taste, Isabella ultimately lacked the resources and personal clout, especially after Francesco died in 1519. She enjoyed a few years as regent, but then her son Federico II took the throne, and she decided in 1525 to go to Rome. There she passed two years – holding her own little court, searching for new antiquities and working non-stop to persuade Leo's cousin Pope Clement VII to make a cardinal of her second son, Ercole. At this she succeeded, although it took so long that she was nearly taken hostage by the renegade Imperial troops who captured and sacked Rome in 1527. She escaped only thanks to the timely intervention of her third son, Ferrante, an Imperial captain who still had some control over his men. Shaken and feeling marginalized, she returned to Mantua, having lost many of her Classical artworks. After years of effectively running her own court and setting Europe's tastes in fashion, music and decoration, Isabella increasingly found herself deserted by her artists and courtiers. Alone and in her sixties, she retreated to her small feudatory at Solarolo to spend her last days admiring the antiquities and the two thousand paintings she had spent a lifetime collecting.

❧

Cesare Borgia

'TO BE IMITATED BY ALL THOSE WHO HAVE
RISEN TO RULE'

1475–1507

Renaissance Italy generated an abundance of cultivated *condottieri* and humanist *signori* – warlords and princes as comfortable in the salon as on the battlefield. Cesare Borgia was not one of these. Consumed by ambition, he made no pretence at cultural refinement and possessed only an unending drive for power. For a decade at the turn of the 16th century he flashed, meteor-like, across the Italian scene. By the time he died at the age of 31, he had built no libraries or monuments yet had permanently reconfigured the political map of the peninsula.

Cesare's family came originally from Valencia in Spain but had gone to Rome and found riches in religion: Cesare was the grand-nephew of one pope and the son of another. His father, Rodrigo Borgia, bought the papacy in 1492, offering benefices and bribes in some of the most blatant simony in Church history. After assuming the throne as Alexander VI, Rodrigo continued his venal and libidinous habits with little subterfuge or shame. Although nepotism – appointing relatives to Church offices – was a well-established means of creating a loyal bureaucracy and cementing family power, Pope Alexander relentlessly schemed to use his children (whose paternity he freely admitted) to establish a Borgia supremacy in Italy. For his daughter Lucrezia and his other two sons, this meant welding alliances through dynastic marriages, but for Cesare, who was clearly the most able, Alexander initially envisioned a life in the Church. He first appointed the boy as archbishop and then in 1493 made him, at the age of just 17, a cardinal.

Although he enjoyed a dissolute life at the Vatican and often served as his father's political agent and legate, Cesare still envied the secular life and opportunities enjoyed by his older brother, Giovanni. In 1497, after Giovanni was assassinated in murky circumstances, Cesare – who almost certainly colluded in the deed – was free to change his life's direction. In August 1498 he renounced his cardinalate – the first person ever to do so – and, in a typically Renaissance piece of political theatre, Louis XII of France promptly named him duke of Valentinois, a bespoke title created on the spot. To exploit this new French–Borgia axis, Alexander sent Cesare in 1499 to subdue the fractious cities of the Italian Romagna, part of the Papal States north of the Apennines, which had for centuries enjoyed the pretence of independence.

In the course of several campaigns Cesare managed, through force, guile, charm or treachery, to overcome – and usually kill – virtually all the petty lords of the Romagna and, for good measure, of the papal Marche as well. Alexander named him duke over all the lands he had conquered, creating a strong new state in the centre of Italy that provided a definitive threat to the fifty-year-old balance of power. With Louis's support Cesare took on first Milan and then Florence. In Rome he thrashed the great baronial families who had squabbled almost unopposed over the city for centuries. Responding in their habitual fashion to unpredictable mercenary captains, the Florentines bribed Cesare to go away. Accompanying the delegation was Niccolò Machiavelli, who wrote a stream of letters back to his superiors marvelling at Cesare's implacable character and the seeming invincibility of his combined French, Swiss and Italian legions.

And then suddenly it was over. In August 1503 Pope Alexander abruptly died – whether of malaria, poison or syphilis no one was sure – at a moment when Cesare was himself too sick to act with his characteristic speed or decisiveness. In October that year, although recovered, Cesare was unable or unwilling to pay the necessary bribes to keep the Borgias' arch-enemy Giuliano della Rovere from getting elected as Pope Julius II and then promptly stripping Cesare of his dukedom. When Cesare fled to Spanish-controlled Naples, Ferdinand of Aragon had him arrested and shipped back to Valencia in chains. After two years in prison Cesare engineered a daring escape, but within a few months he was killed in a minor border skirmish in Navarre.

Although the Borgias had vanished from the scene, they left their mark. While Alexander put his family ahead of the Church, and even God, he did prove a surprisingly able administrator, bringing some peace to Rome and the Papal States. In this he was certainly helped by Cesare, whose years of buccaneering around the Romagna finally reduced an historically anarchic region to something like an orderly and unified state – even if it ended up in the hands of the papacy rather than a Borgia dynasty. Cesare's most enduring legacy, however, lay in the inspiration he provided Niccolò Machiavelli for *The Prince* – the sublimely amoral yet devastatingly effective Renaissance ruler, 'one to be imitated by all those who have risen to rule'.

Pope Leo X

THE CONNOISSEUR POPE

1475–1521

Fully 18 members of the extended Medici family were made cardinal at one time or another, but the first and youngest of them all was Giovanni, son of Lorenzo the Magnificent. His climb up the ecclesiastical hierarchy began as classic Renaissance family politics – when Pope Innocent VIII arranged to marry his bastard son to Lorenzo's bastard daughter, 13-year-old Giovanni was appointed cardinal-deacon as part of the deal. For the sake of propriety the Medici scion was not fully admitted into the Sacred College until he turned 16, but instead sent to tutors in Pisa to study canon law. His main interest, however, was humanism and classical literature.

A year later, Giovanni's programmed career was derailed when, in the course of just three months, both Lorenzo and Innocent died. Just two years later, the entire Medici clan was expelled from Florence by a popular revolt, and the still-teenage cardinal had to sneak out of town disguised as a Franciscan friar. Reduced to wandering, Giovanni made the best of the situation, solidifying ties with old Medici friends, first in Italy and then abroad – though in Rouen, in Northern France, he and his entourage were humiliatingly imprisoned for a while as spies. Making it back to Rome in 1500, he was content to set himself up as a cardinal more interested in cultural than religious or political affairs.

Despite his youth, relative detachment from matters of state, and not even being a priest, Giovanni de' Medici was easily elected to the papacy in 1513, as Leo X. His main appeal to those who voted for him was his conciliatory nature, which contrasted sharply with that of his contentious predecessor,

Julius II. He was also supposedly in ill health, and although only 39, was not expected to live too long. For most of his eight-year pontificate, Leo struggled to preserve some vestige of independence for the Papal States and promote the fortunes of the Medici dynasty in the midst of the ongoing struggle between France and the Empire for control of Italy. In reality, he was not very successful, though he did manage to return his native Florence to family control. Instead, the often tortuous diplomatic positions into which Leo was forced by his own timidity served only to win him a reputation for deviousness while distracting him from the larger threat posed by the rise of Lutheranism in Germany and Scandinavia.

He was also distracted by his enthusiasm for playing the part of a prince – as he famously exclaimed, upon election, 'Since God has given us the Papacy, let's enjoy it.' Although the Medici had long been a key players in Italian finance and politics, Leo was the first in the family to exercise formal lordship over a domain, and he was determined to make the most of his powers as pope. He turned his training in the classics to good use, establishing oversight of archaeological finds in the city, revitalizing the moribund University of Rome, and moving the center of Greek learning and publishing from Florence. He also opened and greatly expanded the already vast papal bureaucracy to create sinecures for the scores of poets and dramatists who flocked to the city and made Rome Italy's literary capital. At the same time, Leo indulged his own desires for pomp and splendour, which derived much of their inspiration from the stories about Imperial Rome he had read as a boy. He gave banquets for a hundred or more guests, offering as many as 65 courses, enhanced by large orchestras, legions of buffoons, and small boys jumping out of the pies and puddings. Although corpulent and unhealthy, he loved taking part in the annual papal hunt – an enormous affair – and in formal processions across Rome that featured contortionists, panthers, and a white elephant named Hanno.

Such opulence did not come cheap, though it was the wars Leo waged to advance the Medici dynasty that truly bankrupted the papacy. To fill his increasing shortfalls, he created and sold papal offices at a dizzying rate – over 2,100 in all; in 1517 he named no fewer than 31 (paying) cardinals in a single conclave. He sold benefices and indulgences so enthusiastically that, even if he never actually said – as was later claimed – 'It has served us well, this myth of Christ,' his cynicism and irreligion became articles of faith among Luther's followers. When he died, at just 45, it was mockingly said of Leo that he had burned through the resources of three papacies – 'the treasure [left to him by] Julius II, the revenues of his own reign, and those of his successor.'

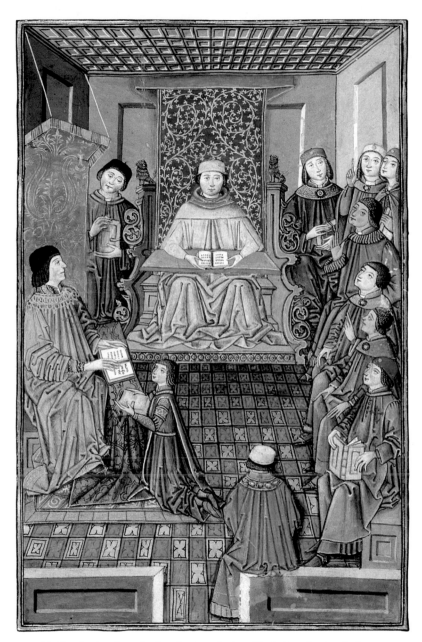

11 This illumination from the *Introductiones Latinae* ('Latin Introductions') shows Antonio de Nebrija teaching a group of Spanish grandees the rudiments of Latin grammar – their first step in Renaissance humanism.

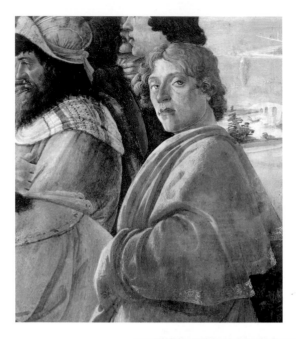

12 Botticelli's self-portrait: a detail from *The Adoration of the Magi* (1475). In the 1490s – the period when Savonarola's apocalyptic visions gripped Florence – Botticelli's art grew darker. While other painters embraced the High Renaissance, his style stagnated.

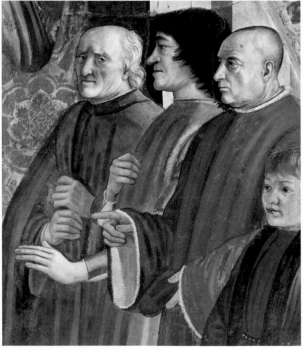

13 Detail from *The Confirmation of the Franciscan Rule* by Domenico Ghirlandaio (1482–85). Lorenzo de' Medici is flanked by two of his Florentine patrician clients, Antonio Pucci and Francesco Sassetti, who commissioned the fresco.

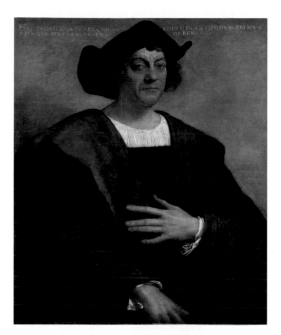

14 "The Ligurian Colombo, the first to enter by ship into the world of the Antipodes 1519", Sebastian del Piombo (1519). There is no known portrait of Columbus from life; this characterful painting dates from 13 years after his death, and the inscription from later still.

16 Below: Anonymous portrait of Vasco da Gama (1510). The realization of João II's hopes for a Portuguese empire ultimately fell to Vasco da Gama, who was given the job of rounding Africa and reaching India by João's cousin and successor, Manuel I, in 1497.

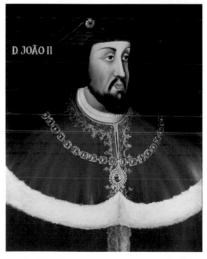

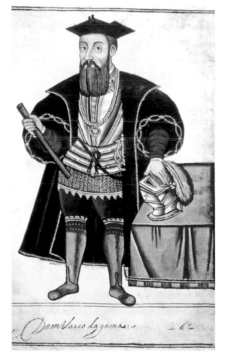

15 João II, in an anonymous portrait of the early 1500s. The first Renaissance ruler to have a truly global strategic vision, João refashioned Portugal's moribund programme of exploration to create an empire.

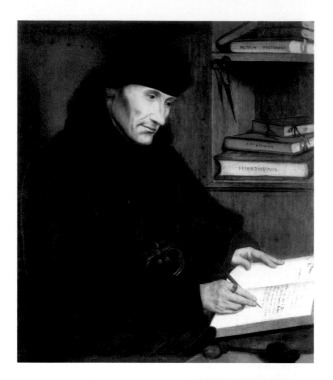

17 Portrait of Erasmus, by Quentin Massys (1517). Desiderius Erasmus rose from poverty to become the leading scholar of his time. In retranslating the New Testament for a new Latin Bible, he bypassed Church-approved scripture, drawing instead on earlier Greek texts.

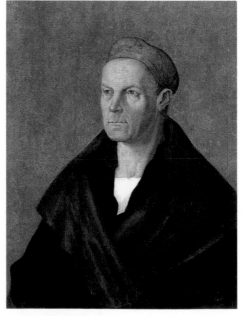

18 Jakob Fugger, by Albrecht Dürer (*c.* 1519). An imperial count at the time this portrait was made, Fugger was also probably one of the richest and most powerful men in Europe.

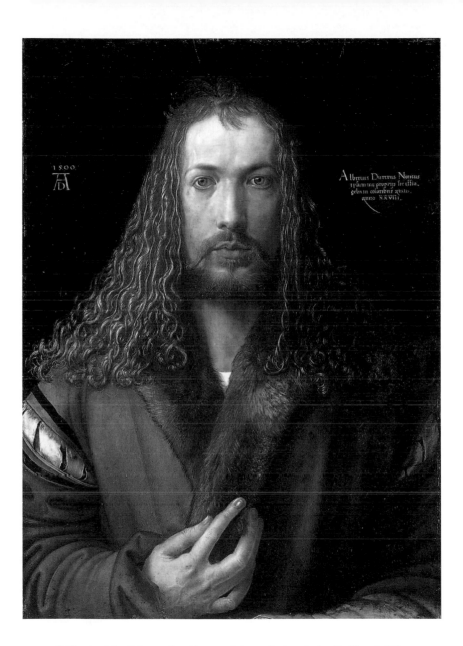

19 Self-portrait by Dürer, painted in 1500. It bears the inscription 'I, Albrecht Dürer of Nuremberg, have painted my likeness at the age of 28 years in my proper colours'. He was the first artist to produce a series of stand-alone self-portraits, paving the way for Rembrandt and others.

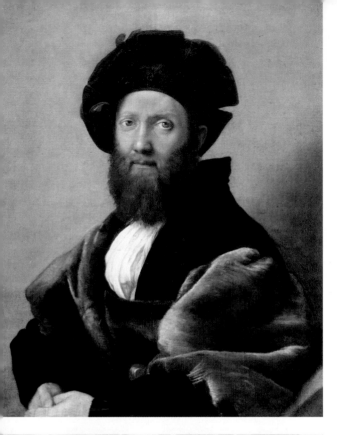

20 Raphael's famous portrait of Baldassare Castiglione, painted 1514–15, shows the courtier dressed with an understated magnificence. Yet there is also a certain pathos in his pose: his gentle gaze is directed perhaps at the painter, who was his good friend.

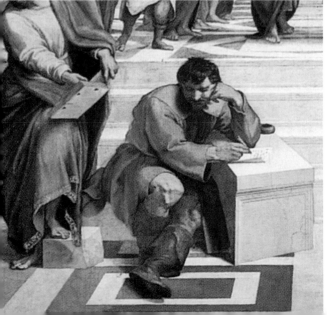

21 Detail from Raphael's *School of Athens*, (1510). This rendering of Heraclitus, known as 'The Weeping Philosopher', is generally considered to be a lifelike portrait of Michelangelo – Raphael's gently teasing tribute to his often dour older colleague.

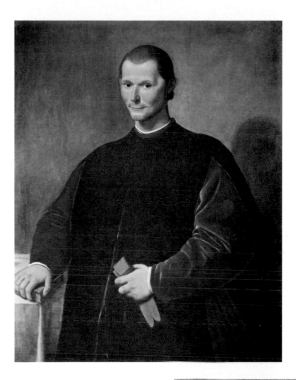

22 This, the most famous painting of Machiavelli, was painted by Santi di Tito in the 1580s, some sixty years after his death. It derives from a terracotta bust of the writer that, in turn, was based on a death mask.

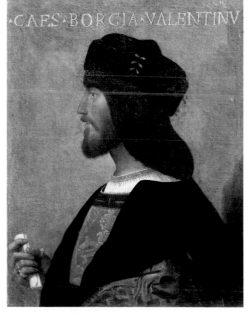

23 Cesare Borgia, painted in the early 1500s. In 1498, as the newly minted duke of Valentinois, Cesare set out to make himself master of northern Italy. With the support of French troops, he nearly succeeded – until his father, Pope Alexander VI, unexpectedly died in 1503.

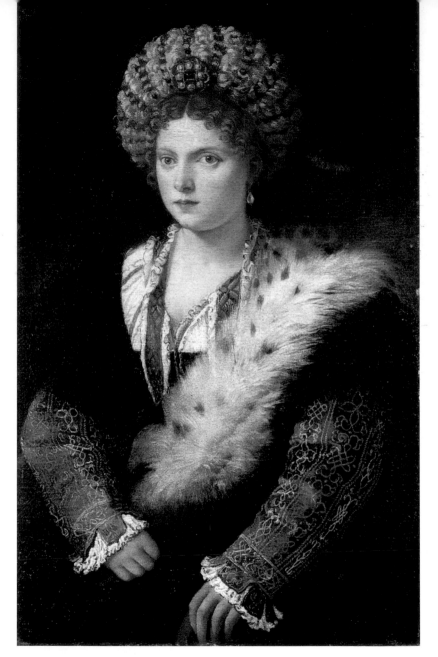

24 Titian's portrait of Isabella d'Este (1534–36). The great artist originally painted
Isabella to look her true age – around 60. She was so enraged with the results, however,
that he changed her face to that of a 20-year-old.

CR

Michelangelo Buonarroti

MIRACLES IN PAINT AND STONE

1475–1564

H ailed as 'the man whose amazing art made art the rival of nature on Earth', Michelangelo Buonarroti was also irascible, tormented in his relations with both patrons and fellow artists and even touchy about having to make a living in the dirty business of stonecarving. Much as Leonardo had done, Michelangelo outperformed and humiliated his first and only teacher – the genial painter Domenico Ghirlandaio, who was only too happy to release him, at the age of just 15, to join Lorenzo de' Medici's Platonic Academy. This ongoing symposium, where humanists argued about Classical letters and arts, represented the only serious schooling Michelangelo ever received. Although the scholars there allowed him to abandon painting for the more Classically grounded art of sculpture, no one bothered to teach him Latin or Greek.

It was a short-lived idyll. Lorenzo died in 1492, and Florence, under the sway of the zealous Girolamo Savonarola, proved too judgmental for Michelangelo's artistic, and perhaps sexual, tastes. By 1496 he was in Rome, beginning a lifelong connection with leading churchmen through his *Bacchus*, commissioned by Cardinal Raffaelle Riario and representing Michelangelo's first, yet substantially complete, realization of the Classical ideas of the human form. The *Bacchus* struck many as too sensual and pagan (Riario rejected it), but the youthful Michelangelo enjoyed much more enduring success with his *Pietà*, carried out between 1497 and 1499 for a French cardinal. This work, on a theme largely unknown in Italy, spread the sculptor's name throughout the peninsula. When the post-Savonarolan

Republic of Florence was casting around for someone to turn a weathered and partially carved block of marble into a monumental statute of *David*, Michelangelo got the commission.

With this work, carved between 1501 and 1504, Michelangelo, although only 28, entered the pantheon of immortal Renaissance artists. Even more than with his *Bacchus*, he captured the essence of the Classical male nude with a seamless, sinewy musculature and dynamic *contrapposto* stance that struck viewers as equal or superior to the best of ancient Greece or Rome. Although the *David* had been commissioned for one of the elevated niches of Florence's cathedral, it was instead placed directly before the seat of government, the Palazzo della Signoria, as a monument to defiant Florentine liberty.

After finishing the *David*, Michelangelo returned to Rome, summoned to carve a grandiose family tomb for Pope Julius II. In 1508 Julius changed direction, however, ordering Michelangelo to give up sculpting and instead to paint the enormous ceiling of the Vatican's Sistine Chapel. Finally accepting the commission on the condition that he had complete artistic licence, Michelangelo came up with his own elaborate, daring statement: a visual depiction of mankind's need for a covenant with God. The resulting work centred on nine major scenes from the Book of Genesis, creating some of the most iconic images in Western art. Michelangelo also included fourteen lesser scenes, a dozen prophets and sibyls, a selection of Jesus' forebears, and twenty muscular male *ignudi* – more than 300 figures in all, in a breathless epic of sin, suffering and the human desire to reach God.

The Sistine frescoes took Michelangelo over four years to finish and were instantly hailed as a monument to the Church, the Renaissance and the human spirit: a contemporary noted how, 'When the work was thrown open, the whole world came running to see what Michelangelo had done; and certainly it was such as to make everyone speechless with astonishment.' Afterwards, though, Michelangelo returned to sculpture. He never finished Julius's tomb, but back in Florence, from 1519 to 1534, he worked on the Medici parish church of San Lorenzo, designing the façade and a funerary chapel, filling the latter with myriad statues of Medici scions and various allegorical and saintly figures.

Even as he grew older and more irascible, Michelangelo continued to receive large commissions. At nearly 60 he returned to the Sistine Chapel to paint his great *Last Judgment* (1537–41), which, with its swirling design and contorted figures, set High Renaissance art on a path towards Mannerism and eventually the Baroque. Michelangelo's sculpture, which became less finished and more introspective as he aged, marks the full integration of Classical norms into Renaissance figural representation. Although an unwilling painter, Michelangelo revolutionized the art form, introducing a monumental clarity, a bold use of colour and a sculptural rendition of forms. His technique broke with the textured, blurry *sfumato* that Leonardo and some Venetian painters had made fashionable, ushering in a last, heroic age of Renaissance art. At his death Michelangelo was busy in yet another field, as architect of the great St Peter's Basilica in Rome. Many who heard the news agreed that, in a life dedicated to art, he had restored 'light to a world that for centuries had been plunged into darkness' and saw his death as marking the end of Italy's artistic Renaissance.

Baldassare Castiglione

THE PERFECT COURTIER

1478–1529

The son of a wealthy lord in the marquisate of Mantua and closely related to the ruling Gonzaga family there, Baldassare Castiglione was groomed from childhood to succeed in courtly circles. He was given the best humanist schooling, but unlike most aspiring humanists chose not to study law at university; instead he went into the service of Ludovico Sforza of Milan as a sort of apprentice courtier. In 1499, with the death of his father and the overthrow of Ludovico, he returned to Mantua to take up his inheritance and further his courtly education by serving Francesco II Gonzaga and his wife, Isabella d'Este.

Recognizing Castiglione's social skills, Francesco sent his protégé on a number of diplomatic missions, and while in Rome the young ambassador fell in with the visiting duke of Urbino, Guidobaldo da Montefeltro, and his remarkable wife (and Francesco's sister), Elisabetta Gonzaga. Thinking nothing of poaching her brother's prize ambassador, in 1504 Elisabetta persuaded Castiglione to abandon Francesco and to move to Urbino, where he found himself a willing player in helping the duchess attract a brilliant court to her small, remote realm.

For the next twelve years, first under Guidobaldo (who died without an heir in 1508) and then under the new duke, Francesco Maria della Rovere, Castiglione kept company with the most brilliant thinkers in Italy – men such as Pietro Bembo, Giuliano de' Medici and Cardinal Bibbiena – and became a close friend of the painter Raphael. With the encouragement of Elisabetta Gonzaga, he arranged soirées, plays and concerts, staged competitive debates and recitations, and wrote pastoral poetry and lengthy letters about his companions at court.

For Castiglione and others lucky enough to experience it, Urbino seemed to be Europe's most sophisticated and civilized meeting place. It did not last, however, and in 1516 Francesco Maria was driven out of his duchy by Pope Leo X, who wanted to put a Medici on the throne. Following his deposed patron into exile at Mantua, Castiglione found himself at a loose end but finally able, as a result, to start a family and to write his great work. *The Courtier* was his attempt to explain what sort of men and women it had taken to make the Urbino court – and, by extension, what it would take to make any social group – into a glittering success.

Set as a long, idealized conversation on four successive evenings in March 1507, *The Courtier* involves some two dozen real-life gentlemen, scholars, soldiers, authors and wits, discussing what qualities characterize the perfect man or woman of the court. Under the firm if humorous supervision of Elisabetta and her teasing lady-in-waiting, Emilia Pia, they consider the importance of birth; of skill at sports, musical instruments, the military arts and Latin; and of flattery, chastity, jokes and puns. In the process they come up with a compendium of Renaissance social values and aspirations, personified by the universal man – knowledgeable in many fields but never so involved in any of them as to be self-absorbed, or so conscious of his own skills as to be forced or studied in displaying them. It was this quality of nonchalance that dominated Castiglione's courtly ideal, and he coined his own word for this, *sprezzatura*, which 'conceals all artistry and makes whatever one says or does seem uncontrived and effortless'.

Castiglione had a less happy life after finishing *The Courtier*. His young wife died in 1520, and he decided to enter the priesthood. He returned to the world of diplomacy, but this time as the papal nuncio to Spain, where he died of the plague in 1529, far from the refined courts he loved. His book had a happier fortune. Published in 1528 by the Aldine Press of Venice, it was an immediate success, going through dozens of editions and translations before the century was over. *The Courtier* remains in many ways the definitive work of Renaissance literature, capturing the age's appreciation of polite and knowledgeable discourse, both in its subject matter and in its discursive framework, with spirited yet friendly men arguing eloquently and warmly under the guidance of two gently mocking women. It has often been said that, after *The Courtier*, men and women became more polite but less sincere. Many called such comportment Italian manners; others saw it as plain hypocrisy. But the book sketched out a new model for civilized behaviour, one that would spread from its elite origins down the social hierarchy, later coming to define the idea of the gentleman. Certainly Castiglione was offering a gentler alternative to the warrior priests and crusading monarchs who, in the name of religion and revenge, would soon be sweeping over Europe.

❧

Raphael

MASTER OF THE HIGH RENAISSANCE

1483–1520

I n a profession that attracts stormy temperaments, the painter Raffaello Sanzio – Raphael – was a zephyr, a handsome gentleman whose good nature was surpassed only by his urbane manners. He was the consummate diplomat, both in life and at work, absorbing and then reconciling disparate ideas in his luminous art. His balanced harmony epitomized High Renaissance painting, which began with Leonardo in the 1480s and continued with Raphael himself, Michelangelo and Titian into the 16th century. His rivals began to move on, however, and it is no coincidence that the High Renaissance lost momentum with Raphael's death in 1520, before sputtering out with the Sack of Rome in 1527.

Raphael was born and brought up in Urbino, among the rolling green hills of central Italy, where his father's position as the duke's court painter brought the boy into contact with both art and the social and cultural milieu of the aristocracy (the sophisticated Urbino court was renowned throughout Italy). Orphaned at the age of 11, Raphael moved to Perugia in around 1500 to study with Perugino, one of the first Italians to paint in oil. He recreated his master's work so deftly that the authorship of some of their paintings was debated for years. After completing his apprenticeship Raphael painted several altarpieces in Perugia, most in oil but some in fresco, adding a more geometrical treatment of figures to Perugino's airy, sweet style.

Raphael travelled to Florence some time around 1504 – just before the last years of the city's art boom – bearing a recommendation from the duchess of Urbino, who praised him as gifted, sensible and well mannered.

His work from this time, mostly portraits and small religious paintings, shows the influence of Leonardo da Vinci, who had recently returned to the city. Raphael turned out dozens of Madonna and Child paintings, rendering figures with idealized classical beauty. To Perugino's soft light and colour he added Leonardo's narrative and movement. One painting shows the Christ Child climbing on to a kneeling lamb; in another he is a restless toddler, twisting in Mary's lap. In his secular portraits Raphael was influenced by the *Mona Lisa*, begun in Florence in about 1503. He borrowed Leonardo's innovative half-figure composition, featuring the sitter from the waist up, arms and elbows anchoring the bottom of a well-defined triangle, but he rejected the work's melancholy palette in favour of luminous flesh tones and rich colours.

By 1507 the art world's epicentre was shifting from Florence to Rome, as Italy's foremost artists and architects gathered at the Vatican, then abuzz with excitement over the construction of the spectacular new St Peter's Basilica. Pope Julius II hired Raphael to fresco his private rooms, the papal *stanze*. In one chamber Raphael painted grand allegories of theology, law, poetry and philosophy, where his populous scenes and muscular figures show the influence of Michelangelo, then working on the Sistine Chapel ceiling. *The School of Athens* (*c.* 1510–12) embodies the High Renaissance in both form and meaning. Against a backdrop of Roman architecture, Raphael placed Aristotle and Plato among ancient philosophers and scientists, many of whom he modelled on his friends.

Raphael lived in Rome for the rest of his life, mingling with the highest circles of society and maintaining a very large workshop. Popes and cardinals commissioned portraits, and Leo X asked him to design biblical scenes for large tapestries and to plan additions to St Peter's (later mostly demolished to make way for Michelangelo's alterations). Nearly all of Raphael's work was portraiture or depictions of sacred subjects. When commissioned to paint a mythological subject, such as the story of Galatea, Raphael sought clues in Classical literature to help recreate the lost art of antiquity; this fresco for the Villa Farnesina in Rome (completed in 1512) re-imagines the tale of sea nymph and shepherd with an energy not found in his earlier work.

Raphael was described as an amorous man, 'delighting much in women and ever ready to serve them', but he never married. He was betrothed in 1514 to the niece of a powerful cardinal, but he repeatedly found reasons to delay the wedding until her untimely death resolved the issue. Instead he maintained a long, apparently happy, relationship with Margherita Luti, a baker's daughter, painting her portrait several times. His reputation for love was so well established that when he died of a fever at the age of 37, rumours abounded that he had been struck down by a surfeit of vigorous love-making.

∞

Leo Africanus

Although he was the author of a best-selling travel guide and something of a minor celebrity, Leo Africanus remains historically elusive. Little is known about his life beyond what he himself mentioned in his guide, and centuries of searching by devoted followers have turned up only a handful of archival references and autograph fragments. Born al-Hassan ibn Muhammad al-Wazzan al-Fasi in Granada, around the time it was conquered by the Spanish in 1492, he was taken to Morocco by parents who, like many Moors, refused to live under Christian rule. Possibly he studied at al-Qarawiyyin University in Fez, although by the age of 14 he had already supposedly left Morocco on the first of several long journeys – to Constantinople, Beirut and Baghdad. In 1509–10 he travelled with his uncle, the ambassador of the sultan at Fez, across the Sahara to Timbuktu, to meet representatives of the Songhai emperor. Two years later al-Hassan claimed he passed through Timbuktu again, this time travelling east along the Sahel to Gao, Agadez and, eventually, Sudan and Egypt, returning to Morocco along the north African coast.

There is some question as to whether al-Hassan actually made this second Timbuktu trip or simply repeated what he read of other Arab travellers who had made the journey. He unquestionably returned to Constantinople in 1517, however, for he was the Moroccan ambassador himself this time, visiting the Turkish sultan Selim I. He then went on to the Nile port of Rosetta, just in time to see the Ottomans conquer Egypt. After stopping by Cairo and Aswan, al-Hassan crossed the Red Sea to Arabia – perhaps to make his obligatory *hajj*, or pilgrimage, to Mecca, although this is not mentioned in his writings. On his way home, somewhere near Crete, al-Hassan's developing career as a scholar–diplomat–wanderer abruptly ended when he was captured at sea by Christian corsairs.

Recognizing, perhaps from his maps and manuscripts, that they had seized a prestigious prisoner, al-Hassan's captors took him to Rome as a present for Pope Leo X. After over a year in prison he won his freedom by converting to Christianity. Recent claims have it that al-Hassan's was a false conversion, undertaken only to escape prison and for the chance it offered to explore a society that had become largely impenetrable to Muslims; all that is certain is the highly public and festive nature of his baptism. With Pope Leo and several high churchmen serving as his godfathers, the grand ceremony was staged on 6 January 1520, and al-Hassan al-Wassan, as was customary in these events, took the name of his chief sponsor, Giovanni Leone de' Medici, later shortened to Leo Africanus, or 'Leo the African'.

Freed from confinement, the newly minted Leo Africanus moved between Rome and Bologna, where he taught Arabic and set to work on a manuscript he called 'Cosmographia et geographia de Affrica'. Working from his original notes, he produced a mixed travel narrative and geographical study of a region and a culture that fascinated Europeans as intensely as it excluded them. Leo never published his work, but it was brought out – in a Westernized form, with books, chapters and correct punctuation – by a Venetian printer in 1550, as *Della descrittione dell'Africa*.

Della descrittione went through dozens of editions, and was an instant best-seller in one of the Renaissance's most popular and enduring literary genres. The English version, *A History and Description of Africa*, taken from a bad Latin translation, came out in 1600. The title belied the work's content, however, for it traced only Leo's travels in north Africa, barely reaching the southern edges of the Sahara. Even so, it introduced Europeans to many hitherto unknown realms and cities such as Timbuktu, which Leo described as pleasant, well governed and fabulously rich, sparking a fascination for this distant outpost that lasted for centuries. His accounts of Islamic Africa were of tremendous importance in filling in what for most readers was a blank immensity. The region was rapidly becoming both more threatening and more mysterious, as once reliable Arab–Christian intellectual exchanges, through Spain and the Levantine trade, were broken by the Spanish *Reconquista* and Ottoman ascendancy.

Leo Africanus was probably unaware of the success of *Della descrittione*. Some time soon after 1527 – and long before the work was published – he effectively vanished from the historical record. Some maintain that he made his way back to the Maghreb and there returned to Islam. Others claim that he settled into European life and even travelled north of the Alps. This, along with his final faith, his resting place and much else about him, remains as unknowable as the cities he once so tantalizingly described.

CR

5. Collapse of the Old Order

1510–1535

Writing around 1513, Niccolò Machiavelli cautioned those who might hope to profit from the great events then roiling Italy: 'There is nothing harder to deal with, more doubtful of success, nor more dangerous to manage than taking the lead in introducing a new order of things.' No one really knew what this new order might be, although Machiavelli himself feared one thing: that the balance of power in Italy, and the peace it had produced for over forty years, had been swept away by foreign invasion and would not return soon. Ill-disciplined armies — French, Spanish, German, Swiss and Italian — ravaged their way back and forth across the peninsula, pillaging the countryside as they slaughtered each other. The traditional Italian powers — Florence, Milan, Naples, Venice and the papacy — so lost control of the situation that, together or separately, they could not stop the tragic finale. In 1527 a mob of German and Spanish soldiers, nominally fighting for Emperor Charles V, mutinied and wandered south, finding Rome itself an easy target. Breaking through the poorly defended walls, the Spanish and German marauders visited more destruction on Rome than the Turks had ever caused in Constantinople. When they finally straggled off a month later, bloated with booty, they quite literally took the Italian Renaissance with them.

Many of the Germans who looted Rome were proto-Protestants, disciples of Luther pillaging in his name, even after he had disowned them. For them, the papacy had lost its legitimacy by becoming too Italian – too busy warring with its neighbours and too beguiled by the humanist fantasies of Classical Rome actually to save any souls. This revulsion with an excessively

Italianate papacy had long been gaining strength in Europe, although adroit monarchs in Spain (in 1482) and France (in 1516) had successfully channelled such hostilities into state-building, by establishing their own 'national' churches and clergy. Germany had no such centralized control, however, and its semi-independent principalities, archbishoprics and char- tered cities found cohesion in Lutheranism as they claimed independence from their nominal overlord, the Holy Roman Emperor (and champion of the Church) Charles V.

The Protestant Reformation, which in its first years had seemed to pope and emperor alike a mere quarrel among monks, soon became a quarrel among princes. It was taken up by the Swedish king, Gustav I, in 1523, and by 1533 all of Scandinavia was Lutheran, as were large swaths of the eastern Baltic. Yet Luther's initial demands for a more local and personalized Christianity slipped from princely control. Germany in particular was racked by populist religious uprisings, from the Peasants' War of 1524–25 to the fleeting establishment of an apocryphal Anabaptist theocracy in the Rhenish city of Münster, in 1534–35. Between 1525 and 1534 England's Henry VIII also broke with Rome. Unlike Gustav in Sweden, however, Henry initially aimed less at Church reform than at obtaining a divorce from Catherine of Aragon, something that Charles V, who was her nephew, kept the pope from granting. As a result, the Anglican Confession, as it came to be known, remained – at least during the rest of Henry's reign – closer theologically to Rome than either to Luther or to the more evangelical form of Protestantism founded by Jean Calvin.

The political and religious earthquakes of this generation were further intensified by a wave of new technologies. The gunpowder revolution, which had begun in the 1440s with the use of cannon in siege warfare, was extended to the battlefield in the early 16th century, through the matchlock musket, or arquebus. Although a familiar weapon by the 1490s, it was only in the early 16th century that matchlocks were fully integrated into battle, by the Spanish infantry regiments, or *tercios*, who coordinated their musketeers with pike and sword men. That such a combination could take on either cavalry or any other form of infantry was famously and repeatedly demonstrated during the Italian Wars. The Imperial *tercios* had their greatest success at the Battle of Pavia (1525), losing only 500 men as against 10,000 of their opponents, wiping out much of the French nobility and even capturing King François I. Even as Pavia secured a place for the matchlock musket that would last over a century, German watchmakers were putting the final touches on its eventual successor – the wheel-lock. Already in the early 1530s Benvenuto Cellini could boast of owning several of these newfangled devices, which allowed a man to fight from horseback, in all weather, and at night.

Training musketeers, casting cannon and investing in the new generation of complex fortifications were expensive propositions that only the wealthiest nations could take on. The changing technology of war thus accelerated the shift in power away from many small cities and states towards a few larger ones. The rising dominance of Spain, France and England was balanced to some extent, however, by the expansion of print technology that could favour weaker powers. The success of the Protestant Reformation in particular can be linked to the publishing industry, which helped realize in very practical terms Luther's profession of the supremacy of God's Word by producing vernacular Bibles, hymnals and catechisms for both theologians and the general public. The printing press also served as a more aggressive element in the increasingly tense religious atmosphere of the 1520s and 1530s. Both Catholics and Protestants churned out cheap pamphlets, broadsides and screeds attacking the other confession with parodies and woodcut cartoons that appealed to a mass audience. Although at the beginning of the 16th century the printing press had been a great innovative force for spreading learning, literature and music, by the following generation it had proved a potent weapon the first great propaganda war of modern times.

Hayreddin Barbarossa

KING OF THE CORSAIRS

died 1546

Barbarossa's rise from near obscurity to almost boundless wealth and power can be traced in the names he carried. He was born Yakupo-lu Khīzr, or Khīzr, son of Yakup – a Turkish *sipahi* ('knight') who had taken part in the Ottoman conquest of Lesbos (Mytilene) in 1462. Receiving a fief for himself on the island, Yakup also took a Greek Christian wife there and then settled down to run a pottery business. Khīzr was the third son of their six children. The family operation grew to include a modest ship, captained by Yakup's second son, Oruç, who carried pottery around the Levant while indulging in a little piracy when the occasion arose. Before long Khīzr, who had originally worked the kilns, fell into piracy as well. At the age of 20, Khīzr had a ship of his own, and from his base in Thrace he began hauling – and hijacking – goods all around the Aegean.

Casual piracy was common around the eastern Mediterranean in the 1490s, a time of unusual instability. The Ottomans were consolidating their hold on the region, but older powers such as the Venetians and the Knights of St John still held territory and maintained large navies in the area. It was a dangerous time for small fry such as Oruç and Khīzr, but they soon found powerful patrons among the Turkish and Egyptian elites to protect them and furnish them with war galleys.

Eager for loot and ready to wage a holy war, the two brothers moved into the western Mediterranean to contest Spanish encroachments along the Barbary Coast of Africa. Oruç gained a leadership role in establishing an Islamic military presence there, especially in Algiers. His *nom de guerre* was a conflation of terms bestowed by friends and opponents: he was called Baba Oruç, or 'Father Oruç', by the grateful Moors, while the Italians knew him as 'Barbarossa', because of his signature red beard. Although Oruç was killed in battle in 1518, his name continued to inspire terror among Christians, and when Khı̄zr assumed his brother's authority, he took his name as well, even dyeing his own auburn beard red.

The new Barbarossa rapidly surpassed the old one. Pillaging Christian coasts and sea lanes from Spain and the Balearics to Sicily, Sardinia and Italy, he grew rich on plunder and enslaved so many Europeans that they said it was 'raining Christians in Algiers'. At the same time Barbarossa worked tirelessly to spread Ottoman power and was rewarded by Sultan Suleiman the Magnificent with Oruç's old positions – *pasha* ('governor') of Algiers and *Kaptan-ı Derya* ('admiral of the Turkish fleet'). Suleiman also honoured him with the Arabic title *Kheir-ed-din* ('Goodness of the Faith'), and he was known thenceforth as Hayreddin Barbarossa. Such was his reputation for relentless ferocity – he commanded up to 200 ships with 30,000 janissaries – that many a coastal town surrendered simply at the sight of his sails. He established semi-permanent naval bases on nominally Christian islands off Sicily and Naples, and for nine months he virtually annexed the French port of Toulon, turning the town's cathedral into a mosque. He refused to leave until King François I, Suleiman's ally, paid him off with the equivalent of nearly three metric tons of gold.

In 1545, having carried out a last devastating sweep along the Italian coast, Barbarossa retired to Istanbul. He took with him immense treasure, some 20,000 slaves and a new, 18-year-old wife, whom he had captured while sacking Reggio Calabria. The Turks greeted him wildly, calling him 'King of the Sea' – which in a sense he had been. When he died of a fever barely a year later, a magnificent mausoleum, designed by the great architect Sinan, was erected in his honour.

Hayreddin Barbarossa was only one of many corsairs who started from nothing to rise high in the Ottoman world. For such men Spain was the enemy, but Italy was the preferred target. They pillaged the country throughout the 16th century, eradicating entire coastal villages, cutting off commercial centres such as Naples and Genoa for months at a time, and even dropping anchor in the mouth of the Tiber – nearly capturing the pope while he was out hunting, not an hour's ride away. Even as French and Imperial troops ravaged their countryside in endless wars over the peninsula, Italians found themselves faced with this second threat coming from over the horizon. Between 1520 and 1600 they saw their legendary wealth, which had once fuelled the Renaissance, evaporate – looted, bartered to ransom captives or spent to build a thousand watch-towers along the coasts. As the soldiers contended and the corsairs grew rich, the Italians themselves became destitute, weaker and fewer.

Lucas Cranach the Elder

THE REFORMATION'S ILLUSTRATOR

1472–1553

Because of Lucas Cranach, we know how Martin Luther looked in disguise. In a painting done in 1522, Cranach depicts a fugitive who had grown out his monk's hairstyle and sprouted an impressive beard while holed up in a castle under the alias 'George'. A wealthy artist, mayor and town apothecary, Cranach produced many portraits of his friend Luther as well as of other important Reformation figures. He was the son of a painter and trained in his father's workshop in Kronach, about 80 kilometres (50 miles) north of Nuremberg, and around 1501 he made his way to Vienna. There he mingled with humanists, painting their portraits in the Danube School tradition, an expressive style with dramatic backgrounds that vie for attention with the central figures. The forests and hills behind Cranach's subjects almost vibrate with meaning as symbolic flora and fauna transmit information about the sitters.

In 1505 Cranach went to Wittenberg as court painter to Duke Frederick III of Saxony, one of the seven German electors charged with choosing new Holy Roman Emperors. Courtly portraits, hunting scenes and altarpieces make up much of Cranach's work from this time, but he took on other jobs as well, designing coins, costumes, carnival masks and coats of arms, and even painting fences when necessary – all at an astonishing pace. He met Luther in Wittenberg, where the two became very close: the artist was best man at Luther's wedding in 1525, and each served as godfather to the other's children. Cranach made Luther's vision visible through religious paintings, book illustrations and propaganda cartoons. He provided art for

Luther's landmark German Bible of 1522 and created many 'law and gospel' paintings with the Protestant message that faith, not ritual, led to salvation. His polemical works include *The Passion of Christ and Anti-Christ* (1521), a booklet with pairs of scenes contrasting Christ with the pope. In one set Christ is crowned with a ring of thorns while the pope receives the triple tiara; in another Christ kneels to wash Peter's feet as the enthroned pontiff permits a supplicant to kiss his shoe.

Like their master, members of the Cranach workshop produced art with impressive speed. The artist's sons Hans and Lucas the Younger turned out thousands of copies of Luther's likeness, for example, to meet the increasing demand. Also popular were Lucas the Elder's female nudes. Italian artists sanitized female nudity – or so they pretended – by rendering women in idealized, heroic forms; Cranach, on the other hand, dispatched with coyness. His *Venus and Cupid* of 1509 features a voluptuous goddess wearing just a wispy piece of drapery and a knowing gaze. Similarly, his *Venus* of 1532 is simply a lovely blonde, *à la nature*, on a plain black background, with neither symbols nor setting to legitimize her state of undress. It was so racy that certain authorities in London balked at displaying it publicly – in 2008. (The image was eventually approved, and appeared without controversy in posters promoting an exhibition of Cranach's work.)

More than a thousand paintings from Cranach's workshop survive today, which suggests a great number of commissions. Not all his clients were reformists: well after Cranach was established in Lutheran circles, he still accepted orders from Catholic patrons, painting more Virgin and Child compositions after 1520 than he had before. In the 1520s and 1530s Cranach even received commissions from Cardinal Albrecht of Brandenburg, the very cleric whose support for selling indulgences drove Luther to assert his 95 theses in 1517.

Cranach's great appeal and productivity ensured a handsome income throughout his life, as did nearly fifty years as court painter to three successive German electors. He also excelled outside the art world, winning terms as Wittenberg's mayor in 1537, 1540 and 1543, and running successful businesses that further enhanced his fortune. In 1520 he secured a lucrative apothecary's licence, becoming the town's sole provider of medicines, spices, sealing wax and ink. To satisfy the growing interest in Reformation tracts, he opened a bookshop and, with a colleague, launched a profitable publishing house. Luther himself never took payment for his writings, but Cranach became one of Saxony's wealthiest men in part by selling them.

In 1550 the artist handed over his workshop to his son; in 1552 he moved to Weimar, where he died the following year. Marking his grave is a full-length relief sculpture showing Cranach in peaceful repose, painter's palette in hand, with text hailing him as *pictor celerrimus*, 'the swiftest of painters'.

∞

Thomas More

DEFENDING THE 'GOOD CATHOLYKE REALME'

1478–1535

With his quick wit and wicked sense of humour, Thomas More could reduce the most dour colleague to fits of laughter. As he joked with friends, however, a hair shirt excoriated his skin until blood stained his clothing. He was a brilliant man who nonetheless valued order and obedience above all; he once argued that even a bad law should not be questioned. As England began to lean away from Rome, More remained his country's most prominent defender of Catholic orthodoxy, and his devotion to tradition ultimately led to his death.

More grew up in a wealthy, influential London family and attended Oxford University, where, along with his liberal arts studies, he wrote comic sketches that he performed with dramatic flair. While his peers completed their degrees and began humanist studies in Italy, however, More dropped out of Oxford. He chose to study law, which, like religion, was for him a predictable construct that corralled life's chaos. While he ultimately did not embrace all of humanism, he was well versed in the Classics and learned ancient Greek, a hallmark of the humanist movement. He and his friend Desiderius Erasmus especially enjoyed Greek satirists, and they translated several ancient texts together. More himself wrote hundreds of satiric epigrams – short, sharp poems with a twist – on everything from bad breath to the brevity of life. In one case he even offers flatulence as a metaphor for political expression. 'To breake a little winde, sometimes ones life doth save,' he wrote, arguing that bodies and states alike must be permitted to vent freely for optimum health.

In a letter written in 1519 Erasmus reported that his friend had considered the clergy but feared he could not remain chaste; More's later polemical writings dwell on lechery, suggesting it was much on his mind. In 1505 he married a wealthy young country girl, Jane Colt, who died after bearing at least four children in six years. Known for his practicality and quick decisions, More was married again within a month, this time to a spirited, well-to-do widow named Alice, who was eighteen years older than Jane and eight years older than More himself. As Erasmus put it, Alice was 'not precisely beautiful', but she was devoted to his children and ran the household with a plucky aplomb that both amused and exasperated her husband.

Between 1510 and 1518 More prosecuted criminals in London, ran a private legal practice, served the king in several roles – he would eventually rise to become Chancellor in 1529 – and (in 1516) completed his most famous book. He called it *Utopia*, a term he coined from the Greek for 'no place'; it imagines an ideal world 'diametrically opposed to ours', both geographically and morally. In the 1520s he used his increasing influence as one of the king's foremost counsellors to oppose the Lutheran movement, banning Protestant books and prosecuting heretics, and a number of both perished by fire. As More enforced canon law, however, the king began challenging Rome over his 'great matter' – his seven-year quest to divorce his first wife, Catherine of Aragon, and to marry Anne Boleyn. When the pope forbade Henry to take a new bride, the king declared the Catholic Church irrelevant and established himself as supreme head of a new Church of England. The anguished More could no longer obey both his conscience and his king, and in 1532 resigned the chancellorship. He was the last important figure in the realm during Henry's reign to advocate the burning of heretics.

More retreated to Chelsea and churned out anti-heresy tracts, his playful sense of satire hardening into sour polemic. Hoping to avoid trouble, he kept silent about Henry's marital issues, but he was forced into the open in 1534. That year Henry required citizens to swear an oath that recognized Anne as queen and acknowledged England's break with the Catholic Church. While More was willing to accept Henry's new wife, he politely and repeatedly declined to comment on his country's relationship with Rome.

More was sent to the Tower of London to reconsider, but being confined to a cell was more of a reward than a punishment. More would happily have adopted an ascetic life years earlier, he told his daughter, had it not been for his love of his family. During a year in the Tower he waved away pleas to swear Henry's oath, and on 1 July 1535 he was at last put on trial for treason. More, who knew the law better than anyone, calmly refused to explain his objections to the oath, still hoping to avoid conviction by recusing himself. But the court found him guilty of high treason and sentenced him to die on 6 July. Remaining calm until the end, he climbed the rickety scaffold that day and forgave his executioner. 'Pluck up thy spirits, man,' he reportedly said, 'and do thine office.' Adding a last request, he asked the axeman to aim well for, as he put it, 'my neck is very short'.

Martin Luther

A NEW CHURCH

1483–1546

The Reformation began with a bolt of lightning. One day in July 1505 a thunderstorm outside the German town of Erfurt knocked the young Martin Luther to the ground. Terrified, he vowed to become a monk if he survived, and two weeks later he entered the order of the Augustinian Hermits. Catholicism held that to deny oneself pleasure pleased God, and the Augustinians offered many opportunities for pious discomfort.

As a monk, Luther went to extremes, even by ascetic standards he took up to six hours to detail his sins in confession, for instance, but still worried that his efforts were inadequate. The prior ordered him to begin a doctorate in theology, thinking it would give Luther's intellect something to gnaw on. Luther scoured scripture and found no evidence that Church-sanctioned 'good works' brought grace. In fact, they began to seem like self-serving acts to extract divine reward. The ledger system at Catholicism's core, he decided, had been invented by the Church to make itself seem necessary for salvation. A radical new notion occurred to him: grace was a gift from God to the faithful. It could not be purchased through prayer or cash payments to the Church.

Thus the stage was set in 1517, when an indulgence-selling Dominican, Johann Tetzel, arrived in Saxony to raise funds for the lavish new St Peter's Basilica being built in Rome. Luther, by then a professor at the University of Wittenberg, was appalled. He compiled nearly one hundred objections to the selling of indulgences and invited his colleagues to a discussion – probably by nailing his statements and a notice on the doors of the church.

Not one person showed up to debate his 95 theses. Luther's treatise took on a life of its own, however, as printers produced and sold copies without his knowledge. Within eight weeks the text had spread throughout Europe. As his ideas gained influence, Rome proclaimed it heresy to question indulgences, and in 1518 Luther was summoned to an assembly in Augsburg and ordered to recant. He refused, unless his accusers could cite a biblical passage that endorsed indulgences. The incensed officials cut the interview short, and Luther's friends, hearing he was to be taken to Rome in chains, whisked him back to Wittenberg.

Previous efforts at reform had mostly originated – and been rejected – among the Latin-speaking elite. But Luther's teachings, written in German, spread beyond those insular circles, and the new printing technology allowed reformers to distribute his ideas farther and faster than earlier dissidents dreamed possible. Luther was famous by the time he was ordered to another assembly, in 1521, this time in the city of Worms. Questioned before Charles V himself, Luther again refused to recant, and the emperor formally declared Luther a heretic, eligible for a heretic's death. To keep Luther from harm's way, his supporters staged a kidnapping on his way back to Wittenberg and bundled him off to Wartburg Castle, owned by a sympathetic prince.

While in hiding, Luther wrote prolifically and produced one of his greatest achievements: a German vernacular Bible. Working mostly from Erasmus's new Greek Bible, he used colloquial prose rather than high-flown churchly language. It proved hugely popular: the first edition of 1522 sold out quickly, despite costing 1½ florins – 50 per cent more than a well-fed pig ready for market.

When Luther surfaced in Wittenberg nearly a year later, his movement had taken root throughout much of northern Europe. He mapped out a new church doctrine, one with no clerical gatekeepers between God and the laity, and continued to define Lutheranism throughout the last two decades of his life. He insisted, for example, that lay worshippers receive both the bread and wine of the Eucharist; in Catholicism, only priests were permitted wine during the Mass. An accomplished musician, Luther wrote German hymns so the faithful could worship in song rather than listen passively to clerics'

Latin chants. He also advocated education for all social classes – girls as well as boys – and dismissed the 400-year-old policy of priestly celibacy, arguing that a husband and wife in the act of love were just as holy as a nun at prayer.

At the age of 42 Luther himself took a bride – Katherine von Bora, a former nun who had escaped her convent hidden in a herring barrel. Family life seemed to agree with him. Although he was in some ways a difficult man, who enthusiastically insulted his opponents – including the pope, the king of England, even the reform-friendly Erasmus – Luther's tone softened when discussing his wife and children. After his wedding, for example, he described the pleasure of waking to see his wife's two pigtails on the pillow beside him. He was also deeply involved in the day-to-day lives of his children. After one infant had wailed inconsolably for an hour, Luther, at his wits' end, announced: 'This is the sort of thing that has caused the Church fathers to vilify marriage.' But of his first son he wrote that 'Hans is cutting his teeth and beginning to make a joyous nuisance of himself. These are the joys of marriage of which the pope is not worthy.'

Bartolomé de Las Casas

APOSTLE AND MISSIONARY TO THE WEST INDIES

1484–1566

When Christopher Columbus returned to Seville after discovering the New World, 9-year-old Bartolomé de Las Casas was in the crowd cheering Spain's imperial triumph. Barely a year later young Bartolomé began a more profound encounter with the Americas when his father, Pedro, who had accompanied Columbus on his second voyage, brought him back a souvenir – his own personal Indian slave. Eight years later the Las Casas family joined the tide of Spanish emigrants to the island of Hispaniola, to become part of the local planter aristocracy and to manage their own *encomienda* – a plantation staffed with Indian slaves. In around 1510, however, Bartolomé was moved to take holy orders. For a while he combined sacred and secular activities – even running his personal *encomienda* – but he found it increasingly hard to reconcile the inherent contradictions between his faith and the realities of colonial power.

As Las Casas saw it, the New World's natives were 'humble, patient, and peaceable ... devoid of rancours, hatreds or desire for vengeance ... poor people, because they not only possess little but have no desire for worldly goods. For this reason they [were] not arrogant, embittered or greedy.' The *conquistadores*' greed made short work of such innocence, he noted, for 'into this sheepfold ... came some Spaniards who immediately behaved like ravening wild beasts ... killing, terrorizing, afflicting, torturing and destroying the native peoples'. From the earliest days settlers who needed labourers to dig for gold and work their plantations had felt free to seize and enslave any natives they could, killing those who resisted or tried to flee.

As a chaplain during the *conquistadores'* capture of Cuba in 1513, Las Casas witnessed such behaviour at first hand and became convinced that the entire Spanish enterprise in the New World was both immoral and illegal. While preaching to natives on his own plantation in 1514, he had a sudden revelation – that 'no one with a clear conscience could enslave Indians' – and he consequently liberated his own slaves and sold his *encomienda*. Finagling leave from his parish, he sailed to Spain, where he preached his new-found passion for Indian rights to Cardinal Cisneros, who responded by naming him 'Protector of the Indians'. His pleas so impressed the young King Charles V that the monarch granted Las Casas a stretch of Venezuelan coast to establish a Utopian settlement and develop a new model for colonial relations. There, it was hoped, Indian and Spanish farmers could thrive together, sharing agricultural techniques and selling their produce for profit. The colony was a dismal failure, however: none of the Spaniards Las Casas recruited actually wanted to farm, and the neighbouring warriors soon attacked and destroyed his small village.

Troubled by this setback, Las Casas joined the Dominicans, who were speaking out against the ongoing genocide. Spending the next two decades on Hispaniola and touring Spain's newly conquered territories in Mexico and Central America, he collected detailed accounts of what he considered Spanish atrocities against the Indians. In 1537 he persuaded Pope Paul III to issue the bull *Sublimis Deus*, making it Church policy that American Indians, as a rational people, had inherent sovereignty over their own land and could not be arbitrarily enslaved, even though they were heathens. In 1542 Las Casas presented his *Brevísima relación de la destrucción de las Indias* ('A Brief Account of the Destruction of the Indies'), his essay on the mistreatment of the Caribbean Indians, to Charles V, who was so horrified by its lurid stories that he hastily passed the so-called 'New Laws', which banned both the enslavement of peaceful Indians and the *encomienda* system. Eight years later Las Casas enjoyed the crowning moment of his career: he publicly and successfully defended the New Laws against the humanist Juan Ginés de Sepúlveda, an advocate of the Aristotelian argument that Native Americans were 'natural slaves'.

Despite official support for his arguments, Las Casas's campaign was not an unalloyed success. Attempts to impose the New Laws on the American colonies almost drove Spanish settlers to civil war. When trying to implement them, the governor of Peru was overthrown and murdered. Las Casas himself, when granted the bishopric of Chiapas in southern Mexico, rejected the position as too dangerous and instead retired to Spain with a pension. Settlers loudly protested that without forced labour they would never grow rich in the New World, and Las Casas himself only made a bad situation worse when he offered his own solution to the problem: instead of using Indians the Spaniards should import African slaves.

Titian

DYNAMIC COLOUR IN VENICE

c. 1485–1576

W hen the great Giovanni Bellini died in 1516, there was no painter
left in Venice to rival his student Tiziano Vecellio, known today as
Titian. Eventually eclipsing his late master, Titian reigned as the republic's
leading artist for over half a century and won regard throughout the peninsula
and beyond. The first Italian master with an international base of clients,
he delighted patrons with his typically Venetian style. Painters of Florence
and Rome focused on balance and harmony, plotting out sculptural forms
with mathematical precision; Venetian artists, on the other hand, organized
their more lyrical compositions with colour rather than geometry. Titian's
palette comprised an unusually vast range of colour – often with very
intense pigments – which he applied in innovative ways to portray highly
realistic textures.

At the age of 10 Titian left his village in the Dolomites and travelled
110 kilometres (68 miles) south to study in Venice with Bellini, whose new
technique captured light and evoked mood in scenes with softly edged
figures. To this style the young painter added a greater sense of passion and
energy, and works from the first half of his career fairly burst with verve
and colour – his *Bacchus and Ariadne*, for example, which he completed
in 1523. His vigorous brushstrokes are more suggestive of the late 18th
and early 19th centuries, and many of his mature works seem to anticipate
Impressionism's blurred softness.

Titian replaced Bellini as the official painter of the Republic in 1516, and in
the next fifteen years he painted several important altarpieces in and around

Venice. One commission, the *Assumption of the Virgin*, still ranks among the world's largest panel paintings. Completed in 1518 for the Franciscan church of Santa Maria dei Frari, it covers a space nearly 7 metres (23 feet) tall and 3.65 metres (12 feet) wide. In it Titian dispenses with the symmetrical order of his southern colleagues and stacks three tiers of riotous figures: the earth-bound apostles looking up to the sky; Mary, buoyed heavenward by a team of chubby putti; and at the top, a welcoming God the Father. In the two years Titian worked on the painting he endured regular criticism from one Fra Germano, who worried that the apostles were much too large compared to the Virgin and the Father. Titian tried to explain that the figures would be in proper scale when viewed from a distance, but the monk was not convinced until an outside authority persuaded him otherwise.

In 1526 Titian supplied the same church with another major altarpiece, the *Pesaro Madonna*. Its figures are traditional – patrons kneel dutifully before a seated Virgin – but the composition was radical for the time. Unlike Leonardo's *Last Supper* or Raphael's *School of Athens*, which both contain strong horizontal lines and central focal points, this painting features a striking slanted arrangement: Mary, the dominant figure, rests off-centre at the top of a diagonal, and Titian uses high contrast, bright colours and perspective lines to draw the viewer's eye towards her. His later works often employ palettes more complementary than contrasting; many seem less frenetic yet remain charged with emotion and even eroticism. His worldly nude *Venus of Urbino* (1538), for example, seems to be painted in soft focus; she lies fetchingly on a bed, head tilted at a coquettish slant, gazing directly at the viewer.

Working nearly all his life in Venice, Titian travelled relatively little. He made one year-long visit to Rome (where Michelangelo reportedly praised his colours but ridiculed his drawing skills), some brief visits to other Italian cities and two trips to Augsburg for one of his most important clients, Charles V. There the emperor commissioned paintings of himself, which Titian completed in the 1540s. Charles held the artist in very high esteem: when Titian dropped his brush one day while working on Charles's portrait, the Habsburg ruler was said to have knelt down himself to retrieve it. Such portraits made Titian famous and put him in great demand – he painted the likenesses of so many important men and women of the 16th century that one early biographer reported that it was difficult to count them all.

Towards the end of his life Titian worked as a studio painter, often creating new versions of his earlier works. He was well into his eighties when a wave of plague swept into Venice, killing him along with 51,000 others – nearly a third of the population. His vision influenced his Venetian contemporaries Tintoretto and Veronese as well as the 17th-century artists Rubens, Rembrandt and Velázquez. Later still, Titian's feathery brushstrokes and glowing light inspired Edouard Manet, one of the earliest Impressionists, who spent hours in the Louvre studying and copying Titian's masterpieces.

ॐ

Nicolaus Kratzer

ROYAL WATCHMAKER AND ASTRONOMER

1486/87–after 1550

By the early 16th century the classical and secular values that had
triumphed in Italian cultural life had also gained a wide following
in the Holy Roman Empire, France, the Low Countries and Hungary.
When it came to humanism, however, England lagged behind the continent.
A century of wars and dynastic squabbles – first with the French and then
among themselves – had left the English with little appetite for mastering
Latin rhetoric or Greek science. A sclerotic scholasticism dominated Oxford
and Cambridge, while the few Italians active in London or Southampton
were less likely to be humanists than sharp-dealing bankers, whose business
practices regularly provoked xenophobic riots.

The conservative and marginalized cultural life of England began to
improve with the early Tudor kings. The young Henry VIII was especially
eager to catch up with the decorative arts and the fashionable thoughts that
were current in intellectual circles across the Channel, and he often invited
outsiders versed in the New Learning to his court. One who responded was
Nicolaus Kratzer. The Munich-born son of a sawsmith, Kratzer enrolled at
the University of Cologne and received his first degree in 1509. Afterwards,
he studied astronomy for a time – which is to say, he copied out manuscripts
– at a monastery near Vienna. His learning was apparently enough to
impress Erasmus, who in turn put him in touch with Thomas More and the
churchman Cuthbert Tunstall when the two were emissaries of Henry VIII
to the Low Countries. Tunstall then wrote to Henry about Kratzer's native
fluency in 'High Almayn' (High, or Upland, German), suggesting he might

be useful as a go-between, diplomatic courier or spy among those Imperial princes who spoke the language.

Evidently Kratzer had other ambitions, for in around 1517 he made his way to England furnished with enough scientific instruments – astrolabes, armillary spheres, books on Ptolemy – to support his claims to scientific knowledge. He seems to have succeeded in passing himself off as more than just the son of a sawsmith, for by 1520 he had landed a job tutoring Thomas More's children in astronomy and mathematics. The next year he began lecturing on elementary astronomy and astrolabe construction at Oxford as Cardinal Thomas Wolsey's protégé. That appointment ended in 1524, however (perhaps he was spending too much time in London and abroad, on his own or the king's business). Thereafter Kratzer had to get by on his stipend as Henry's 'estronomyer' and 'deviser of the Kinge's horologes' – designer, that is, of the royal clocks and sundials.

The modest pay of £20 a year that Kratzer received – the royal falcon master earned twice as much – reflected his lowly status at court. Perhaps there was a language problem – even after Kratzer had served Henry for thirty years, the king still mocked him for not speaking better English. Yet even while he was teaching at Oxford, he was apparently less prized for his scientific lectures than for his skill at incorporating the latest astronomical theories into complex timepieces. He put up his first sundial, at St Mary's Church, to commemorate a meeting of Oxford divines called by Cardinal Wolsey to condemn Luther. He celebrated gaining his Oxford master's degree by crafting another dial with multiple faces that could tell the time all day long. On it he wrote of being 'the astronomer of King Henry, the eighth of that name, who held [me] very dear', insisting that 'at the time I was the admiration of that generation', even though '[I] always drank in the German fashion and could swallow whatever liquor there was'.

Kratzer also designed mechanical clocks. One of these he built with the French clockmaker Nicholas Oursian for Henry at Hampton Court. Based on Copernican theory, the clock told not only the time, but also the day, the month, the sun's place in the zodiac and the age of the moon, as well as the high tide at London Bridge – useful when Henry set off for town on his barge. Unfortunately, the mechanism and decorations of this grand Renaissance artefact have been completely reworked over the centuries, and almost nothing remains of the original. Kratzer's many sundials have also mostly vanished. The only survivor is a fist-sized polyhedron of gilded brass conserved at Oxford and reproduced in a pair of paintings by Hans Holbein. Perhaps Holbein himself was the most significant humanist discovery that Kratzer brought to England – supposedly he persuaded his fellow Bavarian to seek a place at Henry's court. Certainly it was Holbein, and not any of his teachings or devices, that gave Kratzer his lasting fame, for he is the subject of one of the paintings – surrounded by his craftsman's tools and grasping the engraved bulk of his polyhedral sundial.

Bernard van Orley

WEAVER OF PAINTINGS

c. 1488–1541

When Henry VIII of England died in 1547, his treasures included enough tapestry to stretch for 5 kilometres (3 miles) if laid end to end – more than 2,700 pieces. Many were small bedspreads and the like, but several were enormous sets covering hundreds of square yards. They were staggeringly expensive, with one set running to more than £1,500 – enough for a well-equipped battleship. In Italy the tapestries designed by Raphael for the Sistine Chapel cost Pope Leo X nearly 16,000 ducats, five times what Michelangelo earned for frescoing the entire ceiling. When Renaissance rulers wanted to dazzle the world with a show of wealth and power, they deployed tapestries.

Sharing Henry and Leo's taste for luxurious weavings was the Holy Roman Emperor Charles V. His magnificent collection featured many works by the Brussels native and tapestry master Bernard van Orley, who had begun his career as a painter. Van Orley was a member of the Romanism school, a group of northern artists who began incorporating Italian elements into their work during the late 15th and early 16th centuries. It is unlikely that van Orley ever studied in Italy himself: his father, Valentin, was also an artist and is assumed to have been his teacher. In 1515 Bernard entered the service of the Habsburgs, and in 1518 Margaret of Austria commissioned several portraits of court members, including Charles V. Van Orley also painted a number of large altarpieces that incorporated Renaissance-style ornament and architectural design, which he probably learned by studying engravings of Italian works.

By the early 1520s van Orley had become a leading artist in the Low Countries and was running a large, prestigious workshop in Brussels that specialized in portraits, altarpieces and stained glass. Perhaps drawn by the lavish sums that woven work commanded, he turned to textiles, and by blending Italian trends with Flemish innovation he created a style that redefined Netherlandish tapestry.

Before van Orley's time, woven pieces were often busily patterned, more like wallpaper than coherently composed art. Tapestries were typically designed by painters, and, like that era's frescoes, woven scenes lacked a realistic sense of depth and volume. *Mille-fleurs* and fruit vied for backdrop space with rabbits, monkeys and unicorns. An artist painted a cartoon, a blueprint of sorts for weavers, on to paper or linen the size of the intended tapestry – about 8 metres (26 feet) by 4.25 metres (14 feet), in the case of van Orley's grandest Habsburg commissions. To begin, workers loaded the loom with plain, sturdy warp threads and outlined the design on the resulting taut-string surface. Using the cartoon as a reference, they then began passing colourful weft fibres across the warp threads, under and over, back and forth, coaxing a pattern into view one slim line at a time.

By the time van Orley took up textiles in the 1520s, the weavers of Brussels were using Flemish advances to achieve painterly effects – contours, shading and fine detail down to individual eyelashes. Van Orley created sophisticated designs that took full advantage of the new methods, specifying elaborate draping, tangles of hair and visible veins on the backs of figures' hands. Inspired by his friend Albrecht Dürer, he created realistic landscapes behind scenes infused with an intense emotion that was new to tapestry. He also drew from Raphael, whose tapestries for the Sistine Chapel were woven in Brussels between 1516 and 1530, incorporating the Italian's realistic proportions and perspective that gave figures new volume and heft.

As functional luxuries, tapestries both insulated and brightened dank castle interiors; as a bonus, they could be rolled up, thrown on to a wagon and moved from palace to palace, or even to luxurious tents during the hunting season. In 1520, when Henry and France's François I peacocked onto a field near Calais for a seventeen-day summit, each tried to out-swagger the other in various ways – including aggressive textile displays. So sumptuous were the weavings brought along for the meeting that the site was dubbed the 'Field of the Cloth of Gold'.

Tapestries signalled wealth and could also serve as portable propaganda, as in van Orley's *Battle of Pavia* (*c.* 1526–31), a seven-piece set of combat scenes glorifying an Imperial victory over the French. It had been a humiliating defeat for François, who was taken prisoner on the battlefield; the centrepiece to the series, which measures 37 square metres (400 square feet), shows three men dragging the French king backwards off his dying horse. Van Orley's most famous set, *The Hunts of Maximilian* (*c.* 1530–33), comprises twelve tapestries showing Habsburg notables in lush settings of hunting, harvesting and feasting. All feature identifiable spots around Brussels, and one, *Departure for the Hunt*, offers a spectacular panoramic view of the city in the background. So accurately detailed are the buildings that a particular chapel is shown under renovation – its temporary thatched roof dates the scene to the years between 1528 and 1533.

Within decades of van Orley's death the luxury textile industry began to unravel, as the Catholic King Philip II of Spain put pressure on the reform-minded Low Countries. Weavers and textile merchants, most of whom had Protestant leanings, dispersed to various cities beyond the king's reach. In 1567 Philip invaded with 10,000 men, further disrupting tapestry production and commerce. Nearly 60,000 people fled the area after the invasion, mostly to neighbouring Germanic states. There the scattered weavers set up new, smaller workshops, but the Netherlands' golden age of tapestry never regained its former splendour.

ℂℛ

Cristoforo da Messisbugo

CLASSIC ITALIAN COOKING

c. 1490–1548

The rise of Renaissance court culture began in Italy and the low countries during the 15th century and spread throughout Europe in the 16th. Such *arriviste* princes as the Medici, the d'Estes, the Sforzas and the Gonzagas vaunted the ideals of Classical rhetoric and medieval chivalry, but the abiding value of their time was the conspicuous display of great wealth. This they accomplished in ways that were guaranteed to shock and astonish: from the mammoth equestrian sculpture commissioned by Ludovico Sforza from Leonardo da Vinci to the dizzying collections of antique coins, medals and statuary assembled by Isabella d'Este; from encyclopaedic Classical libraries whose owners read neither Greek nor Latin to the kennel of 5,000 hounds maintained by the dukes of Milan; and from extravagant mock battles staged between hundreds of costumed Medici lackeys to the 20-year-old Beatrice d'Este's personal collection of eighty-four pearl- and gold-encrusted dresses.

A vital component of a large and voluptuous lifestyle was food. Literally an occasion for conspicuous consumption, a grand banquet turned the most traditional form of social bonding into an opportunity to impress. As they grew less interested in fighting with each other on the battlefield, the Italian princelings of the late 15th century began waging an endless food fight – competing over who could set the most sumptuous table, offer the greatest variety and peculiarity of dishes and provide the most elaborate amusements between courses.

Inevitably, this culture of competitive excess produced its own heroes: master chefs and banquet managers known as *scalchi*. As these grand, theatrical dinners grew increasingly notorious, admiring or envious princes elsewhere in Europe sought to recruit their own *scalchi*, or at least a good book on the subject. One of the first to provide a guide to the princely dining arts was Cristoforo da Messisbugo, head chef for nearly three decades to the d'Este family of Ferrara. His origins are unclear: although the name Messisbugo may indicate a Flemish background, he seems to have been as well versed in the tastes, pretensions and foibles of the people of Ferrara as any native.

Messisbugo kept exhaustive notes of his work and put together a compendium of his most notable dinners, along with many recipes for individual dishes. Soon after his death these were assembled and published as *Banchetti, compositioni di vivande et apparecchio generale* ('Banquets, preparation of dishes and general arrangements'). A Messisbugo banquet generally ran from about nine in the evening until three or four the next morning and consisted of eight or nine courses. These each featured a dozen or more individual dishes, with broiled, baked, boiled and fried meats and fish mixed in seeming abandon with various pies, soups and pastas, beginning with a scattering of cold antipasti and ending with fruits, salads, sweets and several thousand oysters. At the end there were also elaborate sugar sculptures, known as *trionfi*. The culinary and logistical results could be astonishing: one banquet, held in 1529 for 104 guests, featured 2,835 plates and required a small army of cooks, pages and servers, including three whose only job was to 'clear the table, [then] wash, sweep, and perfume the locale' between courses.

Messisbugo often emphasized the French or German origins of his dishes, and although it was infused with the cosmopolitan spirit of a Renaissance court, his *Banchetti* also maintained certain medieval tastes, such as sauces based on cinnamon, cloves and pepper mixed with sugar and vinegar. The apparent cacophony of dishes, with the same meat or fish repeated in successive courses, aimed at overwhelming guests with abundance while periodically startling them with unusual combinations. In this Messisbugo's cuisine had much in common with the polyphonic music that was its contemporary, where competing and sometimes discordant themes all enjoyed an equal place in the ensemble. Not surprisingly, such music also featured prominently in these feasts. A band opened the festivities, introduced each new course and played *divertimenti* in between. In larger affairs Messisbugo included a play as well, put on in sections throughout the evening.

His *Banchetti* makes it plain that Messisbugo was as much an impresario and stage manager as a cook, which may explain how he was able to rise socially from an otherwise servile profession. In the course of his long attachment to the d'Este household he managed to marry a local noblewoman, and in 1533 the emperor Charles V made him a count palatine. By the time he died he had established himself as Europe's first celebrity chef, his fame guaranteeing that his posthumous book would be a best-seller.

CR

Vittoria Colonna

THE DIVINE RHYMER

1490–1547

I t is said that Vittoria Colonna's parents chose her name because of the victories that would supposedly accrue from their two families. The Colonna were one of the great Roman dynasties, and Vittoria's father, Fabrizio, was one of the great *condottieri*, or professional warriors, of the age. Her mother, Agnes da Montefeltro, was the daughter and granddaughter of two even greater *condottieri* – Federico da Montefeltro, duke of Urbino, and Francesco Sforza, duke of Milan. Their progeny, it was expected, would usher in a new and glittering era for Italy in arms, culture and magnificence.

In fact, the family triumph was more nuanced. Vittoria's brother Ascanio, although a warrior in his own right, spent most of his life fighting successive popes, his nominal liege lords, over taxes. Vittoria, who received the lion's share of her family's artistic and spiritual gifts, had fewer weapons with which to resist the shifting politics of her day. Under intense pressure from Ferrante, the Aragonese king of Naples, the Colonna family betrothed her, at the age of just 4, to Fernando Francisco d'Avalos, the 6-year-old son of Ferrante's Aragonese captain-general. The two were married in 1509 on the island of Ischia, one of the many feudatories of the d'Avalos family and part of the growing Spanish territories in Italy. The marriage went extremely well, although the two usually had to express their affection at a distance – after a year with his new bride Fernando Francisco went off to fight the French in northern Italy. Except for brief visits for funerals and other formal occasions, he never returned to live on Ischia; in 1525, wounded in the Battle of Pavia, he died.

Left a widow without any children, Vittoria was bereft to the point of considering suicide. She railed against an age where men, 'driven by a frenzy, thinking of nothing more than honour, plunge into danger, shouting with rage, [while] we, timid in our hearts, with grief on our brows, wait for you'. Fortunately, she had her devoted circle of courtiers, admirers and sometime suitors – poets and scholars of the rank of Ludovico Ariosto, Pietro Aretino and Baldassare Castiglione – along with several female cousins, permanently in residence, to help her recover. On her idyllic isle, anchored in the Bay of Naples, she turned to developing her literary skills, spending much of the next twenty years writing lyric and epistolary poetry. Most of her early efforts were love poems – by the mid-1530s she had written at least 130 of these *rime amorose*, which were published in 1538 under the title *Rime de la diva Vettoria Colona*. About this time she struck up a deep friendship with Michelangelo, who was in Rome to work on the *Last Judgment*. The two exchanged poems and intimate letters for nearly a decade, and Michelangelo included her likeness in several paintings.

Although her love poems established Colonna's reputation – Ariosto exclaimed that she had 'a sweet style that has not been surpassed' – she gradually became more interested in questions of faith. Jesus, she decided, would replace d'Avalos as the rudder for the 'frail bark' of her lyric poetry. She corresponded with friends about Christendom's broadening religious gulf and wrote over 200 meditative poems that she called *rime* (or *sonnetti*) *spirituali*. She moved to Rome and set up house in a convent, although she never took vows. Instead she formed ties with some leading theologians, including reformist clerics such as Bernardino Ochino and Cardinals Reginald Pole and Pietro Bembo. Attracted by their calls for a conciliatory approach to Martin Luther, she adopted Pole as her spiritual counsellor and virtually moved in with him at his country retreat in Viterbo.

As the clash of empires and faiths intensified during the 16th century, Vittoria Colonna's world of well-bred courtliness and spiritual serenity appeared increasingly inopportune, if not slightly ridiculous. The reformists she had supported with such high hopes in the 1530s became the targets of a Catholic reaction spearheaded by Cardinal Pietro Caraffa in the 1540s.

When Bernardino Ochino fled to Switzerland in 1542 and declared himself a Calvinist, the era of reconciliation ended abruptly, and everyone who had kept company with reformers – including Colonna herself – was now suspect. She lamented this 'cursed century and evil harpies, where honour, life, time and riches delight the eye but are absent in the heart', but her time was clearly past. When she died, the Council of Trent was already under way. It was rumoured that she too was under investigation by the Inquisition.

CR

Marguerite of Navarre

ROYAL WRITER, AUXILIARY QUEEN

1492–1549

When Marguerite d'Angoulême was born in 1492, her parents were deeply disappointed. Her father, the count of Angoulême, was second in line to the throne and had hoped for a boy, since the crown could pass only to a male heir. When Marguerite's brother was born, in 1494, it changed the course of her life. Her father died just two years later, leaving the infant François as heir apparent. Marguerite's mother, Louise of Savoy, devoted her life to ensuring that the boy became king and essentially raised Marguerite as another mother to him. Unusually well educated herself, Louise schooled Marguerite, François and at least two of the count's illegitimate daughters together. She taught the children Spanish and Italian herself, while leading humanist scholars and clerics trained them in Latin, theology and philosophy. It was a rigorous, comprehensive curriculum, challenging even by noble standards, and Marguerite easily outperformed her brother.

For all her education, however, she was most valuable to France as a potential bride – there lay prospects for a political alliance. The ageing Henry VII of England proposed marriage, but the teenage Marguerite protested that the king was too old and England too foggy. Refusing the union, she declared she would one day 'marry a man who is young, rich, and noble – without having to cross the Channel!' Eventually, in 1509, she married Charles, duke of Alençon, in a union that settled a territorial dispute in south-west France. Charles met her requirements but shared few of her interests; in a poem years later she wrote that 'having neither read nor studied,/he would never have been taken for an orator'.

According to contemporary accounts, Marguerite was a tall, striking woman with violet-blue eyes, quick-witted and engaging. She was a great asset to François and played a far more public role than his wife, Queen Claude, who was shy and, thanks to the king, constantly pregnant. Marguerite corresponded with heads of state, tended to civic affairs and even conducted diplomatic missions. The most important took place in 1525, after the Battle of Pavia, when François was defeated and captured by Imperial forces. It was his sister who journeyed to Madrid to negotiate his release; she met face to face with the emperor Charles V, alone in a room save for a female companion for propriety's sake. François lost Burgundy and any claim to Italian territory but ultimately returned to Paris unharmed.

Marguerite's husband also fought in Pavia but was fatally wounded. In 1527 the 35-year-old Marguerite married Henri d'Albret, king of Navarre – a tiny kingdom in the Pyrenees under France's protection. A swashbuckling figure ten years her junior, he had a weakness for gambling and 'Spanish ladies'. But his keen intellect appealed to her, and they enjoyed each other's company. The following year she gave birth to a daughter, Jeanne, the future mother of Henri IV. Pregnant again in 1530, Marguerite was forced to miss out on important events. The woman who had once taken on the Holy Roman Emperor wrote, 'How vexing it is ... to be brought low by a mere baby.' A son was born, but five months later he grew suddenly ill on Christmas day and died within hours. Devastated, Marguerite wore only black from that day on.

A skilled writer with many poems and plays to her credit, she began to compose more serious work after losing her son. In 1531 she published the pious, death-obsessed 'Mirror of the Sinful Soul', a poem that revealed her reformist beliefs and incurred the wrath of conservative theologians. She embraced the evangelical movement of Erasmus, which sought change in, rather than a break with, the Catholic Church. A passionate supporter of French humanist writers, she patronized François Rabelais and Lefèvre d'Etaples, who translated and published the first French New Testament in 1523 – despite a ban by the Sorbonne, the theological college of the University of Paris. To provide progressive scholars with an alternative institution, she persuaded François to found the Collège de France, which is still known today for its unorthodox offerings.

While she wrote a large body of religious poetry, Marguerite is best known for *The Heptameron*, which she conceived as a French version of the Italian *Decameron*, written by Giovanni Boccaccio in 1353. Her book comprises some seventy stories told by travellers trapped on a mountain by a torrential flood. While waiting for the waters to recede, the five men and five women decide to entertain each other with tales. They debate the issues in a way that sheds light on the concerns of 16th-century society, including the deep divide between male and female views: in a dramatic example the women condemn a character who tries to force himself on an unwilling maiden while the men protest that a quest thwarted is honour denied. Mistaken identity, outhouse mishaps, secret trysts – the stories run from thrilling to slapstick to heart-wrenching. Following Boccaccio, Marguerite had planned a hundred tales, but she died in 1549 before completing them. Faced with an unfinished 'decameron', it was a resourceful publisher who dubbed her great work *The Heptameron* before printing it at last in 1558.

Pietro Aretino

'THE SCOURGE OF KINGS'

1492–1556

The bastard son of a cobbler and a prostitute who worked part-time as a model, Pietro del Tura chose early on to call himself simply Pietro Aretino – 'Pietro from Arezzo'. Certainly he had inherited little to be proud of besides his own precocious and contentious mind. Essentially unschooled, he took art lessons for a while in nearby Perugia during his teens but then decided he wanted to be a poet. In 1516 he was in Siena, where one of his squibs – a satirical eulogy on the death of Pope Leo X's pet elephant Hanno – caught the eye of the fabulously wealthy Sienese banker Agostino Chigi. When Chigi's business took him to Rome, Aretino went too.

Rome during Leo's pontificate was fertile territory for satirists: the city swarmed with worldly clerics, conniving bankers and hungry newcomers. Satirists also had an ideal venue for their witty sneers: they pasted their poems and squibs about current affairs on the limbless torso of Pasquino – one of Rome's famous 'speaking statues'. Soon after arriving, Aretino would turn these semi-anonymous works into a racy and popular form of social commentary, while also making a name, and a great many enemies, for himself.

The tolerant atmosphere in Rome ended abruptly with the death of Leo and the election of Pope Hadrian VI in 1522. Aretino, who had wildly defamed Hadrian before his election, had to leave Rome in a hurry. Yet Hadrian's pontificate was brief, and when Giulio de' Medici succeeded him (as Pope Clement VII) in 1523, Aretino returned, expecting this new Medici to be as indulgent as the previous one. Times in Rome were changing, however, with the cultural and religious climate becoming less indulgent. A new crackdown on immorality brought the arrest of Aretino's good friend Marcantonio Raimondi; an engraver, he was imprisoned for printing the highly salacious *I Modi* ('The Positions'; 1524). Aretino led a divisive campaign for his release, in which he published his own *Sonetti lussuriosi* ('Lecherous sonnets'; 1526) to go with Raimondi's copulatory art. Clerics who attacked his openly pornographic poems were skewered in yet more of Aretino's pasquinades, until he and a high-ranking bishop got into a public shouting match that degenerated into slapping, kicking, punching and spitting. Later the bishop sent assassins after Aretino, and when Clement showed little inclination to intervene, the satirist decided to leave Rome again – this time for good.

After a year knocking around the courts of northern Italy, in 1527 Aretino settled in Venice. Renting the modest but well-placed Ca' Bollani on the Grand Canal, he set out to 'live by the sweat of my ink': a risky ambition, for many such died in poverty. Some of his success Aretino owed to his new city. Cosmopolitan and crowded with eager printers, Venice was famous for leaving its satirists and pornographers in peace as long as they did not defame the Republic. Equally important, however, was Aretino's range as a writer. Largely abandoning poetry for prose, he aimed at every imaginable market, churning out essays on manners, morality and theology, tragedies and comedies, and – as a whole new genre – semi-fictitious 'Letters' to the great and the good of Europe. Safe in Venice, he was free to praise or damn anyone he chose and was soon earning as much from the precautionary 'pensions' rulers paid him as from actual book sales. He boasted that 'I have made every Duke, Prince and Monarch that there is pay tribute to my genius'.

Through it all Aretino ran Ca' Balloni like a private bordello open to his many friends. He kept up his unrestrained gourmandizing and fornicating until the day he died – supposedly from laughing too much at the sight of a pet monkey trying to walk in his boots. After his death a famously appropriate epitaph soon circulated:

Here lies the Tuscan poet Aretino,
Who spoke ill of everyone, except for Christ,
Excusing himself by saying: 'I never knew him.'

✑

William Tyndale

SCRIPTURE TRANSLATOR, BIBLE SMUGGLER

c. 1494–1536

Anyone who has used the phrases 'let there be light', 'the powers that be' and 'salt of the earth' is already familiar with William Tyndale's work. A priest with a sense of poetry, Tyndale wrote the first English Bible to be based on the earliest Christian manuscripts, penning elegant prose that still resonates in modern editions. Like Martin Luther, Tyndale strove to wrest the Bible from the Catholic Church, which opposed translating scripture into worshippers' native tongues, insisting on Latin scripture and services. In the view of Tyndale and other reformers, the Church gave less credence to Christianity's founding texts than to doctrines designed and promulgated in the Middle Ages to enhance its power. During Tyndale's lifetime Catholic dominance did begin to falter, but the Church still had influence enough in 1536 to have him executed for heresy.

Born in south-west England, Tyndale earned bachelor's and master's degrees from Oxford University, became a priest in 1515 and probably learned ancient Greek at the University of Cambridge. Like Erasmus, who compiled the first Bible based on original Greek texts, Tyndale believed the earliest manuscripts came closest to the actual Word of God. Luther used Erasmus's Latin version of the New Testament as the basis for his landmark German Bible, and Tyndale envisioned an English version for his own country, a purer text that stripped away what he saw as the Latin Vulgate's distortions to reveal the true 'process, order, and meaning' of the Bible. English officials, rattled by Luther's momentum abroad, had prohibited such translations, and no patron was willing to fund the project, so in 1525 Tyndale went to

Cologne, where he completed his translation and engaged a publisher. Even there, however, Catholic officials raided the shop during a print run, forcing Tyndale and an assistant to scoop up their materials and flee the city.

When Tyndale's New Testament finally surfaced in 1526, it had to be smuggled into England among shipments of tools or glassware, even raisins and figs. It was not only a ground-breaking text but also a compelling piece of writing, which added to its power. In addition to English, Latin and Greek, Tyndale knew German, French, Hebrew, Spanish, Italian and probably a few other languages as well: the man had a way with words. To appeal to a wide readership, he used vivid, everyday Anglo-Saxon words to produce memorable, rhythmic prose that remains readable today. The book confirmed conservatives' fears, however, as Tyndale, like Erasmus, saw passages in the early texts that conflicted with Catholic doctrine and threatened the established order. Where the authorized Latin Vulgate Bible used the terms 'priest' and 'do penance', for example, Tyndale thought the original Greek context called for 'elder' and 'repent', both of which implied that Church hierarchy was irrelevant.

Thomas More, England's most ardent defender of orthodox Catholicism, singled out Tyndale for special vitriol. As a young man, More had himself championed vernacular Bibles, but as the reform movement gained a footing he wrote a treatise against heresy, denouncing translations in general and Tyndale's in particular. The priest answered with a slim book that, among other things, identified where More's beliefs conflicted with scripture. Tyndale must have touched a nerve: More exploded with a 500,000-word response – more than 2,000 pages – that mixed logical argument with personal attacks and mocking taunts.

In 1534 Tyndale released a revised New Testament from Antwerp, which, despite its location in the Catholic-dominated Holy Roman Empire, was a major centre of Christian humanism and therefore relatively safe for reformers. A fellow expatriate named Henry Phillips, however, managed to prise him from his protective circle. Phillips, a bankrupt anti-Lutheran, received payment from some like-minded authority for flushing Tyndale into the open. After befriending the preacher, Phillips invited him to dinner in another part of town and informed Imperial officers where their quarry could be found. Tyndale, looking forward to a hot meal with his friend, was arrested en route and carted off to a castle outside Brussels.

He was held captive for more than a year, and in August 1536 he was tried for heresy, found guilty and delivered to the secular authorities for execution. His status allowed him a quicker death than the average heretic's: once his captors tied him to a stake surrounded by kindling, they were kind enough to strangle him before lighting the fire that consumed his body. His Bible, however, lived on, and with few changes it was adopted as the Church of England's authorized text. In the King James Version his writing constitutes about 84 per cent of the New Testament and 75 per cent of the Old Testament. Nearly every subsequent English edition reflects his influence, and, given such lines as 'give up the ghost', 'filthy lucre' and 'fight the good fight', the English-speaking world is still hard pressed to avoid him.

François Rabelais

GARGANTUAN TALENT

c. 1494–1553

François Rabelais studied theology, mastered multiple languages and embraced Classical literature; he went on to earn a medical degree and a reputation as a leading physician. What fixed his place in history, though, were his bawdy satires *Gargantua* and *Pantagruel*, which juxtapose complex philosophy and controversial theology with giant genitalia and copulating couples 'joyfully rubbing their bacon together'.

Around 1510 Rabelais joined the Franciscans at Fontenay-le-Comte, near France's west coast, where the curriculum included recently resurrected studies in ancient Greek. For progressive humanists Greek allowed access to the earliest known versions of the New Testament, but early texts often contradicted the Latin Vulgate Bible, the only authorized version of scripture. As a result, the language was deemed heretical by the theological college of the University of Paris – the Sorbonne, a powerful body that monitored religious orthodoxy in the region – and Rabelais's monastery dutifully confiscated all related materials.

The young friar transferred to a less restrictive Benedictine monastery in the nearby Vendée region, where he continued his Greek, fathered at least three illegitimate children and probably began his medical studies. He was among the few student physicians who could read the ancient Greek writings of Galen and Hippocrates, then regarded as cutting-edge texts despite being over a thousand years old. Because monks were forbidden to practise medicine, in about 1530 he left his order to become a physician. His choice was considered an act of apostasy, and absolution required papal dispensation.

It took several years and a substantial sum, but Rabelais eventually regained good standing with the Church.

Rabelais served as personal physician to the bishop of Paris – a moderate cleric who became an important patron – and was eventually appointed to a prestigious hospital in Lyons, a humanist hub in eastern France. *Pantagruel*, which he composed in Lyons and published in 1532, seemed to reflect a physician's orientation. The prologue's wine-loving narrator, Alcofribas Nasier (an anagram of François Rabelais), hails the healing power of humour and boasts that his stories have comforted both gout sufferers and the pox-ridden. The tales themselves take an earthy, straightforward approach to bodies and their functions: the young giant Gargantua, for instance, climbs to the top of Notre-Dame Cathedral and, '*par ris*' ('for a laugh'), doffs his codpiece and 'bepisses' the unfortunate townspeople below, accidentally drowning 260,418 citizens. The incident, Rabelais jokes, gave the city its name: Paris. Genitalia figure prominently, but in a slapstick rather than an erotic way. Gargantua's male ancestors sport magnificent 'digging tools' long enough to be 'tied around their waists five or even six times'. Less fortunate men wear 'hypocritical codpieces' that are 'stuffed with nothing but wind – to the great regret of the feminine sex'. Female anatomy, on the other hand, is frightening or even dangerous, as when an old woman drives a devil away by flipping up her skirts or when a character proposes building a protective wall around Paris using diseased pudenda.

Beneath the ribaldry in *Pantagruel* and *Gargantua* (1534/35?), however, lurked hostility toward the Church, the upper classes and the fusty scholars who clung to medieval scholasticism. Rabelais ridicules a famously anti-humanist library in Paris, claiming it contained such titles as *How Virgins Shit*, *Bishops' Antidotes for Aphrodisiacs* and *The Art of Farting in Public*. He likewise targets the nobility with characters such as Lords Fartsniffer and Kissmyass, as well as a haughty Parisian lady who, doused with the essence of a female dog in heat, is urinated upon by 600,000 besotted hounds.

Taking aim at traditional Catholicism, Rabelais invokes the patron saint of cuckolds, describes a martyr who suffers death by cooked apples, and invents a female St Nytouche, meaning 'don't touch it'. A race of 'Papalmaniacs' practise empty rituals, privilege canon law over the Bible and line up to kiss the pope's behind. In a famous passage on humanist education, Rabelais rejects the Vulgate Bible in favour of the Hebrew Old Testament and Greek New Testament, and elsewhere he imagines a Utopian monastery with no walls, no rigid schedules and a multilingual library bulging with books.

Written in colloquial French rather than Latin, *Gargantua* and *Pantagruel* were hugely popular with both the scholarly elite and the middle class. As Rabelais's popularity surged, so, too did the consternation of the Catholic authorities. In the 1540s the Sorbonne banned works by writers with heretical leanings, Rabelais included, despite the support he received from Marguerite of Navarre, the reform-minded sister of François I. In 1546, shortly after publishing his third book of tales, Rabelais spent a year in an Imperial town beyond the Sorbonne's jurisdiction. Why he left France is unclear, but his time abroad followed the executions of several French humanist writers and publishers.

As a religious moderate, Rabelais advocated reform rather than a split from the Church, and he took shots at Protestants too. In 1550 Jean Calvin attacked him in print for not going far enough, while Rabelais grouped Calvinists with impostors, liars and 'vile seducers'. His fourth book features the Fat Sausage people, a wild race of northern warriors who worship a mustard-flinging flying pig that seems to resemble Martin Luther. With something to entertain – and to offend – nearly everyone, Rabelais's books flew off bookshop shelves. A hundred editions of his work appeared in the 16th century, and unauthorized copies abounded. Even after he died, Rabelaisian prose continued to appear, as lesser writers cashed in on his fame with their own versions of his raucous stories.

⚮

Hans Holbein the Younger

THE MIRROR OF PRINCES

1497/98–1543

The first great generation of Renaissance German artists was crowded with the likes of Dürer, Cranach and Grünewald, but the generation that followed featured only one true master. Born in Augsburg, Hans Holbein the Younger was trained by his father and uncles before leaving for Basel as a journeyman painter in 1515. In that lively commercial and intellectual centre Hans produced a variety of arts, from woodcuts to stained-glass designs to his first commissioned painting – a small double portrait in 1519 of Basel's mayor and his wife. This early work already bears Holbein's characteristic style – the dominance of line over colour and texture, the adroit creation of a three-dimensional setting for his subjects, and a tranquillity of gesture and expression that contrast strongly with both the traditional German Gothic and the work of his older contemporary Albrecht Dürer.

For the next ten years Holbein flourished in Basel, with perhaps a short trip to northern Italy around 1517. He married a local widow and joined the painters' guild, made woodcuts for books – including Martin Luther's German Bible – and found his first clients for paintings among humanists who frequented local printing shops. Initially, like most artists of his day, Holbein made his living from religious paintings, either for institutions or private patrons. Soon, however, his skill at portraiture, infused with a Flemish realism that prized a sitter's individuality, was proving more profitable. Among his earliest clients was the celebrity humanist Desiderius Erasmus, who was staying in Basel at the time. Erasmus ordered several poses, in multiple copies, with the idea of sending them to friends and admirers as tools of self-promotion. Holbein's portraits perfectly answered his needs, showing the writer as studious, serene and solitary.

By the mid-1520s the citizens of Basel had become more concerned with religious reform than with commissioning paintings, either sacred or secular. As Erasmus himself put it, 'the arts are freezing in this part of the world.' Erasmus encouraged Holbein to try England and supplied a letter of introduction to his good friend Thomas More; Nicolaus Kratzer, a tutor in More's family, may have written a similar recommendation. After being given leave by the burghers of Basel, Holbein spent the next two years painting More (who called him 'a wonderful artist'), More's family and members of his intellectual circle. Well paid for his work, Holbein was able to return to Basel and buy a house for his family. He was now admired and loaded with commissions, but after four years he nevertheless left again, possibly because of his lack of interest in the religious disputes that continually rocked his adopted city.

On his return to England in 1532 Holbein found that More had fallen from favour, so he quickly abandoned his old patron – much to the annoyance of Erasmus, who complained how 'he deceived those to whom he was recommended'. Such a talented artist, however, found new networks easy to forge. Among Holbein's new clients were the German Lutheran merchants of the city, for whom he did a number of portraits in the early 1530s, and the courtly circles surrounding Henry's new wife and new chief minister, Anne Boleyn and Thomas Cromwell. His portraits grew larger – often life-size – and ever more remarkable for the artist's miraculous ability to render the books and other objects that his sitters held, or the silk, velvet, gold, embroidery, leather and fur that they wore.

In 1536 Holbein was taken on as the king's artist, and he was soon involved in all the design aspects of Henry's court, from murals and state robes to buttons, buckles, armour and bookbindings. His greatest contribution remained his portraits, however. With over 150 depictions, life-size and miniature, of royalty and courtiers, Holbein provided a minutely detailed mirror in which the elite of Henry's world could see how they could – or should – appear. One of Holbein's more peculiar tasks for his famously uxorious monarch was to visit potential wives, sketch them and bring the results back for Henry's evaluation. One such was the recently widowed Christina of Denmark, whose sketch so pleased Henry that, reportedly, 'since he saw it he has been in much better humour than he ever was, making musicians play on their instruments all day long.' Christina herself was less enthusiastic and supposedly said that only 'If I had two heads, [then] I would happily put one at the disposal of the King of England.' With Jane Seymour, Anne of Cleves and Catherine Howard, Holbein's efforts were more successful, even if the marriages themselves were not.

Niccolò Tartaglia

STUTTERING SAVANT

1499/1500–1557

It is said that young Niccolò Fontana – as he was originally known – was so poor that he could only afford an instructor to teach him his alphabet as far as the letter K. For the rest of the alphabet, and for his mathematics, he was, necessarily and quite proudly, self-taught. Impoverished when his father, a mere postal courier, was murdered in 1506, he was also horribly mutilated on his face and jaw six years later, when the invading French captured and sacked his native Brescia. Left for dead by a slash from a sabre-wielding pillager, Niccolò was slowly nursed back to health by his mother, but he remained horribly disfigured and unable to speak clearly. As an adult, he responded with characteristically aggressive pride – covering his scars with a thick beard and signing his many books as Niccolò Tartaglia ('Niccolò the Stammerer').

Pride, mathematical brilliance and driving ambition were not enough to guarantee Tartaglia a good living in late Renaissance Italy, where real success required a university credential and aristocratic patronage. For a long time he was reduced to teaching merchants' boys in an 'abacus school' in Verona. Tartaglia did attract the attention of local military men, though, entering into their lively arguments over how to position and aim field cannon for maximum range. He realized he could solve these problems by reconfiguring them in mathematical language – an enormous breakthrough in what was then known as 'natural philosophy'. Publishing his insights in his book *Nova scientia* in 1537, Tartaglia was the first to mathematize problems of bodies in motion. Although his Aristotelian background kept him from fully comprehending momentum or gravity – these were first understood by Galileo – he did bring together mathematics and real-world situations in what was indeed a new science.

By the late 1530s Tartaglia had carved out a minor niche for himself, quantifying military problems ranging from the design of fortifications to gunpowder mixtures and methods for raising sunken ships. His true passion remained pure mathematics, however, which was also his only path to a university chair. Tartaglia gained recognition by producing the first reliable translations of Euclid and Archimedes into Italian and by solving problems that had confounded both ancient and contemporary mathematicians. Chief among these was finding a solution to cubic equations, in the form of $ax^3 + bx^2 + cx = d$, an old challenge that his fellow Italians called *il cubo* ('the Cube') and that Tartaglia's predecessor Luca Pacioli had deemed unsolvable.

Working in relative isolation, Tartaglia solved the Cube, although in the tradition of his time he kept his formula a secret. Without revealing the details, he defended his solution in a kind of mathematician's head-to-head, where he and a challenger – who possessed a similar formula but failed to understand its application – publicly sent cubic equations to each other. The results of this and similar 'debates' were gratifying: Tartaglia gained fame for solving most forms of the Cube and was soon receiving gracious letters from such famed mathematical scholars as Gerolamo Cardano. He even won a paid lectureship in his home town of Brescia.

Science and mathematics in the mid-16th century were a cut-throat business, however. Invited by Cardano to Milan in 1539, Tartaglia reluctantly agreed to show him the solution to the Cube, which Cardano swore never to reveal. Yet in his own *Ars magna* (1545) Cardano published the formula, and although he gave Tartaglia full credit, this perceived treachery drove Niccolò into a paranoid loathing. He fired back in 1546 with his own *Quesiti et inventioni diverse* ('Various questions and discoveries'), which rehashed some earlier work on ballistics but mostly focused on the Cube story and vilified Cardano. Tartaglia challenged his nemesis to another of the mathematical head-to-heads in which he normally triumphed, but Cardano would only send a student with whom he had worked out a more general and widely applicable solution to the Cube. A public play-off was arranged, one where smooth rhetoric counted almost as much as mathematical skill, and armed with a superior formula, Cardano's student overwhelmed Tartaglia. Reduced to stammering and unable to solve any equations, Niccolò fled back to Brescia. When word of his disgrace reached his university's administrators, they withheld his salary and then fired him. Humiliated and without any patrons to support him, Tartaglia moved to Venice, where he ended his days again teaching numbers to the sons of merchants, enjoying little benefit from his work on either the mathematical basis of science or his beloved Cube.

6. The New Wave

The final generation of the Renaissance was one of consolidation and redefinition. A century earlier the first humanists, with their Classical texts extolling secular individualism, civil society and rhetorical flourish, had discovered a natural audience in the republican city states of northern Italy. Early 15th-century artists had worked within this social context, finding their patrons among mercantile elites who valued intimacy and tranquillity in a Classical and naturalist setting. Inevitably, both civic humanism and 15th-century art fell from fashion with the decline of those city states. What took their place was a courtly culture that favoured lineage and good breeding over wealth, faith over rhetoric and an imperial rather than a republican Classicism. In both literature and art *la maniera*, the 'manner' in which a work was composed, became more important than its content – and ever since, such lively renditions of action, colour and conflict have been referred to as Mannerist.

Such shifts in artistic and cultural taste reflected the broader retrenchment of secular power. After a few generations spent challenging established authority, the moneylenders, explorers, soldiers, petty nobles and other 'men from nowhere' who had dominated the earlier Renaissance were either marginalized or absorbed into existing elites. Ultimately, the likes of Lorenzo de' Medici, Francesco Sforza, Henry Tudor, Christopher Columbus and Jakob Fugger proved to be less interested in creating a new power structure than in joining the existing one. Repeatedly, land and lineage won out over new money and innovation, as newcomers discovered that almost anyone with enough money could marry into some noble family down on its luck.

The aristocratic obsession with honour, form, display and cultured violence, which had once seemed in decline, was back in force by the mid-16th century.

The settling of earlier turmoil – the withdrawal of marauding armies from Italy and the winding down of religious conflict in the German Empire – freed these elites from their traditional obligations to raise and support troops. They could instead flaunt their wealth on buildings and acquisitions. They rushed to commission architects such as Andrea Palladio to design new town houses, villas and gardens, spreading the elegant neo-classical style from northern Italy to France and eventually England. Their decorative needs soon set off a corollary boom in the tapestry, glass and furnishing industries. Likewise, their desire to travel in grandeur around the crowded cities sparked technical innovations in carriage making. This new industry, pioneered by Hungarian craftsmen, provided elite clients with comfortable, strong coaches that were essentially mobile palaces, able to raise their owners both literally and figuratively above the urban mob. More ephemeral forms of aristocratic self-expression reached their apogee in Florence. There the new Medici grand duke, Cosimo I, and his duchess, Eleanor of Toledo, devoted vast riches to fêtes, masques, jousts and mock battles. For other elites Florence provided the model for the theatrical and ever more hierarchical court that came to predominate in Baroque Europe. It was exported north of the Alps and greatly enlarged on by Cosimo's distant cousin Catherine de' Medici, when she married into the French royal family in 1533.

In the middle of this spreading opulence was Rome. Although badly battered by the Sack of 1527, the city wasted no time embarking on a rebuilding binge of its own. Wealthy bankers holding papal monopolies and worldly cardinals eager to establish themselves as princes of the Church raced to turn unused stretches of urban land into their own villas and parks. These prelates' profligacy and sumptuous frivolity added more fuel to the anger of religious reformers – men and women who saw the world in terms of personal salvation and whose politics were expressed as disputes over dogma. The Protestantism begun by Martin Luther in the 1510s and 1520s became more confrontational in the following generation, as the evangelistic doctrines of Jean Calvin and Ulrich Zwingli won large-scale conversions in

Switzerland, the Rhineland, the Netherlands, Scotland and much of France. It took decades for the papacy – and the Church's defender, Charles V – to stop dithering and confront the Protestant challenge. Only with the election of Pope Paul III in 1534, and the reorganization of the Italian Inquisition by Cardinal Pietro Carafa in 1542, did a Catholic response to Protestantism begin. By this time, however, all middle ground between the faiths had effectively vanished.

The council that finally met in 1545, in the southern Alpine city of Trent, took nearly twenty years to complete its examination and reform of Catholicism. It ended in 1563 with a ringing reaffirmation of the Church's traditional practices and dogma, and the Council's unwillingness to compromise with its critics marked the irrevocable division of Western Europe into Catholic and Protestant camps. Little remained to argue about for the rest of the century, beyond what territories might ultimately end up in whose hands. If it failed to maintain Christian unity, however, Catholic reform at least spawned a host of new religious orders, which directed and strengthened the faith of individuals for generations to come. The Ursulines offered pious women a chance to enter into teaching, while the Theatines, Capuchins and, above all, the Jesuits provided spiritually committed men the opportunity to preach the Catholic doctrine to heretics and unbelievers. Beginning their work in the contested regions of France, Italy and southern Germany, these fervent champions of the Church eventually embarked on religious missions throughout the world. Their proselytizing transformed them into global explorers as they carried their message to peoples previously untouched by Western influence. In the process they often drew European civil and military authorities after them – where Christ led, they liked to say, the armies of Europe were bound to follow.

∞

Pope Paul IV

THE MOST HATED OF POPES

1476–1559

When Giovanni Pietro Carafa was elected to the papacy on 15 May 1555, he was as surprised as anyone. At 71, he was not only rather old to be running the Church, but also extraordinarily unpopular: as he himself supposedly admitted, 'I have never conferred a favour on any human being.' Many assumed that the aged cardinal would turn down the honour, lest he outdo even his immediate predecessor, Marcellus II, who died after a papacy of just twenty-two days. Nevertheless, Carafa accepted the tiara, determined to rule if only because Emperor Charles V had been dead set against his election.

Born into the Neapolitan aristocracy, Carafa was taken under the wing of his uncle Cardinal Oliviero Carafa, who in 1494 got Giovanni Pietro started by giving him the bishopric of Chieti. Recognition and high office left him unfulfilled, however, and an ambassadorship to Spain merely sparked a lifelong hatred of the Spanish. In 1524 Giovanni Pietro and the equally pious Gaetano da Thiene (later St Cajetan) formed a new religious order for non-conventual clergy devoted to charitable work and funded by members selling off their own benefices. Calling themselves the Oratory of Divine Love, they would later be known as the Theatines, after Theate, Latin for Chieti – the bishopric that Carafa sold to help fund the order.

Carafa's own sense of divine love did not extend to those he suspected of heresy. In the 1520s and 1530s, when doctrinal differences between Catholics and Protestants were still being established, even some high clerics seemed tempted by Luther, much to Carafa's fury. In 1542, now a cardinal in his own

242

right, he helped resurrect the Roman Inquisition, which had flourished in the Middle Ages but declined with the coming of the Renaissance. Impatient with the plodding papal bureaucracy and eager to start hunting down waverers and heretics, he bought the necessary chains and locks with his own funds, supposedly boasting that 'Even if my own father were a heretic, I would gather the wood to burn him!'

Initially active enough to persuade many crypto-Protestants to renounce their beliefs or flee Italy altogether, the Roman Inquisition really came into its own only after Carafa was elected pope. He aggressively solicited anonymous denunciations not only for heresy, but also for sodomy, gambling, prostitution and simony; Pope Paul's agents used the Holy Office's broad powers to root out not just heterodoxy but anything else he considered socially deviant. Beggars were driven from town, monks and nuns were returned to their convents, and bishops banished back to their dioceses. Paul also revoked the ancient pacts protecting Roman Jews, corralling them in a walled compound near the Tiber. Elsewhere in the Papal States his Inquisition hunted down the so-called *marranos* – Jews who had been forcibly converted to Christianity but then secretly returned to their traditional faith – burning scores of them at the stake. In 1557 Paul extended the reach of the Holy Office by issuing an 'index of prohibited books' – a list of over 500 authors and dozens of presses whose works were forbidden to Catholics. Books on the index were no longer sources of information but evidence of guilt, and anyone caught with even a single banned work could be condemned for heresy.

Although Paul intended to purify Catholic thought and weed out heretical ideas with the index, its effect was to deaden intellectual discourse in the birthplace of the Renaissance and drive a once thriving printing industry from Italy to Amsterdam and Geneva. The rest of his papacy followed a similar scenario, with his ferocious idealism colliding with political and economic realities. The ill-considered war he declared on Spanish Naples bankrupted the papacy, caused widespread famine in the Papal States and almost provoked a second Sack of Rome. Refusing to accept responsibility for either that fiasco or the failure of social services after the Tiber flooded in

1557, Paul publicly denounced and humiliated his own nephew Carlo Carafa, a vicious incompetent whom he had earlier made his commander-in-chief.

Romans greeted Paul IV's death with a riotous outpouring of joy unusual even for them – they demolished his monumental statue and played football with the head. The Carafa coat of arms was torn from buildings, and many leading members of the family were hunted down, arrested and eventually executed. Although he oversaw the final transition from the Renaissance to the Counter-Reformation papacy, Paul IV went into history as one of the most hated ever to wear the tiara: for years afterwards Romans insisted on ordering their wine by the *brocca*, or pitcher, rather than use the traditional term – a carafe, or *carafa*.

Emperor Charles V

EMPEROR OF THE WESTERN WORLD

1500–1558

At the age of 6 Charles Habsburg already ruled thirteen major principalities. By 16 he had made himself lord of the largest and fastest-growing kingdom in Europe; at 19 he was Holy Roman Emperor. Arguably the greatest Caesar in history, Charles ruled an empire nearly twice the size of Classical Rome at its height, yet he won very little land by conquest. Rather, his realm was built through dynastic matches and adroit political manoeuvring – much of it arranged before he was even born. Although his personal motto was *Plus Ultra* ('further beyond'), Charles passed his life in almost continuous war, less to expand his domains than to defend his inheritance.

That so much power devolved on one man – or boy, really – resulted from marriage policies among European royalty, which routinely used castles, cities and duchies as dowries to cement alliances and concentrate power. By the 15th century, with the emergence of monarchical nation states, whole kingdoms were passed around this way. It all culminated in 1496, with the marriage of Joanna of Trastámara, heir to the newly unified kingdom of Spain, to Philip the Fair, heir to the combined houses of Habsburg and Burgundy. Into the mix the spouses also brought the Low Countries, Milan, Naples and potentially vast territories in the New World.

To many at the time, the emergence of a super-monarch born in the epochal year of 1500 presaged the return of a universal Christian empire. Certainly Charles thought so. While still a teenager he rapidly secured his power in the Netherlands, eased the dotty Joanna off her Spanish throne and bribed his election as Holy Roman Emperor with silver borrowed from the Fugger family. At just 19 he was willing to finance the world-spanning expedition of the Ferdinand Magellan, to secure his dynasty's claim to territories encircling the globe.

Ultimately, however, the promise – or threat – of Charles's universal empire was never realized, thanks to constraints endemic to his time. Flemish in origin, he never became especially fluent in either German or Spanish and so had difficulties exerting his sway in both realms. His power as Holy Roman Emperor was hedged by the position's elective nature, while the Spanish never lost their suspicions of a young outsider and his coterie of foreign advisers. At a time when European monarchs still lacked fixed courts, Charles was constantly on the move, from Spain to Germany to Holland to Italy and even Tunis, as he formed alliances, sought new funds, fought battles and confronted the latest crisis.

And crises there certainly were. Europeans turned out to be more concerned about losing their long-standing freedoms and sources of income than about the vague promises of a universal monarchy. The new French king, François I, felt especially threatened by Charles's super-state and by 1521 began a series of expensive and devastating wars with Spanish and Imperial forces for control of Italy, Flanders and Lorraine. Lesser players such as England's Henry VIII and Pope Clement VII also jockeyed for position, and the need to maintain their support kept Charles engaged in constant diplomatic missions. Much more threatening were the powerful and expansionist Ottoman Turks, who chased the Habsburgs out of Hungary and North Africa and made threatening alliances even with the nominally Catholic François.

Still harder was managing the religious uprising championed by Martin Luther. Long convinced that such doctrinal disputes were little more than petty clerical squabbles, Charles generally ignored the question of Protestant dissent in Germany, usually turning the problem over to his brother Ferdinand I. When he finally persuaded the pope to call the Council of Trent in 1545, it was already too late to avoid a definitive break that sundered not only the Church but also his empire.

Ultimately, the era's weak bureaucracies, glacial communications and poorly managed economics made the job of universal monarch too much for one man. Even with a number of Habsburg relations to serve as his regents, Charles still found the demands overwhelming as he raced around his empire with his expensive (and often unpaid) armies to confront uprisings and invasions. By 1550 he was exhausted, ever more troubled by gout and his jutting, misaligned jaw – the result of centuries of Habsburg inbreeding – which often kept him from chewing his food. In 1556 he finally gave up and, one by one, abdicated his many titles, splitting the vast Habsburg lands back into their original Spanish and German branches and retiring to the silence of a monastery near Madrid for the last few years that remained to him.

◌℞

Reginald Pole

A DIFFICULT COUSIN

1500–1558

Royal blood brought Reginald Pole as many problems as privileges. Great-grand nephew of English King Edward IV, he grew up close to the throne – King Henry VIII personally paid his way not only to Oxford University, but also for four years at the University of Padua. There, Pole received the standard humanist education in Latin and Greek and befriended many of the more liberal and reformist clergy in Italy. When Henry finally summoned Pole back home, in 1526, it was to offer his cousin a high church office – the Archbishopric of York was suggested – provided he would back Henry's divorce proceedings against Catherine of Aragon. Since Pope Clement VII had refused to issue a papal dispensation dissolving Henry's marriage, this put Pole in a painful situation, forced to choose between loyalty to his pontiff or to his monarch.

Unwilling to accept a diocese on such terms, Pole prevaricated and persuaded cousin Henry to send him abroad again, this time to study at the Sorbonne in Paris. The king kept up the pressure on Pole, however, finally pushing him to reject the king's beloved project to his face. Henry's response was to explode with anger and pull a knife on his hapless relative – who saved himself only by bursting into tears. At this point, Pole might well have lost his head, as would happen to Thomas More for much the same reason, but he persuaded the king to again let him return to the congenial surroundings of Padua. There he involved himself in Biblical studies and questions of Church reform, even though he remained inflexible on the considerably more fraught question of Henry's marriage.

This apparently happy interlude was short-lived. Returning to England, Pole expressed increasing opposition to Henry's new wife and the Anglican Church. Then, in 1535 the new pope, Paul III, appointed him to a commission for laying out a path to Catholic renewal. Joining the board gave Pole a chance to promote his relatively conciliatory and reformist positions, but serving on such a high-level body required he be named a cardinal. This he strenuously avoided, for fear of enraging Henry, but in the end, in late 1535, Paul made him a cardinal anyway, virtually against his will. Once again, Henry was enraged, and since Pole himself was safe in Italy, the king arrested the leading members of the Pole family. After long, uncomfortable stints in the Tower of London, virtually all of them – including Margaret Pole, Reginald's elderly and saintly mother – were beheaded, simply for being the cardinal's relatives.

For the next 17 years, Pole lived in exile – a stateless cardinal with no family or national backing, dependant on papal financing. Still, widely known as 'The English Cardinal,' he was repeatedly sent off as Pope Paul's legate, to broker peace between the always warring François I and Charles V or to reconcile Henry VIII back to the Church. Most of these expeditions ended in failure, as neither François nor the Emperor wanted his services or even to be seen talking to him. Henry was less interested in hearing Pole's messages than in sending assassins to kill him. The cardinal's major success in these years was as Paul's representative to the Council of Trent, opened in 1545 to redefine and reform Church doctrine.

Here too, however, Pole was conflicted – his reformist beliefs, especially concerning the key issue of justification, or salvation by faith alone, were uncomfortably similar to those of Luther and Calvin. Some of his closest friends from his Padua days had already deserted Rome and embraced Protestantism. His near-heretical positions made it all the more remarkable that in the papal election of 1549 Pole himself came just one vote short of being elected to the Throne of St. Peter. Had Pole, rather than the dissolute and religiously indifferent Julius III, become pope, Rome's approach to reform might have been radically altered – one of the big What ifs? of European history.

Instead, Pole had another fate. In 1553, Henry's elder daughter became Queen Mary I of England and eagerly invited him to return home, first as papal legate and then as Archbishop of Canterbury. Pole energetically set about returning England to the old faith, by law and persuasion when possible, but also by fire – with his permission, if not directly by his order, around 280 Protestants were burned at the stake during Mary's reign. Such harsh methods showed another facet to this conservative religious reformer, one that was fortunately brief. Barely four years after his return, Reginald Pole died – just 12 hours after the death of Queen Mary herself had ended his cherished hope that Catholicism could be revived in England.

CR

Benvenuto Cellini

GREAT SCULPTOR, BETTER AUTOBIOGRAPHER

1500–1571

After eighteen years of childless marriage Giovanni Cellini was so pleased when his wife bore him a son that he kept crying out *'benvenuto! benvenuto!'* ('Welcome! Welcome!'), until 'that was the name they decided on' – Benvenuto Cellini. When it was time to decide the boy's career, there was some initial disagreement. Giovanni, an instrument maker and player in Florence's town band, naturally assumed that his son would follow a musical calling, while Benvenuto himself complained that 'I hated every minute of it and would only sing or play the flute to obey him'. Finally the young Cellini convinced his father to apprentice him to a goldsmith.

As a maker of jewelry and figurines Benvenuto thrived. Like many another craftsmen of middling origins, he reached the heights of his profession through skill and good connections – such was the cultural and social mobility that characterized Renaissance Italy. Working first in Rome, then in Florence, France and finally back in Florence, Cellini filled the decorative needs of the lay and clerical autocrats who flourished so conspicuously in the 16th century, supplying them with vases, statuettes, jewelry and medals in gold, silver and bronze. The most famous of these was, and remains, the Classically inspired golden *saliera* or salt cellar he created for the French king François I in 1543.

Although Cellini believed he had the talent to become his generation's Michelangelo, only in middle age did he start landing the large-scale commissions necessary to become a major sculptor. In 1540 King François contracted him to embellish the royal residence at Fontainebleau with an entrance, fountain and twelve large silver statues of Greek gods. Cellini only finished three of this pantheon, however (and those have since been melted down), and failed to complete the fountain. He was more successful with subsequent commissions from Florence's Duke Cosimo I, for whom he cast several large portrait busts and the monumental *Perseus Holding the Head of Medusa* (1545–54), which still stands magnificently where it was originally erected – in the Loggia dei Lanzi in the centre of Florence.

Cellini never became the next Michelangelo. What lasting fame he won came instead from his conviction that 'all men of every sort who have done something that is or seems truly worthwhile should, being upright and truthful, write down the story of their own life.' At the age of 58, Cellini did precisely that – he set out to compose his *Vita*, or autobiography. When he ended his tale five years later, he had filled nearly 500 manuscript pages. Although he spent as much space denouncing his opponents as detailing his accomplishments, he had inadvertently produced a work of art whose fame would eclipse virtually all the medallions, reliquaries and statuary he had ever created.

Autobiographies were not new in Europe, but the existing approach was to cast one's life as a spiritual journey. Cellini's *Vita* offered no such narrative arc: his account ends abruptly, in the middle of a paragraph: 'and then I set off for Pisa.' Instead, his is the story of a recognizably modern man, an autonomous individual flawed with temper, arrogance and lust, striving not only to overcome his weaknesses but also to convert them into creative art. The *Vita* is an artistic autobiography, filled with Cellini's passions for design, craftsmanship and aesthetics; the clashes of wills between artists and patrons; and the nuts and bolts behind the making of great art. A deeply social tale, it plots the shifting and unclear relationships that Cellini had to navigate, whether among his fellow artists or in princely courts.

Yet his was also a life of adventures. During the Sack of Rome in 1527 Cellini defended the Castel Sant'Angelo; eleven years later he was imprisoned in the same fortress, on supposedly trumped-up changes. In 1533 he joined midnight séances held in the Roman Colosseum and proved so stalwart in facing down unexpected hordes of demons that the necromancer 'tried to persuade me to join him in consecrating a book to the devil'. Over the years he took both men and women as lovers and had at least five children. He was quick to form friendships and even quicker to make enemies. He learned tennis and owned one of the first wheel-lock muskets; he admitted to murdering three rival craftsmen and assaulting many more, usually over questions of honour. From the *Vita*, Cellini emerges as a boastful, daring, inspired, self-confident and passionate man of his time. When the book finally found widespread publication in the early 19th century, readers were quick to hail Cellini the man, rather than his statuary, as the true Renaissance masterpiece.

ℂℛ

St Francis Xavier

APOSTLE AND MISSIONARY TO THE EAST INDIES

1506–1552

The 16th-century evangelical enthusiasm that led many Europeans to
Protestantism also impassioned many others who stayed within the
Roman Church. One of these was Francisco de Jaso y Azpilcueta, born
to Basque nobility in Javier, in the Pyrenees. Orphaned and deprived of
his birthright after the Spanish conquered his homeland in 1512, Francisco
emigrated to Paris, where, known as Francis of Xavier, he enrolled in philosophy at the Sorbonne. While there, he met another Basque and fellow
student, Ignatius of Loyola, who took Xavier under his charismatic spell.
Submitting himself to the transformative experience of his new mentor's
Spiritual Exercises, Xavier joined with Ignatius and five other companions
to found the Society of Jesus, or Jesuits, swearing mutual religious vows
on 15 August 1534.

One of these vows promised unquestioning obedience to the pope,
'whether [he] sends us among the Turks, or among those who live in realms
called the Indies, or among all kinds of heretics and schismatics, or elsewhere'. Their dedication was promptly put to the test: João III of Portugal
asked Pope Paul III for missionaries to the East Indies, and Paul chose
Xavier for the job. On 7 April 1541 Xavier left Europe forever and, after
a wearisome voyage of thirteen months, reached Goa, on the west coast
of India. Although King João had originally intended him to evangelize
among Portuguese merchants and sailors who had taken Indian wives and
gone native, Xavier preferred working with their racially mixed offspring.
These he attracted to his mission by walking the Goan streets and ringing

a small bell. Discovering that his missionary work irritated many of the Portuguese in Goa, Xavier withdrew from the city to spend several years ministering and preaching in Ceylon and southern India, where he allegedly baptized over 20,000 pearl fishers.

Officially both papal nuncio and apostle to the East Indies, Xavier was more interested in working with Indians than with his fellow Europeans – eventually he became so impatient with the Portuguese Goans that he asked the Inquisition to come and punish their heresies. In 1544 he left India, travelling east to seek 'a plentiful harvest [of souls]' among more amenable pagans unspoiled by Western values. Malacca, the Portuguese imperial capital in western Malaya, struck him as little better than Goa, so he continued eastward, to the Maluku Islands. There he found the pagan communities he had been seeking, for although 'the place is very dangerous, because indigenous tribes are wicked and put various poisons in the food and drink', the people were still willing to heed his preaching, and many converted to Christianity.

In 1549 Xavier headed to Japan, where he found a society virtually untouched by Western influence – the Portuguese had been trading there for less than a decade. The Japanese, he felt, were 'led by reason in everything more than any other people', and although highly bellicose, they were also culturally sophisticated, polite and very curious about Western practices and beliefs. They avidly listened to – but also challenged – Xavier's attempts to convey such Catholic fundamentals as a merciful creator God who still allowed evil and a Hell that doomed all their ancestors to eternal torment. Although hampered by having to rely on translators and pictures for his preaching, Xavier still made a notable impression on both the elite and commoners, using his medical and scientific knowledge to attract the attention of listeners, whom he then baptized, if not exactly indoctrinated. The tangible success of his method – he baptized thousands – obscured significant spiritual weaknesses, however. Even more than the Malukus, the Japanese respected Xavier as a cultural advocate of the novel technology and superior firepower of the West. In a Japan riven with civil war, many who accepted his teachings did so for manifestly political reasons, looking to strike an alliance not only with Christ but also with the Portuguese traders, who offered the very worldly advantages of muskets, warships and coined silver.

Japan was Xavier's greatest apostolic venture. Unable to commit himself permanently to even such promising beginnings, he was soon on the move again, however. He declared that, 'We have decided at all costs to open a way into China', which he concluded was the true centre of law, politics and religion in East Asia. He returned to Goa in 1552 to organize a China mission, but then his plans went terribly awry. While waiting for permission to enter Canton, he was abandoned by his fellow Portuguese on the little island of Shangchuan, not far from Macao. There, alone save for a Chinese acolyte named Antonio, he fell ill and died, on 3 December 1552, on the threshold of the Chinese Empire and the Jesuits' greatest missionary challenge.

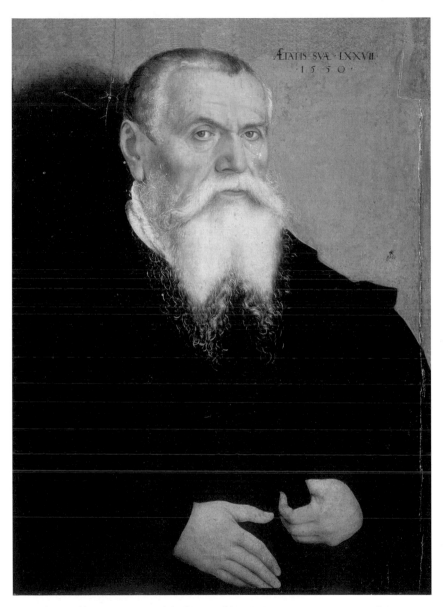

25 Either a self-portrait or a work by his son, this painting captures Lucas Cranach in 1550, three years before his death at the age of 81. During his long life, the prolific artist painted many Reformation leaders, including Luther and his wife.

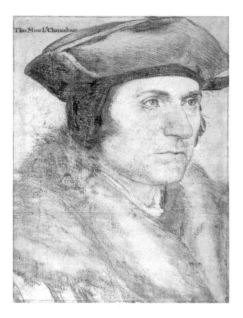

26 Thomas More, in a drawing by Hans Holbein the Younger (*c.* 1527). A serious, devout man, More nevertheless excelled at practical jokes: he once answered his daughter-in-law's plea for a pearl necklace with an elegantly boxed string of white peas.

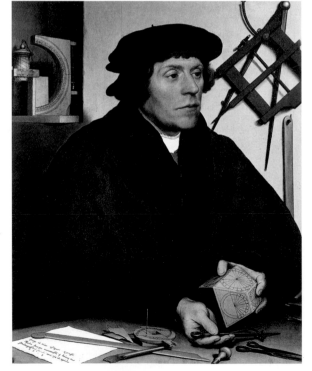

27 In 1528, Holbein painted Nicolaus Kratzer surrounded by the tools of his orologist's trade and holding what was one of his favourite creations: the bronze polyhedral sundial that could be considered the first portable timepiece.

28 Marguerite of Navarre, in a drawing by François Clouet (*c.* 1540). More intellectual than her brother, the king of France, Marguerite was a lifelong scholar widely admired by humanists. In addition to writing well-regarded books, she protected religious reformers and supported such authors as François Rabelais.

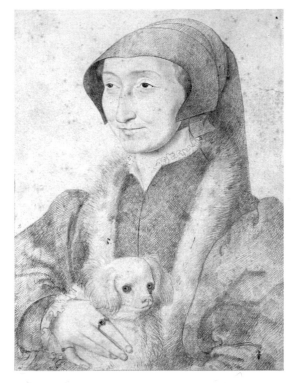

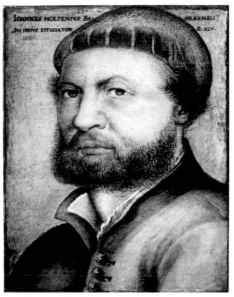

29 Self-portrait by Hans Holbein (1542–43). Holbein executed this small image in pen and coloured chalks shortly before he died. Perhaps a work of self-promotion, it captures his weariness.

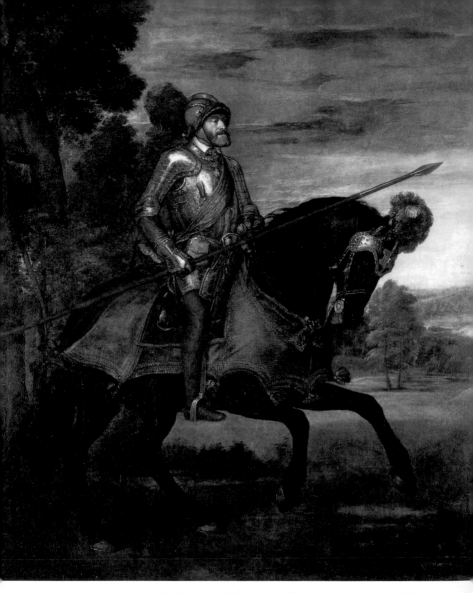

30 Holy Roman Emperor Charles V at Mühlberg, painted by Titian (1548). One of the most powerful monarchs of the age, he ruled an empire twice the size of Classical Rome – but secured through dynastic union rather than conquest.

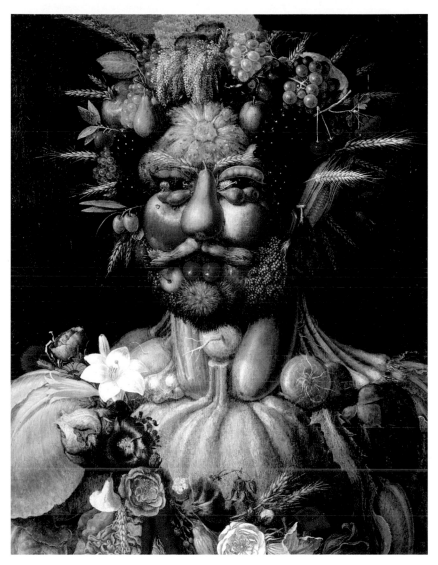

31 Rudolf II, as depicted in one of the most exuberant, even optimistic, of Arcimboldo's composite portraits (detail; 1591). Looted by the Swedish troops who sacked Prague in 1648, this painting, together with many others by Arcimboldo, now resides in Stockholm.

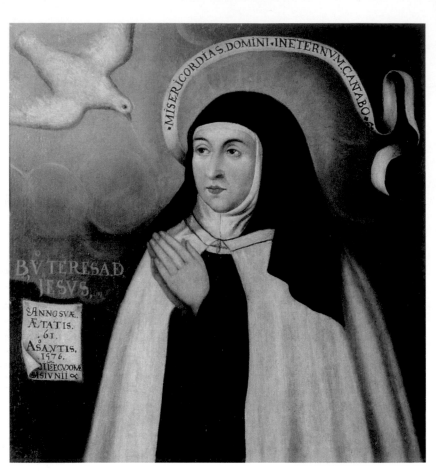

32 A copy of the only known portrait of St Teresa of Avila made from life, by Fray Juan de la Miseria. The original was painted in 1576, when Teresa was 61 years old. The ribbon reads: 'I shall forever sing of the mercies of the Lord.'

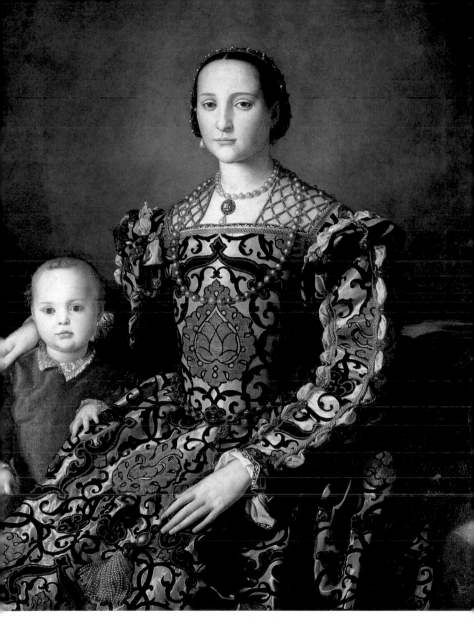

33 Angelo Bronzino's portrait of Eleanor of Toledo and Giovanni de' Medici (1545). Eleanor tried to overcome her outsider status among the Florentine nobility through paintings and other public gestures that vaunted her domesticity, propriety and wealth.

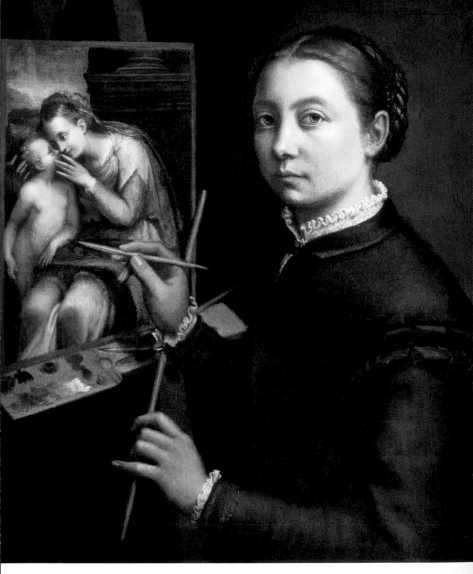

34 Self-portrait by Sofonisba Anguissola (1556). Painted just after her time with Michelangelo in Rome and before her departure for Madrid, this work radiates wit, intimate charm and self-confidence.

⍟

Andrea Palladio

PERFECTION IN STONE AND BRICK

1508–1580

In 1535 the Italian nobleman Gian Giorgio Trissino, a poet and humanist, decided to renovate his family's old villa just outside the northern Italian city of Vicenza. Excited by the Classical writings of Vitruvius, Trissino decided to keep a close eye on the project, acting as something of an amateur architect. He was pleased to discover that one of his workers, a middle-aged stonecutter named Andrea di Pietro della Gondola, was unusually talented – both in his own craft and in picking up the Vitruvian principles that Trissino championed. Fancying himself another Pygmalion, Trissino took Andrea under his humanist wing, to turn this son of a charwoman and miller into an adept of the noble arts of architecture. So avid and capable did Andrea turn out that the two soon collaborated on new projects. Trissino introduced the stonecutter to his friends – other humanists with some building projects of their own – and then took him to Rome so that he could study surviving Classical monuments at first hand. Convinced of his acolyte's genius, Trissino even gave him a new name – Palladio, from Pallas Athene, the Greek goddess of wisdom.

Very quickly Palladio made his new education and connections pay off. By 1537 he was running his own studio and had received the first in what would be a long line of commissions, mostly from Vicentine or Venetian nobles looking to have their villas done in the Classical manner. Working with furious energy, Palladio designed a dozen such villas in the next decade, and he went on to produce around thirty in his lifetime. Mostly scattered over the idyllic countryside around Vicenza, they have come to represent a unique artistic patrimony – and a UNESCO World Heritage Site. Some, such as the villas La Rotonda (1567–91) and La Malcontenta (1558–60), were primarily programmed as pleasure houses in the Classical Roman style – places where nobles could seek refuge and relax during the hot summer months while they played at being farmers. Others, such as the Villa Barbaro (1560–70), were intended to grace actual working estates. In either case Palladio, recognizing the wish of an owner to lord it over his servants and peasants, always made a point of putting the airy and proportionally gracious homes he designed on a pedestal, giving them hierarchical dominance over the surrounding outbuildings.

Palladio's talent for private villas was something new, both in architecture and in society. It was triggered by growing personal wealth and the increasing competitive urge for self-expression among the Italian elite. He also carried out more traditional commissions, however, including a few civic buildings, such as the Teatro Olimpico (1580) in Vicenza – the first covered theatre built since the Classical age. After Trissino died in 1550, Palladio quickly moved on to more exalted patrons – in particular, the brothers Cardinal Daniele Barbaro and Marcantonio Barbaro, from one of the most venerable Venetian noble families. As enthusiastic about their rustic disciple as Trissino had been, the Barbaro brothers worked with Palladio on several publishing projects, escorting him back to Rome and eventually introducing him to the inner circles of Venice's ruling elite. Soon he was at work on prestigious churches for the Republic and, in particular, three that would permanently leave his mark on the Venetian cityscape – San Francesco della Vigna (1564), San Giorgio Maggiore (1565) and Il Redentore (1577). In 1570 he was named *Proto della Serenissima* ('chief architect of Venice') – responsible for every building project in the city.

That same year, after a lengthy preparation, Palladio published perhaps the most important book ever written on designing buildings: *I quattro libri dell'architettura* ('The four books of architecture'). In it he not only clarified the principles of Vitruvius but also provided the practical means for employing them – the proper application of the Golden Rectangle, aesthetic rules for mixing different architectural forms and a guide for scaling all of a building's elements based on multiples of a central feature. The book, illustrated with Palladio's own works, called for simple compositions that achieved grandeur through a careful juxtaposition of formal elements in highly symmetrical display. Although the resulting villas, palaces and churches can seem somewhat unadorned and severe, they fit perfectly with the standards and aspirations of a new generation of occupants and patrons – members of the elite who were in the process of leaving the world of commerce to settle down as gentleman farmers, in emulation of Cicero and Virgil. Soon after Palladio died – neither rich nor ennobled – *I quattro libri* was eagerly received in Britain and Holland. There, its neo-classical models were rechristened 'Palladian' and became a primary guide for generations of merchant princes until well into the 19th century.

Jean Calvin

PREDESTINED BY GOD

1509–1564

Although usually associated with Geneva, Jean Calvin was not from Switzerland and spent only the second half of his life in the Swiss city. Born far from the Alps, in French Picardy, he abandoned his early preparation for the priesthood when his father sent him to a humanist school in Paris and then to Orléans to study civil law. While at Orléans, at about the age of 20, Calvin had a religious revelation, and although he finished his law degree and even published a humanistic study on the writings of Seneca, his true passion in life never wavered from this conversion experience.

By the early 1530s Martin Luther's proposals for reforming Christian dogma and Church organization had gained a wide following in the German Empire. They were much less acceptable in France, however, where a unified monarchy and strong religious institutions put up firm resistance. Having involved himself in a clamorously unsuccessful attempt to reform one such institution – the University of Paris – Calvin was forced by a Catholic backlash to go into hiding and then exile in 1534. For a while he found a safe home in Basel, a university town and the northernmost city in the Swiss Confederation. After just a year of furious writing he produced the first version of his *Institutio Christianae Religionis* ('Institutes of the Christian religion'). This explanation and defence of the reformed faith, filling as it did a need among reformers for clarity and unity, established Calvin's fame on both sides of the rapidly widening religious divide. Within a year, more by accident than design, he found himself in Geneva, where fellow French exiles begged him to stay and reform the local church.

In matters of doctrine Calvin argued against the Church's long-accepted dogma that participation in the sacraments, good works and personal merit contributed to a Christian's salvation. Sin, Calvin wrote, whether Original or personal, could be 'justified' only by God's infinite grace, accessible only through Scripture and not by any comparatively minuscule human effort. In this Calvin largely agreed with Luther, although he was more rigid, perhaps because of his background in the law, in insisting on the logical consequence of this doctrine – that an omnipotent God had necessarily predestined the salvation or damnation of all humans, regardless of how they behaved during their lives.

This stark dogma had a certain appeal to the burghers of Geneva, not least because it replaced the age-old Christian obsession about personal salvation with the more immediate, if also more restricted, duty of contemplating the power and majesty of God through reading scriptures and attending sermons. But if 'Calvinists' – as they became known – could contribute nothing towards their own salvation, they were still part of a community whose covenant with God required group discipline and social organization. At Calvin's urging, the Genevese governing council expelled the Catholic bishop, suspended celebration of the Mass, abolished convents and confiscated their property and declared that the city would 'live henceforth according to the law of the gospel and the word of God, and ... abolish all papal abuses'. Although claiming no authority for himself beyond that of preacher, Calvin persuaded the Genevese to accept an expanded ministry to regulate their civic morality. Ruling in parallel with the secular government, this theocracy had four distinct branches: pastors, to preach and give the sacraments; theologians, to teach doctrine; elders, to judge and administer religious discipline; and deacons, to run public charities.

As it happened not all, or even most, of Geneva always supported this theocratic state. In 1538 those who found Calvin's visionary society too strict had him expelled, and he moved to the German Imperial city of Strasbourg. Invited back in 1541 to a Geneva now swollen with reformist exiles from France, Calvin remained unofficial head of the new congregation there for the rest of his life. He wrote and published numerous commentaries on almost every book of the Bible, greatly expanded and translated the *Institutio*, and preached relentlessly – daily sermons, an hour or more in length, delivered without notes. In 1559 he founded a college and seminary for aspiring Calvinist theologians, whose many graduates brought the reformed message back to their homelands in France, Holland, Scotland and England. In their discipline, determination and secrecy this corps of Calvinist evangelists operated much like – and often came into conflict with – the Jesuits, who competed with them in many of the same countries. This, and Calvin's willingness to take on dissenters and condemn his theological opponents to death, gave Geneva a reputation as the Protestant Rome – ideologues, Inquisition and all.

❦

Gracia Mendes Nasi

LA SEÑORA OF THE SEPHARDIM

1510–1569

I f a portrait of Gracia Nasi existed, it would probably show a shrewd, tough-minded yet sympathetic face. However, since for Renaissance Jews it was normally unacceptable to sit for a painting, it is necessary to settle for the picture we get of Nasi from her correspondence and business records. From these sources she emerges as one of the most successful financiers and politicians of the 16th century – this at a time when having no fixed country or declared religion could be dangerous, or even fatal, handicaps – especially for a woman.

Although she became the most powerful non-aristocratic woman of the Renaissance, little is known about Gracia Nasi's early years. She may have been descended from Jews of Spanish origin who emigrated to Portugal, but how long the Nasis had lived there and what they did are complete speculation. The only certainty is that in 1528, under the Spanish name of Beatriz de Luna, she married a wealthy *converso* merchant, a Christianized Jew named Francisco Mendes, in Lisbon. During their marriage both Mendes and his brother and partner Diogo grew still richer as financiers in the Portuguese Empire, trading in spices, silver and slaves. A daughter, Ana – known privately as Reyna ('Queen') – was born to Francisco and Beatrice around 1534.

In early 1536 Francisco Mendes died, leaving his half of the partnership to Beatrice. The young widow had to master her husband's business quickly while also dealing with the newly arrived threat of the Portuguese Inquisition. In mid-1536 the Inquisitors entered Lisbon to root out 'judaizers'

– Christianized Jews who practised their former religion in secret. In reality, however, the Inquisition went after all *conversos*, especially the wealthier ones, whose goods could be impounded on their arrest.

Moving decisively, Beatrice relocated most of the Mendes fortune – along with her daughter, sister and several nephews – from Lisbon, first to London and eventually to a large community of *conversos* in Spanish Antwerp. Alongside them in their new home was her brother-in-law Diogo, running a profitable bank with his half of the partnership. Beatrice stayed in Antwerp for around eight years. Through her agents around the world, she efficiently ran and strengthened the family business, even arranging for Diogo to marry her sister Brianda. Then, in 1543, Diogo died, willing control of his considerable wealth to Beatrice. Although she now commanded one of largest and wealthiest commercial firms in Europe, the challenge of running her business was often the least of Beatrice's problems. Rich, single and female, she was a magnet for predators, who tried various schemes to relieve her of her wealth – forcibly marrying her daughter to a Spanish nobleman, charging her dead husband with judaizing and coercing her into making interest-free loans to Emperor Charles V. Convinced she could find no protection in Antwerp, Beatrice decided she could not stay put; she took Brianda and their two daughters, along with what treasure she could carry, and secretly decamped to Venice.

Since they were officially Christians, the de Luna sisters could rent a palace on the Grand Canal rather than squeeze into the city's insalubrious Jewish Ghetto. Living among Gentiles made Beatrice more open to accusations of judaizing, however. These were promptly forthcoming, from none other than Brianda, who was determined to reclaim her share of the Mendes fortune, even if it meant sending her sister to the Inquisition. This family squabble soon dragged in the Venetian state, and, fearful for her life and fortune, Beatrice fled again, to nearby Ferrara. There she renounced her Christianity, taking the Jewish name Gracia Mendes Nasi. Finally, in 1555, aware that the conservative Pope Paul IV was intent on making all of Italy dangerous for Jews and *conversos* alike, she packed up and moved one final time – to Constantinople.

Settled at last, Gracia Nasi retained her profitable business, if not all of her original fortune. She spent much of her remaining wealth helping fellow Iberian Jews and *conversos* resettle in safer lands, endowing synagogues and yeshivas, and supporting rabbinic scholarship. She bought land on the Palestine coast at Tiberias to establish the first Zionist resettlement in the Holy Land. Although this petered out after her death, her other endowments, such as the Spanish translation of the Tanakh, or Hebrew Bible, proved of lasting value for diaspora Jews. The publisher of this work, known as the Ferrara Bible, sang her praises in his introduction, calling her 'the Heart within the Body [of] Our Portuguese [*converso*] Nation'. The many Jews who had benefited over the years from her care and generosity had a simpler name for Gracia Nasi, however – to them she was just known as *La Señora* ('The Lady').

CR

Andreas Vesalius

PHYSICIAN OF THE EMPEROR, DISSECTOR OF THE DEAD

1514–1564

Even in an age known for peripatetic geniuses Andreas Vesalius stands out. The son of the personal physician to Charles V and the grandson and great grandson of court doctors, Vesalius was groomed for a medical career from his birth in Brussels. Enrolled at the prestigious University of Louvain at the age of just 16, he followed a course of philosophy and philology while teaching himself rudimentary anatomy by dissecting dogs, cats and rats. At age 19 he moved on to the University of Paris, where he trained under the renowned professor of medicine Jacobus Sylvius. Although securing human cadavers for study was a somewhat shady business, Vesalius found a steady supply by bribing custodians at the local foundling hospital. He became so familiar with the human skeleton that he took bets that he could identify any bone while blindfolded. His passion for hands-on study put him at odds with the traditionally minded Sylvius, who preferred to teach sitting at his professor's cathedra, reading aloud the appropriate passages from the Classical anatomist Galen while a hired surgeon performed the actual autopsy, holding up body parts as they were mentioned.

Finding this approach both timid and uninspiring, Vesalius left for the Venetian university at Padua. There he passed his exams in just three months and was named Doctor of Medicine at the age of just 22. The day after his graduation he performed such an impressive public dissection that the Venetian authorities offered him Padua's chair of anatomy and surgery on the spot. For six years Vesalius taught and perfected his dissecting skills

– helped out by an obliging Paduan judge who supplied him with the cadavers of executed criminals. Increasingly convinced that Galen's dissecting experience had been limited to the bodies of apes, he lost his reverence for this god of Classical and medieval medicine and began to question the entire basis of the anatomical sciences. Brash and self-assured, the young Fleming complained about:

> How many often absurd things are accepted in the name of Galen … [for example, human structures] the existence of which are constantly supported by his writing and of which the doctors speak constantly. They have never seen [them], but nevertheless they continue to describe them, guided by [his] teachings. I myself am now really astonished at my previous stupidity … caused by my devotion to Galen.

Vital to Vesalius's teaching method were accurate drawings of the human body, and from 1540 to 1543 he put all his findings, both prose and illustrations, into one magisterial volume, *De humani corporis fabrica* ('On the structure of the human body'). The *Fabrica*, as it became known, featured strikingly accurate, often aesthetically pleasing, etchings that were supposedly produced by the workshop of Titian. Meanwhile, Vesalius continued his textual assault on entrenched Galenic dogma. He refuted a host of long-cherished teachings, both trivial (whether women, made from Adam's rib, had one more of these than men) and profound (the nature of blood circulation, the workings of the nervous system and function of the kidneys). To theologians who asked him if the soul was located in the heart, he replied that his studies had only revealed that the heart (despite Galen's claims) had four chambers and was not the originating point of the nervous system. This, like consciousness, he located in the brain.

Not surprisingly, the *Fabrica* was hotly contested, not least by Sylvius himself, who insisted that there could be no anatomical knowledge beyond Galen. The collapse of medicine's most cherished paradigm shocked the scientific world. Even Vesalius's Paduan colleagues turned against him, and people punned on his name, calling him 'Vesanus' ('the Madman'). Repelled by his colleagues' mulish response, Vesalius left his teaching post and returned to his family's traditional work, as the Habsburg court physician. He joined the entourage of Charles V in 1543 – but only after the Emperor's theologians declared that human dissection was acceptable.

Vesalius spent the remainder of his life treating battle injuries and courtly illnesses for Charles and then for the Emperor's son Philip II. He found life in Madrid with his new monarch less congenial than Brussels, however. His envious Spanish colleagues constantly undermined him, circulating rumours that the Inquisition was investigating his work because he had begun dissecting a body that was still alive. In 1562 Vesalius left Spain, ostensibly for a pilgrimage to the Holy Land but also hoping to get back his old job at Padua. He did visit Palestine, but on his return he fell ill and died, far from both courts and universities, on the Venetian island of Zante (Zakynthos).

∽

Roger Ascham

THE ENGLISH TEACHER

c. 1514–1568

The humanist scholar Roger Ascham defined education for young men and at least one young woman in Tudor England – in the late 1540s he tutored a teenage Princess Elizabeth. Famous for his progressive philosophy of learning, he condemned classroom beatings (then a common pedagogical tool) and exhorted teachers to treat children with love and patience.

A Cambridge graduate, Ascham taught Greek and mathematics at the university for several years. To supplement his meagre income, he wrote a treatise on archery titled *Toxophilus*, 'lover of the bow'. A keen archer himself, he promoted it as a manly pursuit, a boon to national defence, and a healthful form of exercise. It was a time-honoured Ciceronian dialogue, but composed in English to prove that the language could be as scholarly as Latin.

Toxophilus was a patriotic project in many ways: archery had gained popularity as a proper English pastime, and he touted the book as covering 'this English matter, in the English tongue, for Englishmen.' Following Aristotle's advice to speak like a common man and think like a wise man, he spurned terms from French and Italian, explaining that 'strange words ... do make all things dark and hard.' He dedicated the work to King Henry, an avid archer himself, and sent copies to important leaders of church and state in hopes of netting a patron. The strategy worked. Henry invited him to Greenwich in 1544 and granted the grateful scholar a royal pension.

Hired in 1548 to tutor the 15-year-old Elizabeth, he designed a rigorous curriculum of classical studies, theology, and foreign languages. Fluent in Latin and Italian by age 10, the talented princess also mastered French,

Spanish, and a good bit of Greek with Ascham's guidance. He believed a thorough education went beyond books, however, and arranged lessons for her on the lute and on the virginals, a relative of the harpsichord. Young people also needed fresh air and exercise, and he set aside time each day for the princess to take walks or ride horses around the palace grounds.

His approach with Elizabeth formed the basis of the groundbreaking book on education that established his fame. He began *The Scholemaster* after hearing of Eton College students who had run away to escape their master's floggings. Ascham argued that beatings kept students from doing their best; even worse, they instilled a hatred of learning. In a novel stance for the time, he emphasized a teacher's role in students' success, pointing out that children learn in different ways and at different rates and that lessons should be tailored accordingly.

The book includes advice on subjects and readings, and deals at length with moral education, revealing a deeply conflicted attitude toward the birthplace of his beloved humanism. Italians had given 'greate good' to the world, but 'that tyme is gone' – lechery and vice had corroded their once-great traditions. He writes that in Italy he saw in nine days more sin than occurs in London over nine years. Travellers returned with 'worse manners,' 'lesse learning,' and a shocking assortment of Italian vices – lying, vanity, 'Papistrie, or worse.' Having been 'free in Italie to go whither so ever lust wil cary them,' men resented England's superior moral standards.

The Scholemaster, published two years after Ascham's death, marks a significant shift in England's attitude toward Italy that resonated throughout the culture. His notion of Italy as a cultural toxin, for example, filtered into the era's literature: an 'Italian sallet,' or salad, was code for secret poisoning, Shakespeare wrote of 'drug-damn'd Italy,' and scheming Italian villains wrought havoc in Tudor and Stuart drama. Such plays allowed theatre-goers an Italian experience in the safety of England, which is much in keeping with Ascham's advice: students could acquire all they needed from Italy through reading. To avoid the fate of an 'English man Italianated,' he instructed students to stay home and read Castiglione's *The Courtier*, which 'would do a yong gentleman more good ... than three yeares travell abroad in Italy.'

CꙄ

St Teresa of Avila

GOD'S ECSTATIC DISCIPLE

1515–1582

When she was a girl, Teresa of Avila recalled, 'I was very adroit in doing anything that was wrong.' She avidly read her mother's chivalric romances and passed hours with her more louche cousins, learning 'to make much of dress. Wishing to please others by my appearance, I took pains with my hands and hair, used perfumes and all the vanities within my reach.' During that time it seemed, she thought, that 'the fear of God had utterly departed from me', leaving her open to a life of gossip, vanities and childish follies.

Teresa's turn from frivolity to faith began with the death of her mother, when she was aged 13. Thereafter she abandoned her romances for religious texts, but hers was a slow, often halting journey. She wished to enter a nunnery, but poor health and her father's opposition thwarted her until finally, at the age of 20, she ran away from home to join the local Carmelite convent. Even in the cloister, however, her spiritual path was difficult. The Carmelites of Avila, like many unreformed orders, followed the 'Mitigated Rule', in which the wealthier sisters enjoyed quite secular lives, with servants, lapdogs, jewelry, perfume and the freedom to socialize and even travel. Seemingly troubled by the lack of religious conviction she found in her new home, Teresa fell so gravely ill that she nearly died. Wracked with intense pain, she was almost completely paralysed, but she later saw the experience as breaking down her childish egoism and opening her spirit. Certainly she maintained her spirited ways. Legend has it that in the midst of great agony she asked God why she had to suffer so. In a vision, the Lord assured her that he treated all his true friends that way, to which Teresa supposedly shot back that it was no wonder he had so few friends.

In 1543 Teresa recovered from the worst of her pain and paralysis, and she found the strength to explore her relationship with God through prayer and contemplation. Drawing on her experiences while sick, she developed a progression of spiritual exercises designed to liberate her from both external attachments and the internal noise of consciousness. Working through these stages of contemplative prayer, she was often infused with ecstasy, bathed in tears and catatonic with rapture. Among her sisters she was known for reaching states of such intense spirituality that, while hearing Mass, she supposedly levitated and had to be held down.

Teresa's mystical attainments both excited and repelled her contemporaries. Some of her sister Carmelites felt threatened, both by the rigour of her discipline and by the obvious manifestations of her raptures. Word began to circulate outside the convent walls, even among her friends and relations, that her ecstasies were provoked by pride and demons. Some whispered that her grandfather, Juan de Toledo, had been a Jew forcibly converted to Christianity – a glaring irregularity in Teresa's parentage that allowed them to cast doubt on the source of her inspiration. In demonstrative recompense Teresa set out on a campaign of self-mortification that continued until her confessor intervened. Her doubts about the spiritual nature of her experiences persisted until 29 June 1559, when she underwent a mystical union with Christ. That visionary moment – famously immortalized by Gian Lorenzo Bernini in his *Ecstasy of St Teresa* (1647–52) – provided a certainty of purpose that would guide her for the rest of her life.

Teresa channelled her sense of mission into reforming the Carmelites. Inspired by similar efforts in male religious orders, she petitioned the ecclesiastical authorities to establish her own discalced, or barefoot, Carmelite house in Avila. Her new rule, which included much stricter obligations of poverty, prayer and penance, mirrored the rigorous spirit of reform sweeping Catholic Europe after the Council of Trent; still, the Discalced Carmelites attracted as many opponents as disciples. Wealthy nuns objected to forgoing their luxuries, of course, but others also complained that Teresa, in founding new convents based on her mystical faith, was transgressing the Council's new rules on spirituality and on the role of women in the Church. After she had founded a flurry of new convents all over Castile, the papal nuncio abruptly reined her in, and the Inquisition opened an inquiry into the orthodoxy of her mysticism. It took several years of careful coaching by her (male) spiritual advisers for her to learn to present herself in a less threatening fashion. Allowed to return to reforming, Teresa largely devoted her last years to writing detailed accounts of her own spiritual journey. It was an experience that so captured the Catholic Reformation religious ideal that she was canonized just forty years after her death.

CR

Catherine de' Medici

MACHIAVELLIAN QUEEN

1519–1589

On her wedding night, the 14-year-old Catherine de' Medici shared her bridal chamber not only with her equally young husband, Henri, but also with her father-in-law, the French king François I, who made himself comfortable and stayed to make sure that the newlyweds 'showed valour in their joust'. Apparently they did: in the morning François happily changed places with Catherine's uncle Pope Clement VII, who came in to give the Church's blessing to a successful coupling. Such close supervision was not surprising, since this was a profoundly important union – Clement called it 'the greatest match in the world' – between the Italian House of Medici, rich with both material and spiritual wealth, and the House of Valois, rulers of France for over 200 years.

Catherine was not especially beautiful; she was short and thin, with wide lips and 'the protruding eyes peculiar to the Medici family'. French courtiers disdained her as a 'merchant's daughter', and Clement had to promise an enormous dowry of golden écus and Italian duchies to qualify her to wed even the second-in-line to François's kingdom. Then, less than a year after the wedding, Clement died, and his successor, Pope Paul III, reneged on all the promised swaths of land and much of the cash, leading François to declare, 'The girl has been given to me stark naked!' It took all of young Catherine's social graces to win any sympathy from the French court, and her situation only worsened. Prince Henri, perhaps never recovering from his wedding night, soon abandoned Catherine for other women. Because of his neglect and perhaps some supposed anatomical difficulties, the royal couple failed to conceive – a shortcoming that grew more serious in 1536, when Henri's older brother abruptly died. Now that she was dauphine, Catherine needed a son quickly or risked a royal divorce. She consulted a host of magicians, astrologers and physicians, and finally, at the age of 34, she bore a son. Thereafter, even though Henri, who succeeded François in 1547, lived openly with his mistress, Catherine still managed to give him nine more children. Seven of these reached adulthood: three became kings, and two queens.

Peripheral during Henri's reign, Catherine was thrust into prominence when her husband died in a jousting accident in 1559. For the next sixteen months her 15-year-old son François II ruled as a weak figurehead for his in-laws, the Guise family, who had designs on the throne. Then François died of an ear infection, and suddenly Catherine de' Medici was queen regent of France. She effectively held the title for most of the next thirty years, ruling first in the name of her next-in-line, the 9-year-old Charles IX, and then, with Charles's death at the age of 24, for her adult but incompetent third son, Henri III.

These were daunting times for France, split between Paris and the provinces, between Catholic stalwarts and Huguenot followers of Calvin, and between two great families that each claimed the throne that Catherine's sons so weakly held – the Guise, on the Catholic side, and the Bourbon, on the Protestant. 'What could the woman do?' asked Henri IV, the Bourbon claimant and eventual winner. '[She was] left by the death of her husband with five little children on her arms, and two families of France thinking of grasping the crown.' She tried but failed to understand the depth of religious passion dividing her kingdom and sought instead to arrange political truces, of the sorts her great-grandfather Lorenzo the Magnificent had imposed so artfully on his fellow Italian princes. When that failed, she was willing to have the leaders on one side or the other assassinated or ambushed – most famously on St Bartholomew's Day in 1572.

The French, both then and later, accused her of cruelty, duplicity and depravity, of being a woman and of being foreign. Yet no one doubted her fierce devotion to a France unified and peaceful under her adopted

6. THE NEW WAVE

Valois dynasty. She succeeded – barely – in saving the kingdom, largely by reinventing the royal court as a unifying force, spending lavishly on great festivals, architectural monuments, and royal progresses that wandered through the kingdom for a year or more. With the Valois line, however, she failed. Although she had certainly borne and raised enough heirs, none of her sons was strong, fertile or royal enough for the job. Only in her last weeks did Henri III suddenly realize that he would have to start acting like a king. But just eight months later this last of the Valois was stabbed to death in a pointless assassination by a deranged friar.

❧

Louise Labé

THE JOUSTING POETESS

1520/24–1566

During a tournament in 1524 in honour of Henri, the Dauphin of France, one knight jousted so bravely that the future king called him over to offer his congratulations. When the knight removed his helmet, however, long curls tumbled out, stunning both Henri and the crowd. The day's champion was actually Louise Labé, a poetess from Lyons. This story, which circulated widely around France, is probably true; less plausible is one of her fighting with French forces against the Spanish in the siege of Perpignan. In any case, along with her nicknames 'la belle Amazon' and 'Capitaine Louise', the tenor of the tales conveys the exotic aura surrounding her name.

She was born in Lyons, a cosmopolitan centre of French publishing in the 16th century. Perched on the River Rhone in eastern France, the city was closer to Italy than to the powerful, stern churchmen at the University of Paris, making it easier for Lyonnais humanists to thrive. She was raised in an affluent, bourgeois family, the daughter of a successful ropemaker who, although illiterate himself, allowed her the same education as her brothers. With them she learned Latin, Spanish and Italian, as well as horse-riding and even fencing. Her father was traditional enough to arrange a marriage for her, however, and around 1543 she was wedded to another prosperous, uneducated ropemaker thirty years her senior.

Having little in common with her husband, Labé hosted gatherings for the Lyonnais literati, an unusual role for a merchant-class wife in the Renaissance. The middle classes were not only less likely to educate girls, but were also less tolerant of women's presence in the public arena. But the urban atmosphere of Lyons made it possible for Labé both to participate in literary life and to publish a book of prose and amorous poetry. She was one of the first French writers to compose a Petrarchan sonnet cycle, much of which is scandalously erotic. It did not, one assumes, address her ageing husband:

The lover in the poem is assumed to have been Louise's fellow poet Olivier de Magny, and elsewhere in the sonnets she suggests the affair ended badly. When less lyrically inclined women in the community condemned her transgressions, she responded in verse: 'Ladies, I beg you think of me no ill / that I have loved, and known love's biting pain, / its myriad burning brands, its bitter bane.'

Labé's prose was less pulsating than her poetry. The longest piece was a Classical dialogue called *Debate of Folly and Love*, which draws on several traditions, both medieval and Renaissance: allegory, Neoplatonism, mythology and, in the vein of Erasmus, satire. The goddess Folly accuses the god Love of taking credit for the world's romance, when in fact she is the one running the show. They take their case to Jupiter, who ultimately declares they are inextricably linked and must therefore learn to get along. The most famous part of the work is its preface, dedicated to a young noblewoman of Lyons named Clémence de Bourges. Considered today as something of a feminist manifesto, the preface spurs Mademoiselle de Bourges to revel in Lyons's liberal climate and to embrace learning now that 'men's harsh laws no longer prevent women from applying themselves to study'. Women must challenge themselves to 'raise their minds a bit above their distaffs and spindles' so that men will see women as equals even 'if we are not made to be in command'.

After her collected works were published in 1555, Louise's notoriety spread throughout France and beyond, or at least to Geneva, where Jean Calvin denounced her as a *plebeia meretrix* – a 'common whore'. Some time after 1556 she retired to the country for reasons that are unclear. Her then elderly husband died in the early 1560s, and in 1566 Labé herself passed away, as legend has it, with a former lover at her side.

Alessandro II Farnese

THE GRAND CARDINAL

1520–1589

The High Renaissance was a time of consolidations, where ambitious dynasties established control over both nation states and financial networks. Such family conglomerates were not limited to the Hapsburgs and the Fuggers – the Church too had its share of lineages that produced private little empires based on benefices, properties, and honors. No one knew better how to work holy office for family success than the Farnese, in particular Cardinal Alessandro II Farnese – of whom it was said that, while popes or kings might be called *Magnus*, or 'Great,' only he merited the nickname of *Gran Cardinale*.

Since the earliest Middle Ages, when the Farnese first emerged as minor feudatories north of Rome, they acquired their wealth and expanded their domains by working as *condottieri*, or mercenary soldiers, for whoever bought their services. Then they really struck it rich: Alessandro's grandfather – also called Alessandro Farnese – was named cardinal by Pope Alexander VI. Rumour had it that this was thanks to the intervention (and sexual favours) the pope had received from Alessandro's sister Giulia, which led to the new cardinal getting the nickname 'Fregnese,' or Cardinal Hump. Even so, in 1534 Alessandro managed to win the papal throne for himself, taking the name Pope Paul III. He wasted no time exercising his own nepotistic prerogative, making his 14-year-old grandson, now known as Alessandro II, a cardinal just two months later; by 1536 two more Farnese youths had donned the red hat.

Even while still a teenager Alessandro II was showered with more papal bounty than most clerics would enjoy in a lifetime. First came the administrative posts – 'archpriest,' or dean, in dioceses ranging from Rome (twice), to Tuscany, Spain, Portugal, Germany, and France. By the time he was sixteen, it was time for Alessandro to assume executive powers, beginning with the bishopric of Monreale, in Sicily, and two years later that of Massa, in Tuscany. In 1539 Paul judged Alessandro seasoned enough to serve as papal legate, a sort of combination ambassador and governor, first at high-level peace negotiations and then in various subject cities of the Papal States. By the time Paul died in 1546, Alessandro had received no fewer than 16 permanent or temporary positions, and though his breakneck collecting of offices inevitably slowed down, it never stopped altogether. Later popes, seeking to secure the support of the three Farnese cardinal-cousins, kept rewarding him with new benefices and dioceses for the rest of his life.

Yet the Gran Cardinale never won the real prize – the papacy itself. His great wealth and connections gave him vast influence, but also worried his fellow cardinals when they met to elect new popes. Too many feared his overarching power and close ties with France. So the grown-up Alessandro poured his considerable energies and income into administration and into the arts. Educated by leading humanists, he was a devote student of the classics just when Rome's archaeological excavations – some would say pillaging – were at their height. Astutely and aggressively buying from the treasure hunters, Alessandro amassed the largest collection of ancient statuary, coins, and manuscripts since ancient times, hiring teams of restorers and sculptors to reassemble scattered fragments and reproduce missing pieces. To store and display his acquisitions, he turned the Palazzo Farnese, the family headquarters in Rome, into a museum. Instead he lodged in the nearby Palazzo della Cancellaria – commanding his nearly 400 retainers, disbursing his patronage to painters like Titian and Vasari, and sending a host of architects (including the aged Michelangelo) to build or remodel churches all over Rome.

The Gran Cardinale also had personal building projects, mostly famously the Villa Farnese and gardens at Caprarola, in the countryside north of Rome. Possibly the grandest country home/pleasure palace ever realized in Italy, the Villa Farnese was a riot of fountains, topiary, verandas, balconies, spiral staircases, and halls frescoed to commemorate the glories of the Farnese family. Confronted with the villa's opulent walkways, statuary, and panoramas, the saintly Carlo Borromeo could only wonder, 'But then, what will Paradise be like?'

For when business kept him at Rome, Alessandro prepared another paradise. Having bought the north side of the Palatine Hill, overlooking the Forum, he laid out the Horti Farnesiani. This became famed as Europe's first botanical garden, and also as an exquisite getaway where he and a few select guests could gather on warm evenings, to enjoy the vistas while indulging in learned conversations and sumptuous meals. Delighting in the musical accompaniment of the Gran Cardinale's personal choir, they strolled on the paths artfully running though a succession of coves, aviaries, fountains, and grottos, imagining themselves transported back to the glory days of Imperial Rome.

Eleanor of Toledo

DUCHESS AND PARTY PLANNER

1522–1562

Cosimo de' Medici was only 17 when Charles V picked him as the new duke of Florence in 1537. Despite his imperial backing, Cosimo's claims to rule Florence were none too strong. He was young, raised outside the city and had only a small fortune and few friends to muster against the many Florentines who dreamed of resurrecting their beloved republic. Yet anyone who, like Benvenuto Cellini, thought that here was just 'a young man on a marvellous horse' – an attractive yet easily manipulated figurehead – soon discovered how wrong they were. Quickly collecting an army, Cosimo defeated the republicans before they could get organized and then moved decisively to place his supporters in key positions throughout the duchy. By 1539 Cosimo enjoyed uncontested authority in Florence: all he needed was an heir to secure his lineage.

This required a wife, and Cosimo turned once again to his patron, Charles V, who soon came up with Eleanor Alvarez de Toledo y Osorio, the teenage daughter of the Imperial viceroy in Naples. It proved a felicitous choice. Although Spanish, Eleanor was blonde and blue-eyed, with a perfect oval face and lithe figure – one of the most attractive women to marry into the Medici since Lucrezia Tornabuoni. Her family connections brought Florence decisively into the Habsburg camp, ensuring France's final defeat in the Italian Wars and giving the duchy a stronger place in a peninsula now dominated by Spain. Although not all Florentines were thrilled to have a Spanish duchess, Cosimo was immediately smitten with Eleanor – and she with him. In an era of arranged teenage marriages they proved unusually devoted, and remarkably fecund: in the course of fifteen years they produced eleven children. Unlike most consorts of her day, she expected to accompany Cosimo on his ducal travels – when her endless pregnancies allowed it – and she was said to cry in despair and pull out her hair if left behind. When separated, they wrote each other letters incessantly, sometimes as many as two a day.

Eleanor calmed Cosimo during his often extreme mood swings, and with her enormous dowry she also relieved his initial insolvency. In exchange, she received a leading role in his regime, the first of the new breed of consort, adviser and companion that would soon prevail in European courts. Eleanor also realized before most monarchs that, for the sake of greater security and grandeur, princes needed to maintain a proper distance from their subjects. In 1549 she purchased the Pitti Palace on the south bank of the Arno, thereby removing her growing family from the city's noisome streets to a grand palazzo overlooking Florence. Given his ancestors' proclivity for getting murdered, Cosimo was easily persuaded to withdraw from excessive public contact. To promote his personal safety and regal mystique, he built an enclosed walkway that allowed him and Eleanor to proceed in privacy from the ducal court in the Palazzo della Signoria, through the government offices (the Uffizi), across the Ponte Vecchio over the Arno and up to the Pitti Palace. For her part, Eleanor almost never walked around her city but preferred to have herself carried in a sedan chair, as shrouded and remote as an icon in its tabernacle.

Once established at the Pitti, Eleanor was soon enlarging and embellishing. She added new wings to the palace, then enclosed and landscaped the vast Boboli Gardens, which ultimately extended to nearly 5 hectares (12.3 acres) in a series of grottoes, *faux* temples and pathways. She put on Latin and Greek comedies in the gardens' Classical amphitheatre, while in the courtyard created by the palace wings, the more martial young nobility arranged formal jousts; the same arena, when flooded, became a basin for mock naval battles. In her role as the Medici impresario Eleanor established a prototype of the 'theatre of state' – ostentation and consumption conspicuously and formally displayed. In the hands of absolutist monarchs to come, such codified theatricality would dominate European courts – a means of broadcasting royal magnificence while controlling and rewarding the noble class.

The consort's role that Eleanor of Toledo defined for herself was never fully realized: she died of malaria at the age of just 40. Yet in her succession of banquets, balls and entertainments, as stylized and formal as her own bejewelled and brocaded gowns, she still managed to sketch out the possibilities for aristocratic comportment in an absolutist age – possibilities that queens such as Catherine and Maria de' Medici would exploit to the full in setting up their own theatres of state.

❧
7. The Framing of Modernity
1550–1600

When the mystical physicist and professional gadfly Giordano Bruno was sent to the stake on 17 February 1600, it could be said that the Renaissance was truly over. A 15th-century humanist in spirit who championed the cosmology of Nicholas of Cusa and the Neoplatonic pantheism of Marsilio Ficino, Bruno had the bad luck to run straight into the new and unforgiving norms of the early modern state. Although it was the Inquisition and papal authorities in Rome who actually burned him, others would willingly have done the job. A hapless philosopher, so ready to speak his mind and so inept at winning powerful patrons or sticking to a single dogma, he had spent years getting chased out of various autocratic regimes, fleeing from charges of subversion, treason and heresy. Unable to land a university, clerical or court position of the sort that Ficino, Lorenzo Valla and Antonio de Nebrija had secured with comparative ease a century earlier, Bruno was left as a vulnerable outsider – the last of the Renaissance humanists, for ever exiled in an increasingly polarized age.

Conservative retrenchment was everywhere in post-Renaissance Europe. Charles V, who had been less interested in doctrinal disputes than in maintaining an ecumenical empire, decided to retire in 1556. To his brother Ferdinand he gave the Holy Roman Empire, and to his Spanish-born son Philip II went Spain, Italy, the Americas and the Netherlands. For both realms the transitions brought an end to decades of war. In Italy it was a Spanish peace, imposed by a treaty of 1559, that definitively expelled the French from the peninsula and left Philip and his soldiers in control virtually everywhere. Only the Republic of Venice could be called fully independent, and the Venetians were too busy with Turkish threats to their eastern empire to risk making their new neighbours unhappy.

With Spanish control in Italy came traditional Spanish values – hierarchy, lineage, deference, piety and militarism – that rapidly smothered the vibrant mercantile and university life that had characterized the Italian city states. Following the Spanish model, large landed estates were soon the norm, and much of Italy was effectively 'refeudalized', with economies once based on manufacturing and banking giving way to large-scale farming and stock-raising. Rural princes and barons became laws unto themselves, running private armies and adopting Spain's honour-driven vendetta culture. As a result there was less rural security than under even the most fractious Renaissance regimes, with banditry, rural poverty and urban depopulation rampant throughout the peninsula. Perhaps fittingly, such problems were even a greater blight in Spain, where in addition a lopsided colonial economy, a rebellious Moorish population and the collapse of manufacturing drove Philip's monarchy into bankruptcy four times between 1557 and 1598.

Peace also came to Germany in the 1550s. With Ferdinand's Peace of Augsburg (1555), the empire's seemingly intractable religious conflict was at least put in abeyance. The solution was simple: the scores of independent principalities were parcelled out between the Catholic and Lutheran camps along the straightforward principle of *cuius regio, eius religio* ('Whoever rules, [there it will be] his religion'). For over half a century this agreement held, despite its relying on the whims of so many petty princelings and its excluding the increasingly numerous and restless Calvinists. When the arrangement finally collapsed, in 1618, the underlying religious antagonisms in the region had reached such intensity that a war lasting for thirty years exploded, drawing in much of Europe and nearly destroying both Germany and the empire.

Elsewhere, the post-Renaissance landscape was defined less by the ending than by the beginning of civil strife and religious turmoil. In France, the outbreak of open hostilities between majority Catholics and minority Calvinists – or Huguenots, as they were known – coincided with the last, foundering years of the once promising Valois dynasty. Under her erratic de facto regency the three sons of the Italian-born queen Catherine de' Medici ruled fecklessly for thirty perilous years. Neither producing a viable heir among them nor rising above their kingdom's factional and religious strife, these sterile monarchs and their ageing mother amused themselves with acting troupes, tumblers and court intrigues while massacres, assassinations and uprisings regularly erupted around them. The whole sorry spectacle ended only when the last Valois died in 1589, and the French throne was claimed – and then won in battle – by the king of Navarre and founder of the Bourbon dynasty, Henri IV.

From 1568 on, the same evangelical Calvinism that so disrupted France also galvanized the seven northern provinces of the Netherlands into a full-scale revolt against their Catholic, Spanish overlords. The resulting conflict, with a few truces, lasted eighty years, in good part because the two sides were too ill matched ever to fight a conclusive battle. The Spanish, with their almost invincible army, could ravage the Netherlands but do little to stop the equally vast Dutch fleet from harassing Spain and its empire around the world. Exhaustion and penury as much as anything finally led the two sides in 1648 to split the Low Countries, into the Spanish Netherlands (later Belgium) and a new European nation – the Dutch Republic.

Meanwhile England, during the brief reigns of the Protestant Edward VI (1547–53) and the Catholic Mary Tudor (1553–58), was also riven by factional strife, as first aggressive Anglicans and then resurgent Catholics sought, under their respective monarchs and advocates, to purge the realm of unbelievers. In the course of barely a decade both sides built up an ample supply of martyrs to keep themselves aggrieved and paranoid throughout the long and much more conciliatory reign of Elizabeth I (1558–1603). As in Germany, the ad hoc compromises finally struck between established Lutheran and Catholic regimes failed to accommodate the more decentralized and doctrinaire Calvinists. Elizabeth successfully defended her kingdom against both the Spanish Armada and the suicide missions undertaken by the likes of the Jesuit Edmund Campion, but in post-Renaissance England, as in so many other European states, it was the rising discontent of these 'Puritans' that would ultimately define the course her nation would take.

☙ Laura Battiferra Ammannati

'THE SAPPHO OF HER AGE'

1523–1589

Few people incarnated the shifting values of the northern Italian Renaissance better than Laura Battiferra. By the time she was winning a name for herself, in the 1550s, the last traces of the mercantile, republican and humanist culture that had dominated northern Italian cities for two centuries had faded away. In its place arose a court society that stressed hierarchy over merit and innovation, and titles over talent. Laura's place in this new, stratified world was seemingly less than assured. The bastard daughter of the bastard son of the bastard daughter of a physician who settled in Urbino in the mid-15th century, she had few blood ties to the titled or powerful. She was also, of course, a woman.

Yet despite all this, Laura also had some significant advantages to her position. The Church, especially in the early 16th century, remained open to ambitious men of dubious lineage – a description that could certainly be applied to her father, Giovanni Antonio Battiferri. Having followed his (legitimate) uncle to Rome, the young Giovanni Antonio acquired a first-class humanist education and a place among the followers of Cardinal Giulio de' Medici, later Clement VII. By the time Laura was born to one of his several concubines, Giovanni Antonio had secured a host of Curial benefices, a house in Urbino and another near the Vatican, with the façade decorated by a good friend, the painter Raphael. He much preferred his daughter to his two rather shiftless sons, and personally educated her in the Classics, showering on her the bulk of his affection and, unusually, most of his fortune.

Consequently, despite her three generations of bastardy, Laura Battiferra was a prize catch among those members of the Italian elite just a notch below the titled aristocracy. Her first husband, Vittorio Sereni, was a 'musician and familiar' to the duke of Urbino, and she was a good wife to him – 'docile, obedient, benevolent, dear, faithful and loving' – in their fairly brief marriage. Sereni's death in 1549 evidently first inspired Laura to write poetry, but her true partner would be the Florentine architect and sculptor Bartolomeo Ammannati. The two may have met when Laura was still a girl – according to legend, Ammannati first saw her and fell for her when she was only 15 and he was working for the duke of Urbino near her father's house. They were married in 1550.

Bartolomeo and Laura spent their first years in Rome, living the good life that wealthy, well-connected commoners could enjoy, even in that hierarchical world. Laura's father linked Bartolomeo to the patronage of the new Florentine pope, Julius III, and Laura with the ageing Michelangelo, who admired her budding poetic talent. As Bartolomeo garnered commissions from the Vatican, Laura perfected her sonnet-writing. Both were welcomed by the literary and intellectual circles of the city, where Laura won praise and encouragement in her writing. She enjoyed the city as much as its society and wrote lyrically of how 'I would go contemplating the seven proud hills and the sacred valleys.'

In 1555, however, Julius died, and with him went the couple's font of patronage. Much to Laura's regret, they had to move to Florence, attaching themselves to the court of Duke Cosimo de' Medici. Still childless – as she would remain – she was initially lonely but soon gratified that the city's 'cultured intellects' welcomed her and her husband into their ranks. With the encouragement of Duchess Eleanor of Toledo, Laura turned out dozens of finely crafted sonnets that were admired in refined circles all over Italy and in the courts of Spain and Austria. Most of her poetry evoked individuals she respected, whose characters she praised – or whose passing she mourned – with delicate turns of phrase, allusive metaphors and apt lyricism. In 1560, secure of her place in the poetic establishment, she published 146 of her poems in her first book of *Rime*. The volume enjoyed immediate success, but shortly afterwards Laura abandoned both secular poetry and courtly society – just as both, after centuries of discouraging active female participation, were finally opening up to women of talent. She turned instead to religion, compelled by the sudden deaths of many of those closest to her – including Eleanor and her father. Although Italy's new aristocracy had made her fame possible, for the rest of her life Laura Battiferra reverted to the pious and reclusive model established by leisured Italian women a century earlier – devoting her poetic gifts to her husband, her spiritual quest and the Jesuit order, which she embraced as her new patron and guide.

❧

Pieter Bruegel the Elder

THE PEASANT PAINTER

c. 1525–1569

There is no trace of Pieter Bruegel in the historical record until 1551, when he enrolled in the painters' guild of Antwerp. The consensus that he must have been around 25 years old at the time has produced a plausible birth date, and a 17th-century biographer claimed he was born in or around Breda, in the southern Netherlands. On the other hand, neither of these assumptions is backed up by concrete evidence, so both remain as unprovable as the notion that, because he painted peasants, he must have been of peasant stock. In fact, Bruegel appears to have been both well educated and well travelled. His artistic training came from Pieter Coecke van Aelst, an artist of some repute, with studios in both Antwerp and Brussels. Soon after completing his apprenticeship, Bruegel travelled to Rome and southern Italy as far as Sicily. His later work was clearly influenced both by the art he saw there and by the dramatic Alpine landscapes that became regular features in his paintings.

Returning to Antwerp some time in 1553, Bruegel found work designing engravings for the At the Four Winds publishing house, owned by Hieronymus Cock. In these early drawings, as in his first paintings, Bruegel remained very much in thrall to the style and vision of Hieronymus Bosch, the great Dutch master of the hallucinogenic and bizarre, who died in 1516. The debt was so strong and so obvious that Cock brought out Bruegel's first engraving, *Big Fish Eat Little Fish* (1556), with Bosch's name attached, in the hope of boosting sales. Throughout his career, in his catalogue of human depravity and folly, Bruegel never completely abandoned his reliance on the

Boschian imagery of grotesqueries, hybrid monsters and obscene violence. Yet from the beginning he also tempered this ghoulish bestiary with Italian painterly values and Dutch charm. He often abandoned Bosch's aerial view, with its moralizing and apocalyptic implications, for a lower and more intimate perspective. He used a brighter palette, rich in primary colours, but above all he brought back from his Italian experiences a love of landscape.

Bruegel's visionary treatment of nature and humanity's place within it signalled both a break with medieval figurative traditions and the beginnings of one of Dutch art's most fruitful and characteristic features. In Bruegel's world, men's greatest endeavours shrank to insignificance against vast horizons, towering Alpine peaks or plains pullulating with humanity. Even in such iconic subjects as *The Adoration of the Magi* and *The Procession to Calvary* (both 1564) he diminished the principal figures so much that viewers must search for them in the crush of daily life. His *Landscape with the Fall of Icarus* (*c.* 1555) depicts a ploughman, an enormous sun and just the feet of the supposed protagonist, thrashing in the water beneath a descending trail of feathers.

This off-hand treatment of humankind's epics and follies evidently struck a chord with Bruegel's Dutch public, who eagerly sought his work. He was successful enough to marry Mayken Coecke, the daughter of his old master, and move to the more courtly world of Brussels in 1563. Not content with past accomplishments, he soon carried his art in revolutionary new directions. In 1565 he took a commission for six large-scale representations of the months, building in them a complex sermon on mankind's proper relationship with nature, which he worked into the doings of anonymous peasants labouring in synchrony with the seasons. He grew so attached to village life that people in Brussels called him *Boer Bruegel* ('Peasant Bruegel') and told stories of him going in disguise to rural festivals to sketch country people when their guard was down.

Whether true or not, such tales marked a final shift in Bruegel's work. After 1566 he painted folk culture as it was lived, devoid of any moral judgment beyond his tendency to romanticize rural innocence and the natural world. From his brush came, in short order, *The Wedding Dance* (1566),

The Land of Cockaigne (1567), *The Magpie on the Gallows* (1568), *The Peasant Wedding* (1568) and *The Peasant Dance* (1568). Each was populated with fewer, larger figures than before – highly animated men and women filled with the rhythms and humours of country life. In his brief but intensely productive last years, Bruegel created portraits not of individuals but of a way of life. He responded to the materialism and religious conflict flaring up in the Netherlands with simple harmonies and innate joyfulness. Having set the moral compass of the Dutch artistic Golden Age, Pieter Bruegel then unfortunately died before he had a chance to witness its full expression.

ℭℜ

Dick Tarlton

THE QUEEN'S COMEDIAN
died 1588

When powerful men in England sought advantage with Queen Elizabeth I, they often turned to one of her most trusted courtiers – not to her privy councillor but to her court jester, Dick Tarlton. A relaxed monarch was a more receptive monarch, they must have reasoned, and they frequently asked the comedian to tag along during royal audiences. As one 17th-century historian remarked, Tarlton worked wonders on the queen: he could 'un-dumpish her at his pleasure', and his tonic humour was able to 'cure her Melancholy better than all of her Physicians'.

According to legend, the greatest comic actor of his era was discovered in a field, tending his father's swine. There, his 'happy unhappy wit' impressed a prominent nobleman's servant, who took Tarlton with him to London. In any case, he was an established actor by 1583, when tapped for the newly formed Queen's Men, an acting company established and financed by Elizabeth. The most successful troupe of its time, it was driven largely by Tarlton's talent. In plays he typically took the fool's role – often written specifically for him – but was famous for abandoning his lines and veering off on hilarious tangents.

As a solo performer, Tarlton improvised ribald jokes and social satire while impersonating a gullible country yokel. His famous costume featured a baggy russet suit, buttoned cap, short boots, musical pipe and small drum, which audiences would have recognized as stereotypical bumpkin attire. Very short and slightly hunched, he had a broad, flat nose and a decided squint – a face made for comedy, to paraphrase one early description. Merely poking his head through the curtains before a performance could reduce a crowd to hysterical laughter.

Although Tarlton wrote many plays, books and ballads – nearly all now lost – he was more famous for extemporizing witty verse, which became known as 'tarltonizing'. He riffed fluidly on random topics called out by the audience, inventing rhyming ditties that he punctuated with drum beats. He was also an accomplished fencing master, a skill he put to comic use in his broad, physical humour. Once, taking a wooden staff as a sword and a side of bacon as a shield, he challenged the queen's tiny lapdog to a duel. His swashbuckling moves (and, no doubt, the pork's proximity) excited the poor creature into a barking frenzy, and the mock-terrified Tarlton begged Elizabeth to call off her 'mastiff'. So convulsed with laughter was she that Tarlton was sent off stage to allow her to regain her composure.

As a royal favourite, Tarlton got away with teasing the queen, telling her 'more of her faults than most of her Chaplains'. He crossed the line during one post-prandial performance, however, when he suggested Walter Raleigh and Robert Dudley had undue influence over Her Royal Highness. The gibe triggered a round of applause among the other guests, but the irked queen banished him from her table for the rest of the evening.

William Shakespeare would have been familiar with Tarlton, although it is unclear whether they met – when the comedian died in 1588, Shakespeare was just 24 and not yet established on the London theatre scene. Nevertheless, Shakespearean fools often bore Tarltonian qualities: Falstaff's lines, for instance, seem convincingly improvised, but are in fact expertly scripted 'tarltonizations'. And Hamlet's tribute to Yorick – that 'fellow of infinite jest, of most excellent fancy' – is considered a nod to the great comic actor.

The Queen's Men lost momentum after his death, though Tarlton himself remained popular for years. His name lived on in nursery rhymes, joke books and popular songs, merchants used his image on signs to suggest a rollicking good time, and countless taverns were named after him, as was at least one pugnacious rooster – a cockfighting champion that came to battle 'like a drummer, making a thundering noyse with his winges' and was, like Tarlton, a master of the grand entrance.

Giovanni Pierluigi da Palestrina

SAVIOUR OF SACRED MUSIC

1525/26–1594

As a boy, Giovanni Pierluigi supposedly hauled vegetables from the family farm in Palestrina to sell at the markets of Rome. A charming legend tells how a Roman choirmaster, hearing him singing the praises of his produce, was completely captivated by his perfect voice and promptly enrolled Giovanni in the basilica of Santa Maria Maggiore – and his name does appear in the choir register in 1537. Just seven years later he was appointed organist and choirmaster in his own right, at his home cathedral in Palestrina. Then came a timely convergence of genius and luck, so characteristic of Renaissance artists. In 1550 the bishop of Palestrina, Giovanni Maria dal Monte, was elected Pope Julius III and invited his talented choirmaster to serve as voice instructor in the Cappella Giulia, one of the two liturgical choirs at St Peter's.

Since the early Renaissance the Vatican choirs had been monopolized by the French and Flemish, so Giovanni Pierluigi was an outsider – all the more so as he was a married layman when regulations required choristers to be in holy orders. Julius waived such obligations, along with the Cappella's strict entrance exam, all of which highly annoyed the other singers. Part of their response was to denigrate Giovanni Pierluigi as simply 'the boy from Palestrina', and the nickname stuck. Julius died in 1555, but Palestrina seemed to have found another enthusiastic patron in his successor, Pope Marcellus II. Then things started to go wrong. Marcellus died after just twenty-two days and was followed by the conservative Pope Paul IV, who took a decidedly dim view of any lay encroachment into clerical preserves.

Within weeks Paul had revoked Palestrina's post at the Cappella Giulia, and he was packed off with a modest pension.

For a while this dismissal so traumatized Palestrina that he fell deathly ill, but in October 1555 he landed the position of choirmaster at the basilica of San Giovanni Laterano in Rome and rapidly recovered both his health and his compositional energies. His works in the 1550s included a series of Magnificats, antiphons and responses that were immediately adopted into Rome's Holy Week observances, remaining central to the celebrations today. Palestrina became so self-confident that when he was refused his request for a raise at San Giovanni, he simply decamped for a position with better pay at Santa Maria Maggiore.

By the 1560s Palestrina was the Vatican's master composer, his work shaping a generation of Renaissance sacred music. His liturgical compositions were famously flowing, with straightforward, gliding melodies that owed much to Gregorian chant and a sincerity that replaced the previously fashionable artfulness. It was his compositional technique that earned Palestrina a reputation for having 'saved' church music during the Catholic Reformation, for many clerical puritans, such as Paul IV, condemned the existing Flemish style as intrinsically profane and so elaborately polyphonic that it made the sacred liturgy virtually incomprehensible. There was supposedly talk of banning music from services altogether – as some Protestant sects were doing – but Palestrina's work, especially his mass for six voices dedicated to Pope Marcellus, the *Missa Papae Marcelli* (1562), neither impinged on nor obscured the sacred text. In it Palestrina scrupulously avoided the 'lascivious or impure' themes that his predecessors had adapted from love madrigals or drinking songs, offering instead original melodies and contrapuntal techniques that presented a liturgy both pleasing and easy to follow.

Unlike many Renaissance artists, Palestrina travelled very little, in part because every time he received an outside offer (the dukes of Mantua and Ferrara practically pleaded for his services), the papal establishment would better it.

In 1571 Pope Pius V, who had overseen the standardization of the Roman Missal, brought Palestrina back to lead the Cappella Giulia. There, despite the protests of the clerical singers (who apparently never forgave this upstart Roman), he was kept on for the rest of his life. After his wife died in 1580, he was again profoundly depressed, and for a time he considered taking orders. Although this might have smoothed relations with the choir, Palestrina suddenly chose instead to marry a wealthy widow, which freed him to compose without worrying about money. Serving under no fewer than twelve popes, Palestrina composed more than 700 works, including over 100 masses, 140 madrigals, 300 motets and a vast array of other sacred pieces. Having trained dozens of students, he launched a purely Italian school of sacred music and was honoured after his death with a stone (now lost) in St Peter's, supposedly inscribed with his title in life: *princeps musicae* ('Prince of Music').

℘

Giuseppe Arcimboldo

HEADS OF STATE, HEADS OF CABBAGE

1527?–1593

V ery little in Giuseppe Arcimboldo's early career explains the peculiar
painter he later became. The son of a Milanese artist of modest repute,
he was not especially precocious and got his first commission at the age of
22 to design the stained-glass windows of Milan Cathedral. Over the next
decade or so he painted some ceiling frescoes and composed the cartoons
for tapestries in the cathedral of Como. Something about him must have
caught the eye of Prince Maximilian II Habsburg, however, for in 1562, the
year Maximilian was elected Holy Roman Emperor, Arcimboldo was offered
the post of Imperial court painter. He set off for a 25-year stay in which he
served two consecutive emperors, first in Vienna and then in Prague.

Even in his days in Milan, Arcimboldo was known as a man interested in
'various oddities'. Perhaps these oddities included grotesque human caricatures of the sort that Leonardo da Vinci had drawn in Milan back in the 1490s.
This was, in any case, the sort of art he began to pursue immediately after
arriving in Vienna, a style that was already fully realized with *The Librarian*
(1562), his portrait of a man composed almost entirely of books. Arcimboldo
then turned to other members of Maximilian's court circle, with *The Jurist*
(1566), featuring a face of poultry and a fish tail, *The Cook* (1570), made
up of suckling pig and roast fowl within a covered pot, and *The Gardener*
(*c.* 1590), a bowl of vegetables.

From the beginning Arcimboldo conceived these works to be intellectual
puzzles as much as caricatures. Just as *The Cook* and *The Gardener* could be
inverted to present innocuous displays of meats and produce, so his more

299

ambitious paintings were intended to strike dissonant, even thoughtful, reactions. He painted several versions of his most famous series, *The Seasons* (1563), in which he used the natural bounty of spring, summer, autumn and winter – flowers, fruits, gourds and sticks – to create a man in the four seasons of life, from childhood to old age. In *The Elements* (1566) he presented the classic Aristotelian elements of air, earth and water as still-life portraits composed of birds, game and fish; fire, the fourth element, he rendered anomalously as flames, lit matches and cannon.

Arcimboldo's intentions sometimes remain obscure, but the talent he needed to realize them is obvious. His use of brilliant and contrasting colours and his skilful rendition of still life set him apart from his artistic contemporaries but also reveal a certain debt to the Low Countries and Northern Mannerism. At the same time Arcimboldo's portraits, although charming, can share the nightmarish vision of Hieronymus Bosch. The human images he constructed out of natural elements were partly shown in the process of disintegration, struggling to maintain their forms while decomposing into a mass of teeming birds or flopping fish that writhe like so many maggots.

Repulsive though they may have been, Arcimboldo's caricature portraits were also in high demand, and he brought out many copies of the ever popular 'Seasons' and 'Elements' to sell in Vienna and elsewhere in Europe. The originals, however, were jealously kept in the Imperial *Kunstkammer*, the 'cabinet' of arts and curiosities established by Maximilian and then greatly expanded by Rudolf II, his eccentric son and heir. In this private collection of paintings, antiquities, stuffed animals, monstrosities and geological specimens, Arcimboldo's grotesqueries – each season paired with its corresponding element – enjoyed pride of place, as tortured visions of order imposed on the irrational jumble of nature.

Much of Arcimboldo's energy in Vienna – and later in Rudolf's new capital at Prague – was spent not on painting but on his activities as general court factotum and impresario. The emperors, father and son, delighted at Arcimboldo's skill in embellishing state receptions, balls, weddings and banquets with his characteristically bizarre designs – processions with floats designed as swans or sirens, and extravagant costumes, hats and hairstyles for ladies in the court. Finally, however, this master of masquerade tired of his work and returned to Milan for his last few years. Before he died, however, he made one last composite portrait (*c.* 1590), perhaps his best – of Rudolf II as Vertumnus, the Roman god of gardens, orchards and all the seasons, the mystical combination of abundance and power. Once the painting arrived in Prague, it was said to have delighted the Emperor more than anything in his vast collection. He would supposedly sit and gaze at it rapturously for hours.

◌

Sofonisba Anguissola

THE FEMININE EYE

c. 1532–1625

The Anguissola, minor nobles in the northern Italian city of Cremona, had the habit of naming themselves after ancient Carthaginian heroes. Amilcare, son of Annibale Anguissola, christened his own son Asdrubale and called his eldest daughter Sofonisba. It was she who made the family famous for something besides their names. Precocious in her love of painting, at the age of 14 Sofonisba convinced her father to place her in the studio of the most renowned local artist, Bernardino Campi – not as an apprentice, which was unthinkable for an aristocratic girl, but as a paying guest. For three years she went daily to study with Campi, especially in his chosen field of portraiture, which by the mid-16th century had become quite fashionable among the Italian aristocracy. By 1549, when Campi left to work elsewhere, Sofonisba was capable of highly refined, strikingly intelligent works, and visitors to Cremona were already hailing her as 'among the exceptional painters of our times'.

Despite her obvious genius, Sofonisba's progress as a painter was never straightforward. In Italy virtually no female of significance had ever painted, and it was generally understood throughout Renaissance Europe that women were the objects, not the creators, of art. Forbidden by her sex from hiring strange men as models, much less studying them in the nude, Sofonisba was unable to undertake the large-scale religious or historical subjects that brought a painter prestige. Instead she had to stick to portrait work, a safe and suitable activity for a respectable noblewoman. Initially this meant repeatedly portraying her siblings, her parents and herself, to work out a personal style that emphasized lively, lovingly depicted and highly individualized subjects decked out in luxuriously rendered fabrics. Some of her family portraits show an attention to detail and playful, everyday interaction that prefigure by more than a generation the genre and still-life paintings of Caravaggio and the Dutch *Bamboccianti*.

Keen on promoting his daughter, Amilcare gave her paintings and draw-ings away like calling cards to anyone who might be a potential patron or tutor. He sent a sketch of a laughing woman to the 82-year-old Michelangelo, who responded by asking for a crying boy. Sofonisba, as it happened, had a drawing ready of her brother, bitten by a crab as a sister looked on. Michelangelo was so impressed that he began sending her his own drawings to copy or rework as exercises, and in 1554 she journeyed to Rome to meet the ageing master. Their relationship noticeably influenced Sofonisba's style, helping her attract the attention of Cremona's overlords in Milan. They, in turn, recommended her to the recently enthroned Philip II of Spain, who was looking for a court artist and lady-in-waiting for Elisabeth of Valois, his new child bride of 14. In Sofonisba he found both.

Moving to Madrid, Sofonisba became quite close to the young queen, in part because Elisabeth, the daughter of Catherine de' Medici, was half-Italian. Her work at the Spanish court included commissioned portraits of numerous courtiers, Elisabeth and Philip himself; she also taught the queen painting. When Elisabeth died at only 22, Sofonisba remained in Madrid, painting, helping raise the royal daughters and eventually marrying a Spanish grandee. After losing her husband in a shipwreck, she set out in 1578 to return to Cremona. Yet while she was already in her late forties, widowed and a veteran courtier, her life was far from over.

While sailing north from Sicily, Sofonisba met and fell in love with the much younger captain of her ship, the Genoese patrician Orazio Lomellino. In early 1580 the two were married and settled in Genoa, where, thanks to Orazio's connections and a pension from Philip, Sofonisba enjoyed another forty years as a respected portrait painter: Peter Paul Rubens, who had inherited her place in Madrid as court artist, came to pay her a visit and homage in 1607. Eight years later the couple decided to relocate in Palermo, where Lomellino had investments, and it was there, in 1624, that Sofonisba received her last admirer and pupil. The young Anthony van Dyck, who had seen her work in Genoa, called on her; he sketched her and noted that 'her age is 96, having a very sharp mind and memory, very courtly, though because of her age, her sight is lacking'. Always helpful, she advised him on portraiture, passing on some of what she had learned from Michelangelo. She served as a remarkable bridge from an artist who had studied in the court of Lorenzo de' Medici to another who would serve Charles I and witness the opening salvoes of the English Civil War.

Michel de Montaigne

THE LITERARY ART OF INTROSPECTION

1533–1592

Michel de Montaigne could not tell cabbage from lettuce, preferred glass cups to metal ones, and had a certain admiration for cannibals. These and many other details we know from his famous essays, written between 1572 and 1587. The collection is autobiographical but is not by any means an autobiography – rather than telling the story of his life, it examines the workings of its author's mind. Montaigne titled the collection *Essais* ('Essays') – a word with no literary connotation at the time. French for 'attempts' or 'experiments', it gained its current meaning because of Montaigne's monumental work. His 107 essays marked a new form of literature, radical in his pledge to follow his thoughts wherever they took him. His technique could frustrate readers, but it also fostered flashes of brilliance as he found connections between Classical wisdom, his own experience and the human condition at large.

Montaigne was born into a wealthy, intellectual family in south-west France, and his humanist father allowed him to speak only Latin until he was 6. He later trained in philosophy and law, worked as a judge for many years and held two terms as mayor of Bordeaux. At the age of 37, however, he abandoned 'the slavery of the court and of public employments' and retired to his estate outside town. He moved his study to a stone tower on his castle's grounds, and there he spent the second half of his life writing and, more important, thinking.

Ironically, the very rest and seclusion he craved as a busy judge and mayor proved vexing. In 'Of Idleness' he writes that empty hours allowed his mind to bolt 'like a runaway horse' and conjure 'chimeras and fantastic monsters'. To rein the beasts in, he resolves to put them in writing, 'hoping in time to make my mind ashamed of itself'. The earliest essays, written before Montaigne conceived of himself as his subject, are mostly responses to books he was reading. They become more personal over time, however, and his voice becomes more confident, especially after the first fifty-seven essays were published to great acclaim.

Following a tradition for medals with special mottoes or insignia, Montaigne designed one with 'What do I know?' on one side and a set of balanced scales with the phrase 'I suspend judgment' on the other. Indeed, his open-mindedness permeates the essays. Montaigne, who read avidly about far-off lands, wrote about the Tupi Indians of Brazil, and even featured their poetry in his essays. The tribe's warriors feasted on enemies whom they defeated in battle, but as he points out in 'On the Cannibals', this was no worse than his own culture's customs. At least the Tupi killed men before roasting them – Christian Europeans burned their enemies alive. In 1562 he met a Tupi chief brought to Rouen who was astounded to see some Frenchmen 'fully boated with all sorts of comforts' while others 'were begging at their doors, emaciated with poverty and hunger'. Montaigne circles his beliefs, not espousing them but dissecting them, and concludes that the Tupi were not savages. The problem, he declares, is that 'every man calls barbarous anything he is not accustomed to'.

Montaigne himself loved travelling, which in his view 'keeps our souls constantly exercised by confronting them with things new and unknown'. On a tour through Switzerland, Germany, Austria and Italy he kept a detailed journal of his experiences. When his notebook was unearthed and published in the 1770s, scholars puzzled over his fascination with local people and their bridges, fountains and crops. He stayed in Rome for six months, avoiding other Frenchmen and embracing Roman culture. He witnessed a Jewish child's circumcision, noted local prostitutes' protocol and observed that Italians ate and drank more moderately than the French. When abroad, he asked to be treated in the custom of that country, regardless of the challenges it posed. Asked why he put up with the inconveniences of travel, he remarked that the unknown could bring delightful surprises. 'I know what I am escaping from,' he wrote, 'but not what I am looking for.'

When Montaigne died in 1592, his popularity had spread beyond France. A member of Shakespeare's circle began an English translation of *Essais* in 1598, and Montaigne's notions reverberate in the bard's later work. In fact, a character in Ben Jonson's *Volpone* accuses English writers of stealing from an Italian author 'almost as much as from Montagnié'. Seventeenth-century writers such as Francis Bacon took up the new form, and the genre flourished in the 18th century with Joseph Addison, Samuel Johnson and others. In the 19th century Ralph Waldo Emerson called Montaigne the frankest and most honest of writers, writing that 'the marrow of the man reaches to his sentences ... Cut these words, and they would bleed; they are vascular and alive.'

♋

Arcangelo Tuccaro

ACROBAT TO THE ARISTOCRACY

c. 1535–1602

For the French people to live in peace, their ruler must occupy them with exercise – this was the advice Catherine de' Medici gave her young son King Charles IX of France. Without regular dancing or sport, she cautioned, they might seek 'autres choses plus dangereuses' – more dangerous outlets for their high spirits. To help keep members of the French court fit and out of trouble, Charles brought the Italian tumbler and dance expert Arcangelo Tuccaro to Paris, where he taught acrobatics and helped Catherine stage her 'magnificences' – the Italian-infused, pageantry-filled entertainments that became popular in France during the 16th century.

Born around 1535 in L'Aquila in central Italy, Tuccaro served in Vienna as *Hofspringmeister* ('acrobatics master') to Holy Roman Emperor Maximilian II. In 1570 he travelled to France with the emperor's daughter to perform at her wedding to Charles, who was impressed enough to hire Tuccaro as *saulterin du roi* ('the king's tumbler'). Once in Paris, the Italian taught tumbling to the 20-year-old Charles, his younger brother Henri and the more agile members of court. As master of ceremonies and choreographer, Tuccaro staged elaborate dramas, tournaments, festivals and balls, the lavish events Catherine deployed to dazzle rivals.

What secured Tuccaro's place in history, however, was his treatise *Trois dialogues de l'exercice de sauter, et voltiger en l'air* ('Three dialogues on the practice of leaping and jumping in the air', 1599). The first book on gymnastics since Classical times, it was one of 16th century's many 'how-to' guides and reflected a growing concern with self-improvement and a new secular interest in the physical world. Tuccaro uses the Classical dialogue form: the topic unfolds as several characters discuss the history, benefits and techniques of gymnastics. The bulk of the work is a manual that outlines an elaborate system for teaching young tumblers. It explicates stunts – 'jump of the monkey with a back flip', for example, and many others that range from simple to alarming. In prose sprinkled with Latin and ancient Greek, Tuccaro often cites Classical advocates of acrobatic exercise, particularly Plato, who had praised it as a way to educate the body, develop self-discipline and ensure good health.

After the Classical era, however, gymnastics had lost its wholesome patina. In the Middle Ages tumbling shows attracted large crowds, but the acrobats themselves were considered hucksters or even heretics. Their death-defying feats seemed magical – so amazing, some thought, that if trickery were not a factor, only a pact with the devil could explain them. In *Trois dialogues*, however, Tuccaro demystifies the tricks with step-by-step instructions and dozens of illustrations featuring a bearded, well-muscled athlete – the author himself, presumably. Geometrical diagrams accompany many of the images, and Tuccaro enjoins novice gymnasts to leap in 'proportions stipulated by mathematical measurement'. He often describes stunts in terms of arcs, angles and circles – orbital movements, he observes, that mirror planetary motions. The notion that human events mimicked celestial events guided many spheres of Renaissance thought and influenced artists, scientists, philosophers, kings – and even acrobats. Performed correctly, Tuccaro argued, the gymnast's flips mirrored the very movements of the heavens.

Tuccaro performed until well into his sixties and went on to publish another book – this time a poetry collection – in 1602. At his death shortly thereafter, he was famous throughout Europe, and *Trois dialogues* remained the primary resource for tumblers several hundred years later.

Edmund Campion

'ONE OF THE DIAMONDS OF ENGLAND'

1540–1581

The son of a London bookseller, Edmund Campion was a scholarship student of such brilliance that at the age of 13 he gave the welcoming address to Queen Mary Tudor during her first royal entry into the city. He graduated at Oxford, taking his degree at St John's College, and stayed on as a lecturer so lionized by the undergraduates that they imitated him and called themselves 'Campionites'. In speaking and debating before Mary's sister and successor, Elizabeth I, when she came to Oxford in 1566, Campion so impressed the Queen and her entourage that William Cecil, the royal chief adviser, proclaimed him 'one of the diamonds of England'.

Yet Campion himself was troubled. As a university lecturer, he had already sworn the Oath of Supremacy to uphold his queen and detest the papacy, but he increasingly prevaricated. For Campion, the Protestants who emerged triumphant with Elizabeth's accession to the throne had, in usurping Catholicism, also 'condemned all [their] own ancestors – all the ancient priests, bishops and kings – all that was once the glory of England'. Increasingly, the required rejection of Catholic ritual, tradition and dogma was not a choice Campion was willing to make, but tensions between the two faiths were rapidly coming to a head. In 1569 the Catholic northern earls had raised a rebellion intending to supplant Elizabeth with Mary, Queen of Scots. The next year Pope Pius V excommunicated Elizabeth, giving English Catholics tacit permission to rebel against her government. In response, Elizabeth ended her toleration policy and declared that ministering or preaching on behalf of Rome was high treason, punishable by death.

In 1571 Campion fled Britain for Douai, in the Spanish Netherlands. There he enrolled in the newly established English College, a university-in-exile for Oxonian scholars who rejected Anglican rule. Although he was welcomed with open arms, Campion stayed only long enough to earn a theology degree and then set off for Rome, where he joined the Jesuits. According to the order's traditions, he was sent to preach the faith in a place perceived to be in need of missionaries – the Czech regions of the Austrian Empire. Settling down in Prague and Brno, Campion ministered to the faithful for six years, reconverting as many Hussites as possible.

In 1580, however, Campion and two others were chosen for the first Jesuit mission to England. They were to preach to the nation's many Catholics, especially among the landed gentry, readying them for any possible over-throw of Elizabeth and the Anglican state Church. The mission was a litany of spy versus spy, with double agents, false identities, secret hiding places and narrow escapes from the authorities. The government was informed of Campion's intentions even before he left Douai; still, he evaded the author-ities and issued a thousand-word *Challenge to the Privy Council,* asserting – rather ingenuously, in the face of the 1570 law – that he had come only for religious, not political, ends. There followed a year of preaching, fleeing and ministering, culminating in June 1581, when Campion published his *Rationes decem* ('Ten reasons'), in which he delineated his faith's superiority over Anglicanism. His arguments were not always especially profound – one was merely that Jews and Turks hated Catholicism more. Yet just the fact that an outlawed Jesuit could get his hands on a printing press while inside England was disturbing enough.

Eventually run to ground, Campion was hustled to London, abused by the mob and thrust into the Tower's notorious Little Ease – a cell too small either to stand up or lie down in. He was racked repeatedly, 'to test the truth of his creed', and forced to debate his doctrine while weakened and disoriented. Simply by preaching and ministering he had legally committed high treason, but the judges suborned witnesses to discredit him further, alleging he had plotted to assassinate Elizabeth. Not surprisingly, Campion was condemned, and although he put on a brave face and sang *Te Deum laudamus*, his martyrdom was a brutal affair. He was taken to Tyburn Cross and hanged, eviscerated and quartered on 1 December 1581. Some said he wept with fear at the end, but his death only marked the beginning of the Jesuit mission to England, where news of his martyrdom attracted many volunteers. During the next generation over 300 Jesuits followed Campion into England, and over half of those were publicly executed. Despite all their daring and blood, however, Catholicism continued to lose ground in England, especially after the failed Spanish Armada of 1588. In the end, a stronger challenge to the Anglican Church came not from Campion's Jesuit followers but from the home-grown ranks of the radical Calvinists who called themselves Puritans.

෬

Catena

RUSTLER, ROBBER, BANDIT CHIEF

died 1581

The Roman police did not torture every prisoner they arrested, but they were willing to do so with a certain Mario Paparello. Picked up on 25 November 1580 while on the road to Florence, he was carrying a sword, dagger, pistol, two razors, and a pair of scissors – along with a considerable amount of cash and a satchel containing snake venom and opium. Paparello was taken back to Rome for questioning, but at first he would only bluster and sneer, offering lame excuses for his many illegal weapons. Finally, the authorities decided to hoist him on the strappado, and as they tied his wrists behind him Paparello boasted, 'I'm bold and ready.' Once lifted by the rope, however, he quickly changed his tune and started shouting, 'Blessed Madonna, help me! Let me down! Oh, Lord! Holy Mary! Cut me down, I'll tell you the truth, I want to tell you the truth about everything!' When they left him hanging a bit longer, he finally shouted out, 'I am Catena!'

As it happened, the police had captured one of the most notorious criminals of the day completely by accident. His real name was Bartolomeo Valente, but he was known as Catena, or 'The Chain'. Michel de Montaigne, on hand at the time, described Catena as 'a famous thief and bandit chief, who has held all of Italy in fear and who they say committed dreadful murders'. He also turned out to be exceptionally loquacious. Once the turnkeys let him down, Catena willingly – especially after further hoists on the strappado – confessed everything. His story was a common one in 16th-century Europe. Banditry flourished from Sicily to Spanish Valencia, from the Pyrenees to Limburg and the Scottish Lowlands, wherever centralized authority was weak, clan structures were strong and ex-soldiers or landless peasants abounded. Sometimes hundreds of such men formed virtual armies, marauding the countryside in defiance of the law, robbing at will and hiding out in swamps, hill country or borderlands.

Catena's career had a typical beginning: at the age of 18 he shot a man in a revenge killing and then fled to hide in the countryside. Soon joined by friends and relations on the run for similar crimes, Catena's gang grew to a dozen or so desperadoes. For over a decade they stole livestock, robbed or kidnapped travellers and killed people – Catena alone took credit for fifty-four homicides, usually with firearms, sometimes with a machete. Often these were paid assassinations, but the band also murdered for revenge – anyone who had harmed gang members, their relatives or clients, and anyone suspected of 'acting the spy for our enemies', was a target. The most effective revenge killings were theatrically grisly. Men were routinely decapitated and once, after killing a shepherd, Catena boasted how 'we also hamstrung upwards of 200 of his goats, to show disrespect to [his uncle], who had killed our companion.'

The gang's main business, however, was kidnapping. Catena explained, 'You should know that I was forced to kidnap and ransom in order to pay for my gang, since I have enemies and the Authorities took away all my possessions.' Merchants and travellers were preferred victims, but Catena was also willing to snatch ordinary peasants and those 'who go behind the sheep'. Judging by the hoard of cash Catena was carrying when arrested, the business paid well, allowing all of the gang to dress the part. They swaggered into town, each with multiple pistols, muskets, knives and machetes shoved in his sashes, sporting the brigand's characteristic long, matted hair – '8 or 10 braids longer than the others ... moustaches, one longer than the other ... [and] hats turned to the side'.

After a highway robbery or village assassination Catena's gang often hid within one of the many feudal properties that dotted the Papal States and were largely off limits to Rome's police. The local lord would leave them alone or even hire them for some private thuggery, 'as long as we don't annoy any of his vassals or cause any trouble'. Eventually, however, things got too hot for Catena even to stay with his baronial allies. So he headed for Tuscany, seeking new patrons and a fresh start, which was when his luck ran out and he was arrested. Once he decided to tell his story, his confession took over a month as he described his crimes and informed on his accomplices – though not with hope of a pardon. Yet Catena's execution, when it came on 11 January 1581, offered its own vindication. He was carted through 'a great crowd of people, since everyone wanted to see [him], for the fame that he had'. Some 30,000 spectators turned out, 'showing no emotion when he was strangled, but with each blow of the axe when he was quartered, they made a pitiful cry'. Within a week someone had written a ballad of his adventures.

♋

Veronica Franco

COURTESAN AND WORDSMITH

1546–1591

In the early 16th century around 100,000 people lived in Venice; according to a diarist of the day, 11,654 of them were prostitutes. A century later an English traveller reported that 20,000 such women found employment in the city. The Serenissima was renowned for its sex workers, particularly its elegant courtesans, and the most famous of these was Veronica Franco. Born in 1546 to middle-class parents, Franco was educated by private tutors along with her three brothers. At 16 or 17 she was wedded to a physician, probably in an arranged match, but she left her husband within a year. By 1564 Franco was expecting a baby and had made out a will, which was the custom for pregnant women, given the risks of childbirth. She named a wealthy nobleman as the father, adding that 'only God knows' for certain, which seems to confirm her status as a young courtesan.

Franco was certainly a professional by 1565, when she appears in a catalogue of high-class prostitutes. Produced by the city as a guide to the 'principal and most illustrious Venetian courtesans', it listed the women's names along with their addresses and rates – Franco's entry explained that payment should be made through her mother, a former courtesan herself. Courtesans provided more than sex: they also offered sophisticated company to upper-class Venetian men. While noblewomen were confined to home, educated courtesans infiltrated male domains, holding forth on philosophy, history and literature as they enchanted men with their brains and beauty. A courtesan's companionship wasn't cheap: a single kiss from Franco was said to cost 5 scudi – a week's salary for a Venetian working man – while a full-service rendezvous ran to 50 scudi. And as the French writer Michel de Montaigne noted with dismay on a trip to Venice, courtesans charged extra for conversation.

Almost by definition, courtesans were engaging and eloquent, but Franco went a step further. Outside her role as a courtesan she mingled with leading writers, meeting regularly with a distinguished group to exchange critiques, and eventually published two books: one a collection of letters, the other a book of verse. Her poems are at once frank and measured. Most are addressed to specific men. In one directed to her lover rather than a client, she extols her own erotic talent in bed, where 'So sweet and delicious do I become ... that the pleasure I bring excels all delight.' But she also praises *his* skill, which 'miraculously stands out' and makes him 'the master of my life', while his 'valour' pulls her into his lap and joins them 'more tightly than a nail in hard wood'. Sometimes she deployed poetry in self-defence, as when an anonymous man assailed her with obscene verse, calling her a disease-ridden common whore, 'a cow that could satisfy the entire Ghetto'. It was a double insult: the Ghetto was the Venetian district in which Jews were forced to live, and Christians with Jewish lovers could be beaten and exiled. Avoiding his coarseness, she asserted her virtue and called on all women to resist such attacks. Women had not yet realized, she wrote, that if they 'made up their minds to do so,/ they would have been able to fight you to the death'. Her attacker turned out to be a member of her literary circle, a priest who went on to become bishop of Corfu and to die of syphilis.

Venetian courtesans were prosecuted less vigorously than those in other cities, perhaps because the women in Venice drew tourists from afar and paid taxes enough to maintain twelve of the Republic's warships. In many ways, courtesans' greatest offence was their appearance. With their refined ways and luxurious dress they were indistinguishable from patrician women, and uneasy men could not tell *bone dalle triste* ('the good from the less fortunate'). A ruling in 1562 banned prostitutes and courtesans from wearing silk clothing or adorning themselves with precious jewelry, either genuine or fake, but few courtesans followed the rule – a famous portrait of Franco, in fact, shows her wearing a single strand of large, luminous pearls.

The plague swept through Venice between 1575 and 1577, and when Franco fled to the countryside, vandals ransacked her empty house, stealing much of her treasure. The epidemic killed a third of the population, and Venetian commerce – prostitution included – dwindled considerably, as did her income in the following years. She faced her greatest challenge in 1580, however, when an employee accused her of witchcraft – practising folk magic as well as entering pacts with the devil to enchant certain German merchants. He charged her with breaking a number of other laws, too – eating meat on fast days, playing forbidden games and ignoring the sacraments. She successfully argued her own case before the Inquisition, deftly rebutting each charge. Franco avoided punishment, but her reputation suffered, further eroding her finances. By 1582 she was living in an impoverished neighbourhood inhabited by many poor prostitutes. When she died, in 1591, after twenty days of fever, however, she managed to leave adequate provisions for her two children while still establishing a fund for prostitutes wishing to leave their profession.

❧

Tycho Brahe

THE LORD OF STAR CASTLE

1546–1601

L egend has it that the Danish nobleman Tycho Brahe was lured into astronomy as a boy, after witnessing a solar eclipse that no one had correctly predicted. Although no eclipse is actually recorded in Copenhagen at the time, there is no doubt about Tycho's childhood fascination with the skies, as his library was filled with star charts and planetary tables dating from his student days. Already by the age of just 17 he had studied and compared all the available star charts, finding to his dismay that they were as variable as the astronomers who had made them – they disagreed wildly.

His response was to propose 'a long-term project … of mapping the heavens, conducted from a single location over a period of several years'. He was driven in part by a curiosity that would now be called scientific, but Tycho also worked with the conviction, widespread in his time, that celestial patterns controlled and were reflected in events on Earth. A more accurate sidereal and planetary record, he believed, would make it easier to understand human fortune, predict the weather, control political events and cure sickness. Not surprisingly, Tycho's other lifelong passion was alchemy.

Thanks to his considerable wealth – he supposedly had the largest private fortune in the kingdom of Denmark – Tycho was able to purchase the best in star- and planet-gazing instruments. Travelling around Germany during the 1560s, he found craftsmen able to build sighting devices that could chart stars' positions to within an arc-minute (the full moon averages around 31.5 arc-minutes). Later he designed and built his own giant quadrants, some over 5 metres (16½ feet) in radius and requiring small armies of servants to adjust every time he took a reading. These he established in 1571, in his own observatory at Herrevad Abbey. Barely a year later the gods seemed to recognize his youthful efforts by staging a millennial event for him. A supernova (now known as sn-1572) burst forth in the constellation Cassiopeia and rapidly became brighter than Venus. In 1573 Tycho, who observed the phenomenon carefully for the two years it was visible, wrote the highly influential booklet *De nova stella* ('The new star') to prove that sn-1572 was not a comet – comets were familiar, if still unexplained, objects – since it did not move from one night to the next. Its very existence, he asserted, shattered one of the basic tenants of the Ptolemaic–Aristotelian world view – that the heavens were fixed and unchanging.

His supernova observations vaulted Tycho into the front ranks of European astronomers, and the Danish king Frederick II began worrying about losing one of his richest citizens and most famous scientists to some German university. To tempt Tycho to stay at home, Frederick offered to build him an observatory on the small island of Hven, in the narrow channel separating modern-day Denmark from Sweden. Establishing himself on his new fief, Tycho promptly built what he called Uraniborg ('Castle of the Muse of Astronomy'). A few years later he built a second, larger observatory on Hven, which he christened Stjerneborg ('Star Castle'). Housing more than a hundred students, Tycho's astronomical and alchemical research centre gained a European-wide reputation. By accurately plotting the planetary parallax – the minute shift that the Earth's rotation caused in the observed positions of planets – he was able to answer several problems unsolved in Copernicus's model and, in particular, the distance of the various planets from Earth. Yet, although his data clearly told him so, Tycho could never quite accept the fundamental Copernican hypothesis that the Earth orbited the Sun. Instead, with some considerable cosmological sleight of hand, he produced a Ptolemaic–Copernican hybrid, in which the other planets revolved around the Sun, which in turn orbited a fixed Earth.

It would take Tycho's student Johannes Kepler, working with the observations from Uraniborg, to place the planets and the Sun in their proper relationships. More significantly, not until Galileo Galilei turned his telescope on the Moon, Jupiter, Venus and the Sun could astronomy finally be purged of its astrological heritage; the breakthrough shifted planetary studies from alchemical fantasies to research on physical bodies composed of actual rock and gas, responding to the same laws of motion that applied on Earth. Tycho Brahe missed this discovery by less than a decade, dying just nine years before Galileo published *The Starry Messenger*. Instead, he ended his life still enthralled by those points of light whose mysterious wanderings through the zodiac remained as puzzling to him as they had been to observers since the dawn of time.

CR

Giordano Bruno

A BURNT OFFERING TO SCIENCE

1548–1600

Ordained as a Dominican priest in 1572, Giordano Bruno soon made a
name for himself. His work on memory and recall was so impressive
that he was permitted to leave his monastery in Naples to demonstrate his
method for the pope in Rome. At the same time, however, he denied the
Catholic Trinity, threw away the saints' images from his cell and was caught
reading forbidden texts in the outhouse. Hearing that the Inquisition was
on his trail, Bruno ran off to Rome in 1576 and then fled again six months
later, under suspicion of having killed a fellow Dominican. He set off on
his own tour of Italy – first to Genoa, then Turin, Venice, Padua and finally
Bergamo – always trying 'to put together a bit of cash so I could survive'
and always having to leave town in haste, usually after insulting someone
in power for being 'a jackass'. He had the training for a university chair
in mathematics or philosophy but lacked the social and political skills to
secure more than occasional lectures. Although still a friar, he wore lay
clothing, much to the irritation of the Dominicans with whom his poverty
often forced him to stay.

In 1578 Bruno decided to seek his fortune in France. Passing through
Geneva, he converted to Calvinism and for a few months enjoyed a position
at the university. Then he publicly denounced a senior professor, presumably
seeking some recognition but only getting himself arrested and forced from
the city. Eventually, via Lyons and Toulouse, he made his way to Paris,
where his mnemonic system brought some fame. Like many Renaissance
figures of exceptional talent, Bruno was accused of using witchcraft to aid

his recall, but he turned this to his advantage by gaining an audience with King Henri III to explain how his system worked. Backed by the French court, for a few years Bruno enjoyed the most secure and fruitful years of his uncertain life, first in Paris and then with Henri's ambassador in England.

In 1582, shortly after arriving in Paris, Bruno began publishing on mnemonics and metaphysics. In such works as *De umbris idearum* ('The shadow of ideas') and *Cantus Circaeus* ('Circe's song'), he argued that sharpened memory skills could not only tame information overload, but could also cut through the chaos generated by the infinite images assaulting the mind and locate the ideal forms behind them. In this, as in much else, Bruno was a Neoplatonist, insisting (heretically, according to the Church) that a universal soul or spirit permeated all of nature, manifesting itself to the untrained mind as matter, but to the philosopher as idea.

Arriving in England, where he unsuccessfully sought a place at Oxford, Bruno turned to cosmology. Borrowing Nicholas of Cusa's notion of the plurality of worlds, he argued that, while Copernicus was correct that the Earth moved, the Polish astronomer failed to go far enough. Not only the Earth but also the Sun and in fact all the stars moved, and not in the limited, concentric spheres of Ptolemy and Copernicus but in an infinite universe, composed throughout of the same matter – the logical manifestation of an infinite deity. Despite, or perhaps because of, his histrionic and extravagant style, he found it hard to promote a post-Copernican cosmology to scholars who were perfectly happy in their pre-Copernican world. He was mocked as 'that wretched little Italian [who] tried, among much else, to set on foot the opinion of Copernicus, that the earth did go round and the heavens did stand still, when in truth it was his own head that did run round, and his brains that did not stand still'.

Having failed in England and fallen out of favour in France, Bruno left for Germany, visiting various university towns in search of a lectureship, repeatedly butting heads with ecclesiastical authorities and having to move on. He had the rare distinction of being excommunicated by Catholics, Calvinists, Anglicans and Lutherans alike. In 1591, feeling a 'perpetual foreigner, exile, fugitive, plaything of fortune, small of body, short of resources, deprived of favour, squeezed by the hatred of the mob – hence disposable for the stupid and the very ignorant who only recognize nobility where gold shines or silver tinkles', he made the very unwise decision to return to Italy. There, in very short order, he was picked up by the Inquisition, which gave him a trial that lasted over seven years. After repeatedly refusing to abjure his heretical and blasphemous opinions, on 17 February 1600 the man who called himself 'an academic with no academy' was burned at the stake.

Isabella Andreini

BORN TO THE STAGE

1562–1604

Despite its name, the Renaissance *commedia dell'arte* had little to do with either art or comedy. To actors and audiences of mid-16th-century Italy, *commedia* meant all forms of drama, and *commedia dell'arte* was understood as 'professional theatre', where performers made a living from their acting skills – their *arte*. Unlike more traditional Renaissance stage productions – the *commedia erudita*, generally Classical or Classically inspired dramas put on by dilettantes for courtiers and princes – the *commedia dell'arte* had its roots in the streets, piazzas and fairgrounds. Props, staging and costumes were sparse to non-existent, as were the scripts, at least originally. Instead, the actors largely improvised off one another – and often off the audience – following a loose plot, or *canovaccio*, whose principal turning points were sufficiently well known and informal to allow plenty of space for semi-spontaneous satire, sexual display and social commentary.

The *commedia dell'arte* rapidly gained a broad popular following, especially in cities such as Venice, where it found a permanent home in newly opened theatres in the red light district. Recognizable companies began to form as well. One of the earliest of these was the Compagnia dei Comici Gelosi ('Company of the Jealous [or Solicitous] Comedians'). Started in Bologna, the Gelosi, as they were commonly known, had already become successful enough to have toured France when, some time around 1577, they were joined by Isabella Canali, a 15-year-old from Padua of obscure parentage. Brilliant, loquacious and charismatic, Isabella was such an immediate sensation in the company that the reigning first lady promptly left. Within a year she had married the leading man, Francesco Cerracchi, taken his stage name of Andreini for herself and begun running the Gelosi with him.

In *commedia dell'arte* the stock characters were called 'the usual ten': two pairs of lovers, or *innamorati*; two lustful old men, the *vecchi*; an impetuous and usually enraged Captain; two guileful servants, or *zanni* (who evolved later into the Harlequin figure); and a conniving serving maid, the *servetta*. The roles became so standardized that the male characters, at least, were played in masks, which made everyone instantly recognizable while still allowing even an understaffed company to fill all the parts. Isabella Andreini was famously able to handle any of these roles, male or female, but she generally played to type as one of the unmasked female lovers, the better to display her remarkable beauty. A good hundred years before women were allowed on stage in England or Scotland, actresses such as Isabella were rapturously embraced by the Italian public, despite the mutterings of a few friars that they polluted the thoughts of young men in the audience with their salacious dialogue, loose costumes and looser morals.

Isabella was deemed a cut above the typical *commedia dell'arte* diva, who was part actress and mostly courtesan. She wrote prolifically, both material for the stage and vast amounts of poetry, some of which she also recited. Soon after joining the Gelosi, possibly while still in her teens, she wrote a remarkable comic play, *La mirtilla* ('The blackberry'), in evident homage to the play *Aminta* (1573), by her friend and patron Torquato Tasso. Isabella claimed that 'I began [it] almost as a joke,' but the work – a pastoral drama filled with Classical allusions – gave the Gelosi a *commedia erudita* of their own, suitable for moving from the rough slapstick of the street or public theatre to more refined, courtly gatherings.

By the late 1580s Isabella had expanded her repertory, in particular with a complex, one-woman improvisation known as *La Pazzia d'Isabella* ('The madness of Isabella'), in which she spoke several languages, interacted with the audience, imitated other characters and then became sane again. Continually on tour among the courts of northern Italy, the Gelosi were featured players when the French king Henri III came to Venice in 1574, had a prominent place in the marriage festivities of Duke Ferdinando de' Medici, and went to Paris twice as regular players at the court of Henri IV. It was in Lyons, in 1604, while returning from the second of these French tours, that Isabella, pregnant with her eighth child, miscarried and died. Her husband, Francesco, who for over twenty years had played the Captain and directed the Gelosi, immediately decided to shut down the company, believing it could not continue without its diva. In time, however, Giambattista Andreini, the only one of Isabella's sons who had stayed in the theatre (most of the rest had gone into religious orders), formed the old Jealous Comedians into his own company, which he called I Comici Fedeli ('The Faithful Comedians'), perhaps in honour of his mother.

Further Reading

GENERAL READING

Burke, Peter, *The Italian Renaissance: Culture and Society in Italy*, 2nd edn (Princeton, NJ: Princeton University Press, 1999)

Campbell, Gordon, *The Oxford Dictionary of the Renaissance* (Oxford: Oxford University Press, 2003)

Cohen, Elizabeth S. and Thomas V. Cohen, *Daily Life in Renaissance Italy* (Westport, CT: Greenwood Publishing, 2004)

Cox, Virginia, *Women's Writing in Italy, 1400–1650* (Baltimore: Johns Hopkins University Press, 2008)

Currie, Elizabeth, *Inside the Renaissance House* (London: V&A Publications, 2006)

Hale, John R., *Civilization of Europe in the Renaissance* (New York: Touchstone, 1995)

Kirkpatrick, Robin, *The European Renaissance, 1400–1600* (Harlow: Pearson, 2002)

Levey, Michael, *Florence: A Portrait* (Cambridge, MA: Harvard University Press, 1996)

Mackenney, Richard, *Renaissances: The Cultures of Italy, c. 1300–c. 1600* (Basingstoke: Palgrave Macmillan, 2005)

Nauert, Charles G., *Humanism and the Culture of Renaissance Europe*, 2nd edn (Cambridge: Cambridge University Press, 2006)

Toman, Rolf (ed.), *The Art of the Italian Renaissance: Architecture, Sculpture, Painting, Drawing* (Potsdam: H. F. Ullmann, 2008)

1. OLD TRADITIONS AND NEW IDEAS
• MANUEL CHRYSOLORAS

Wells, Colin, *Sailing from Byzantium: How a Lost Empire Shaped the World* (New York: Delacorte Press, 2007)

Wilson, N. G., *From Byzantium to Italy: Greek Studies in the Italian Renaissance* (Baltimore: Johns Hopkins University Press, 1992)

• CHRISTINE DE PIZAN

Bell, Susan G., *The Lost Tapestries of the City of Ladies: Christine de Pizan's Renaissance Legacy* (Berkeley, CA: University of California Press, 2004)

Pizan, Christine de, *The Selected Writings of Christine de Pizan*, ed. and trans. R. Blumenfeld-Kosinski (New York: W. W. Norton, 1997)

Willard, Charity Cannon, *Christine de Pizan: Her Life and Works* (New York: Persea Books, 1984)

• LEONARDO BRUNI

Bruni, Leonardo, *The Humanism of Leonardo Bruni: Selected Texts*, ed. and trans. Gordon Griffiths, James Hankins, David Thompson (Binghamton, ny: Medieval and Renaissance Texts and Studies, 1987)

Witt, Ronald G., *In the Footsteps of the Ancients: The Origins of Humanism from Lovato to Bruni* (Boston, MA: Brill, 2000)

• JAN HUS

Hus, John, *The Letters of John Hus*, trans. Herbert B. Workman and R. Martin Pope (London: Hodder and Stoughton, 1904)

Spinka, Matthew, *John Hus: A Biography* (Princeton, NJ: Princeton University Press, 1968)

Spinka, Matthew, *John Hus and the Czech Reform* (Hamden, CT: Archon, 1968)

• FILIPPO BRUNELLESCHI

Edgerton, Samuel Y., *The Renaissance Rediscovery of Linear Perspective* (New York: Harper & Row, 1975)

Fanelli, Giovanni, and Michele Fanelli, *Brunelleschi's Cupola: Past and Present of an Architectural Masterpiece* (Florence: Mandragora, 2004)

King, Ross, *Brunelleschi's Dome: How a Renaissance Genius Invented Architecture* (New York: Penguin, 2000)

Walker, Paul Robert, *The Feud that Sparked the Renaissance: How Brunelleschi and Ghiberti Changed the Art World* (New York: Perennial, 2002)

• ST BERNARDINO OF SIENA

Mormando, Franco, *The Preacher's Demons: Bernardino of Siena and the Social Underworld of Early Renaissance Italy* (Chicago: University of Chicago Press, 1999)

Polecritti, Cynthia L., *Preaching Peace in Renaissance Italy: Bernardino of Siena and his Audience* (Washington, DC: Catholic University of America Press, 2000)

• DONATELLO

Avery, Charles, *Donatello: An Introduction* (New York: Westview Press, 1995)

Poeschke, Joachim, *Donatello and his World: Sculpture of the Italian Renaissance*, trans. Russell Stockman (New York: Abrams, 1993)

Pope-Hennessy, John, *An Introduction to Italian Sculpture*, vol. 2, *Italian Renaissance Sculpture* (London: Phaidon, 2000)

• COSIMO DE' MEDICI

Brucker, Gene A., *Renaissance Florence* (Berkeley, CA: University of California Press, 1983)

de Roover, Raymond, *The Rise and Decline of the Medici Bank, 1397–1494* (Cambridge, MA: Harvard University Press, 1963)

Hibbert, Christopher, *The House of Medici: Its Rise and Fall* (New York: Harper Perennial, 1999)

Kent, Dale, *Cosimo de' Medici and the Florentine Renaissance: The Patron's Oeuvre* (New Haven, CT: Yale University Press, 2000)

• JAN VAN EYCK

Hall, Edwin, *The Arnolfini Betrothal: Medieval Marriage and the Enigma of van Eyck's Double Portrait* (Berkeley, CA: University of California Press, 1997)

Harbison, Craig, *The Mirror of the Artist: Northern Renaissance Art in its Historical Context* (Upper Saddle River, NJ: Prentice Hall, 1995)

———, *Jan van Eyck: The Play of Realism* (London: Reaktion, 1997)

Snyder, James, *Northern Renaissance Art: Painting, Sculpture, the Graphic Arts from 1350 to 1575*, 2nd edn, rev. Henry Luttikhuizen and Larry Silver (Upper Saddle River, NJ: Prentice Hall, 2005)

• MASACCIO

Ahl, Diane Cole, *The Cambridge Companion to Masaccio* (Cambridge: Cambridge University Press, 2002)

Cole, Bruce, *Masaccio and the Art of Early Renaissance Florence* (Bloomington, IN: Indiana University Press, 1980)

2. EUROPEANS AT PEACE

• FLAVIO BIONDO

Baldassarri, Stefano Ugo, and Arielle Saiber (eds), *Images of Quattrocentro Florence: Selected Writings in Literature, History, and Art* (New Haven, CT: Yale University Press, 2000)

Biondo, Flavio, *Biondo Flavio's Italia Illustrata: Text, Translation, and Commentary*, ed. and trans. Catherine J. Castner (Binghamton, NY:

Global Academic Publishing, 2005)

Hay, Denys, 'Flavio Biondo and the Middle Ages', *Renaissance Essays* (London: Hambledon Press, 1988), pp. 35–65

• LUCA DELLA ROBBIA

Domestici, Fiamma, *Della Robbia: A Family of Artists* (Florence: Scala; New York: Riverside Book Co., 1992)

Pope-Hennessy, John, *Luca della Robbia* (Ithaca, NY: Cornell University Press, 1980)

• NICHOLAS OF CUSA

Bellitto, Christopher M., Thomas M. Izbicki and Gerald Christianson (eds), *Introducing Nicholas of Cusa: A Guide to a Renaissance Man* (New York and Mahwah, nj: Paulist Press, 2004)

Nicholas of Cusa, *Nicholas of Cusa: Selected Spiritual Writings*, trans. H. Lawrence Bond (New York and Mahwah, NJ: Paulist Press, 1997)

• FRANCESCO SFORZA

Black, Jane, *Absolutism in Renaissance Milan: Plenitude of Power under the Visconti and the Sforza, 1329–1535* (Oxford: Oxford University Press, 2009)

Welch, Evelyn S., *Art and Authority in Renaissance Milan* (New Haven, CT: Yale University Press, 1996)

• LEON BATTISTA ALBERTI

Alberti, Leon Battista, *On Painting*, ed. Martin Kemp, trans. Cecil Grayson (London: Penguin, 1991)

Alberti, Leon Battista, *The Family in Renaissance Florence: Book Three, Libri Della Famiglia*, trans. Renée Neu Watkins (Long Grove, IL: Waveland Press, 1994)

Baldassarri, Stefano Ugo, and Arielle Saiber (eds), *Images of Quattrocentro Florence: Selected Writings in Literature, History, and Art* (New Haven, CT: Yale University Press, 2000)

Edgerton, Samuel Y., *The Renaissance Rediscovery of Linear Perspective* (New York: Harper & Row, 1975)

Grafton, Anthony, *Leon Battista Alberti: Master Builder of the Italian Renaissance* (Cambridge, MA: Harvard University Press, 2002)

• POPE PIUS II

Baldassarri, Stefano Ugo, and Arielle Saiber (eds), *Images of Quattrocentro Florence: Selected Writings in Literature, History, and Art* (New Haven, CT: Yale University Press, 2000)

Mitchell, R. J., *The Laurels and the Tiara: Pope Pius II, 1458–1464* (London: Harvill, 1962)

Piccolomini, Aeneas Sylvius (Pius II), *Reject
Aeneas, Accept Pius: Selected Letters of Aeneas
Sylvius Piccolomini*, trans. Thomas M.
Izbicki, Gerald Christianson and Philip Krey
(Washington, DC: The Catholic University
of America Press, 2006)
Pius II, *Memoirs of a Renaissance Pope:
The Commentaries of Pius II, an Abridgement*,
ed. Leona C. Gabel, trans. Florence A. Gragg
(New York: G. P. Putnam's Sons, 1959)
• LORENZO VALLA
Mack, Peter, *Renaissance Argument: Valla and
Agricola in the Traditions of Rhetoric and Dialectic*
(Leiden: Brill, 1993)
Nauta, Lodi, *In Defense of Common Sense: Lorenzo
Valla's Humanist Critique of Scholastic Philosophy*
(Cambridge, ma: Harvard University Press,
2009)
• ALESSANDRA STROZZI
Brucker, Gene, 'Alessandra Strozzi (1408–1471):
The Eventful Life of a Florentine Matron',
*Living on the Edge in Leonardo's Florence:
Selected Essays* (Berkeley, CA: University of
California Press, 2005) pp. 151–68
Crabb, Ann, *The Strozzi of Florence: Widowhood
and Family Solidarity in the Renaissance* (Ann
Arbor, mi: University of Michigan Press, 2000)
Strozzi, Alessandra, *Selected Letters of Alessandra
Strozzi*, bilingual edn, ed. and trans. Heather
Gregory (Berkeley, CA: University of California
Press, 1997)
• ISOTTA NOGAROLA
Jardine, Lisa, 'Isotta Nogarola: Women
Humanists – Education for What?' in *The
Italian Renaissance: The Essential Readings*, ed.
Paula Findlen (Oxford: Wiley-Blackwell, 2002),
pp. 273–92
Nogarola, Isotta, *Complete Writings: Letterbook,
Dialogue on Adam and Eve, Orations*, ed. and
trans. Margaret L. King and Diana Robin
(Chicago: University of Chicago Press, 2004)
• FEDERICO DA MONTEFELTRO
Osborne, Joan, *Urbino: The Story of a Renaissance
City* (Chicago: University of Chicago Press, 2003)
Simonetta, Marcello, *The Montefeltro Conspiracy:
A Renaissance Mystery Decoded* (New York:
Doubleday, 2008)
• LUCREZIA TORNABUONI
Tomas, Natalie R., *The Medici Women: Gender and
Power in the Renaissance* (Aldershot: Ashgate,
2003)

Tornabuoni de' Medici, Lucrezia, *Sacred
Narratives*, ed. and trans. Jane Tylus (Chicago:
University of Chicago Press, 2001)
• GENTILE BELLINI
Brown, David Allen, and Sylvia Ferino-Pagden,
*Bellini, Giorgione, Titian, and the Renaissance
of Venetian Painting* (New Haven, CT: Yale
University Press, 2006)
Brown, Patricia Fortini, *Art and Life in Renaissance
Venice* (Upper Saddle River, NJ: Prentice Hall,
2005)
Campbell, Caroline, and Alan Chong (eds),
Bellini and the East (New Haven, CT: Yale
University Press, 2005)
Steer, John, *Venetian Painting: A Concise History*
(London: Thames & Hudson, 1980)
• MEHMET II
Freely, John, *The Grand Turk: Sultan Mehmet II
– Conqueror of Constantinople and Master of an
Empire* (New York: Overlook Press, 2009)

3. THE EMERGING NATIONS
• WILLIAM CAXTON
Deacon, Richard, *William Caxton: The First
English Editor* (London: Frederick Muller,
1976)
Painter, George D., *William Caxton: A Biography*
(New York: G. P. Putnam's Sons, 1977)
• HEINRICH KRAMER
Broedel, Hans Peter, *The* Malleus maleficarum
*and the Construction of Witchcraft: Theology
and Popular Belief* (Manchester: Manchester
University Press, 2003)
Heinrich Institoris, *The Malleus Maleficarum*,
ed. and trans. P. G. Maxwell-Stuart (Manchester:
Manchester University Press, 2007)
Levack, Brian P., *The Witch-Hunt in Early Modern
Europe*, 2nd edn (London: Longman, 1995)
Russell, Jeffery B., and Brooks Alexander,
*A History of Witchcraft: Sorcerers, Heretics and
Pagans*, 2nd edn (London: Thames & Hudson,
2007)
• FRANCISCO JIMÉNEZ DE CISNEROS
Rummel, Erika, *Jiménez de Cisneros: On the
Threshold of Spain's Golden Age* (Tempe, AZ:
Arizona Center for Medieval and Renaissance
Studies, 1999)
• FELIX FABRI
Fabri, Felix, *The Wanderings of Felix Fabri*, ed.
and trans. Aubrey Stewart (New York: AMS
Press, 1971)

FURTHER READING

• ANTONIO DE NEBRIJA

García de la Concha, Victor (ed.), *Nebrija y la introducción del Renacimiento en España* (Salamanca: Universidad de Salamanca, 1983)

Percival, W. Keith (ed.), *Studies in Renaissance Grammar* (Aldershot: Ashgate, 2004)

• MATTHIAS CORVINUS

Kaufmann, Thomas DaCosta, *Court, Cloister, and City: The Art and Culture of Central Europe, 1450–1800* (Chicago: University of Chicago Press, 1995)

Tanner, Marcus, *The Raven King: Matthias Corvinus and the Fate of his Lost Library* (New Haven, CT: Yale University Press, 2008)

• LORENZO DE' MEDICI

Hibbert, Christopher, *The House of Medici: Its Rise and Fall* (New York: Morrow, 1974; repr. New York: Harper Perennial, 1999)

Sturm, Sara Higgins, *Lorenzo de' Medici* (New York: Twayne Publishers, 1974)

Unger, Miles J., *Magnifico: The Brilliant Life and Violent Times of Lorenzo de' Medici* (New York: Simon & Schuster, 2008)

• LUCA PACIOLI

Crosby, Alfred W., *The Measure of Reality: Quantification and Western Europe, 1250–1600* (Cambridge: Cambridge University Press, 1997)

Taylor, R. Emmett, *No Royal Road: Luca Pacioli and his Times* (Chapel Hill, NC: University of North Carolina, 1942; repr. New York: Arno Press, 1980)

• SANDRO BOTTICELLI

Dempsey, Charles, *The Portrayal of Love: Botticelli's Primavera and Humanist Culture at the Time of Lorenzo the Magnificent* (Princeton, NJ: Princeton University Press, 1992)

Hatfield, Rab, 'Botticelli's *Mystic Nativity*, Savonarola, and the Millennium', *Journal of the Warburg and Courtauld Institutes*, vol. 58 (1995), pp. 89–114

Lightbown, Ronald, *Botticelli: Life and Work*, 2nd edn (New York: Abbeville Press, 1989)

Schumacher, Andreas (ed.), *Botticelli* (New York: Hatje Cantz, 2010)

• JOSQUIN DES PREZ

Higgins, Paula, 'The Apotheosis of Josquin des Prez and Other Mythologies of Musical Genius', *Journal of the American Musicological Society*, vol. 57, no. 3 (autumn 2004), pp. 443–510

Lowinsky, Edward E. (ed.), *Josquin des Prez: Proceedings of the International Josquin Festival-*

– Conference held at the Juilliard School at Lincoln Center in New York City, 21–25 June 1971 (London: Oxford University Press, 1976)

Merkley, Paul A., and Lora L. M. Matthews, *Music and Patronage in the Sforza Court* (Turnhout: Brepols Publishers, 1999)

Sherr, Richard (ed.), *The Josquin Companion* (Oxford: Oxford University Press, 2001)

• ALDUS MANUTIUS

Barolini, Helen, *Aldus and his Dream Book: An Illustrated Essay* (New York: Italica Press, 1992)

Pettegree, Andrew, *The Book in the Renaissance* (New Haven, CT: Yale University Press, 2010)

• LEONARDO DA VINCI

Bramly, Serge, *Leonardo: The Artist and the Man*, 2nd edn, trans. Sian Reynolds (London: Penguin, 1995)

Capra, Fritjof, *The Science of Leonardo: Inside the Mind of the Great Genius of the Renaissance* (New York: Doubleday, 2007)

Goffen, Rona, *Renaissance Rivals: Michelangelo, Leonardo, Raphael, Titian* (New Haven, CT: Yale University Press, 2004)

Leonardo da Vinci, *Leonardo's Notebooks*, ed. H. Anna Suh (New York: Black Dog & Leventhal Publishers, 2009)

• KING JOÃO II

Birmingham, David, *A Concise History of Portugal*, 2nd edn (Cambridge: Cambridge University Press, 2003)

Boxer, Charles Ralph, *The Portuguese Seaborne Empire, 1415–1825* (New York: Alfred A. Knopf, 1969)

• ANTONIO RINALDESCHI

Connell, William J., and Giles Constable, *Sacrilege and Redemption in Renaissance Florence. The Case of Antonio Rinaldeschi*, rev. 2nd edn (Toronto: University of Toronto Press, 2008)

4. SUDDEN SHOCKS

• INTRODUCTION

Partner, Peter, *Renaissance Rome, 1550–1559: A Portrait of a Society* (Berkeley, CA: University of California Press, 1979)

• CHRISTOPHER COLUMBUS

Columbus, Christopher, *The Four Voyages of Christopher Columbus*, ed. and trans. J. M. Cohen (Harmondsworth: Penguin, 1969)

Heat-Moon, William Least, *Columbus in the Americas* (Hoboken, NJ: John Wiley, 2002)

Sale, Kirkpatrick, *Christopher Columbus and the Conquest of Paradise*, 2nd edn (London: Tauris Parke, 2006)

• JOHN CABOT

Firstbrook, Peter L., *The Voyage of the Matthew: John Cabot and the Discovery of America* (San Francisco: Bay Books, 1997)

Fritze, Ronald H., *New Worlds: The Great Voyages of Discovery, 1400–1600* (Westport, CT: Praeger, 2002)

Pope, Peter Edward, *The Many Landfalls of John Cabot* (Toronto: University of Toronto Press, 1997)

• GIROLAMO SAVONAROLA

Hatfield, Rab, 'Botticelli's *Mystic Nativity*, Savonarola, and the Millennium', *Journal of the Warburg and Courtauld Institutes*, vol. 58 (1995), pp. 89–114

Martines, Lauro, *Fire in the City: Savonarola and the Struggle for Renaissance Florence* (Oxford: Oxford University Press 2006)

Savonarola, Girolamo, *Selected Writings of Girolamo Savonarola: Religion and Politics, 1490–1498*, ed. and trans. Anne Borelli and Maria Pastore Passaro (New Haven, CT: Yale University Press, 2006)

• JAKOB FUGGER

Jardine, Lisa, *Worldly Goods: A New History of the Renaissance* (New York: W. W. Norton, 1998)

Strieder, Jacob, *Jacob Fugger the Rich: Merchant and Banker of Augsburg, 1459–1525*, ed. N. S. B. Gras, trans. Mildred L. Hartsough (New York: Adelphi, 1931; repr. Whitefish, MT: Kessinger Publishing, 2008)

• DESIDERIUS ERASMUS

Bainton, Roland H., *Erasmus of Christendom* (New York: Charles Scribner's Sons, 1969)

Erasmus, Desiderius, *The Praise of Folly and Other Writings*, ed. and trans. Robert M. Adams (New York: W. W. Norton, 1989)

Huizinga, Johan, *Erasmus of Rotterdam, with a Selection from the Letters of Erasmus*, trans. F. Hopman and Barbara Flower (London: Phaidon, 1952; repr. as *Erasmus and the Age of Reformation*, Mineola, NY: Dover Publications, 2001)

• NICCOLÒ MACHIAVELLI

Machiavelli, Niccolò, *The Portable Machiavelli*, ed. and trans. Peter Bondanella and Mark Musa (New York: Penguin, 1979)

Viroli, Maurizio, *Niccolò's Smile: A Biography of Machiavelli*, trans. Antony Shugaar (New York: Farrar, Straus and Giroux, 1998)

• TOMMASO INGHIRAMI

Bonner, Mitchell, *Rome in the High Renaissance: The Age of Leo X* (Norman, OK: University of Oklahoma Press, 1973)

• ALBRECHT DÜRER

Hutchison, Jane Campbell, *Albrecht Dürer: A Biography* (Princeton, NJ: Princeton University Press, 1990)

Panofsky, Erwin, *The Life and Art of Albrecht Dürer* (Princeton, NJ: Princeton University Press, 2005)

Snyder, James, *Northern Renaissance Art: Painting, Sculpture, the Graphic Arts from 1350 to 1575*, 2nd edn, rev. Larry Silver and Henry Luttikhuizen (Upper Saddle River, NJ: Prentice Hall, 2005)

• NICOLAUS COPERNICUS

Gingerich, Owen, *The Book Nobody Read: Chasing the Revolutions of Nicolaus Copernicus* (New York: Penguin, 2005)

Repcheck, Jack, *Copernicus' Secret: How the Scientific Revolution Began* (New York: Simon & Schuster, 2008)

• ISABELLA D'ESTE

Campbell, Stephen J., *The Cabinet of Eros: Renaissance Mythological Painting and the Studiolo of Isabella d'Este* (New Haven, CT: Yale University Press, 2006)

Cartwright, Julia, *Isabella d'Este, Marchioness of Mantua, 1474–1539: A Study of the Renaissance*, 2 vols (London: John Murray, 1903)

• CESARE BORGIA

Bradford, Sarah, *Lucrezia Borgia: Life, Love and Death in Renaissance Italy* (London: Penguin, 2005)

Hibbert, Christopher, *The Borgias and their Enemies: 1431–1519* (Boston, MA: Mariner Books, 2009)

Johnson, Marion, *The Borgias* (London: Penguin, 2001)

• MICHELANGELO BUONARROTI

Goffen, Rona, *Renaissance Rivals: Michelangelo, Leonardo, Raphael, Titian* (New Haven, CT: Yale University Press, 2004)

King, Ross, *Michelangelo and the Pope's Ceiling* (New York: Penguin, 2003)

Nagel, Alexander, *Michelangelo and the Reform of Art* (Cambridge: Cambridge University Press, 2000)

Ryan, Christopher, *The Poetry of Michelangelo: An Introduction* (Madison, NJ: Fairleigh Dickinson University Press, 1998)

Wallace, William E., *Michelangelo: The Artist, the Man and his Times* (Cambridge: Cambridge University Press, 2010)

• BALDASSARE CASTIGLIONE

Burke, Peter, *The Fortunes of the Courtier: The European Reception of Castiglione's 'Cortigiano'* (University Park, PA: Pennsylvania State University Press, 1996)

Castiglione, Baldassare, *The Book of the Courtier*, trans. George Bull (London: Penguin, 1976)

• RAPHAEL

Dacos, Nicole, *The Loggia of Raphael: A Vatican Art Treasure* (New York: Abbeville Press, 2008)

Goffen, Rona, *Renaissance Rivals: Michelangelo, Leonardo, Raphael, Titian* (New Haven, CT: Yale University Press, 2004)

Jones, Roger, and Nicholas Penny, *Raphael* (New Haven, CT: Yale University Press, 1983)

• LEO AFRICANUS

Davis, Natalie Zemon, *Trickster Travels: A Sixteenth-Century Muslim Between Worlds* (New York: Hill and Wang, 2007)

5. THE COLLAPSE OF THE OLD ORDER

• INTRODUCTION

Lindberg, Carter, *The European Reformations*, 2nd edn (Malden, MA: Wiley-Blackwell, 2010)

• HAYREDDIN BARBAROSSA

Bradford, Ernie, *The Sultan's Admiral: The Life of Barbarossa* (New York: Harcourt, Brace & World, 1968)

Heers, Jacques, *The Barbary Corsairs: Warfare in the Mediterranean, 1480–1580*, trans. Jonathan North (London: Greenhill, 2003)

Norwich, John Julius, *The Middle Sea: A History of the Mediterranean* (New York: Doubleday, 2006)

• LUCAS CRANACH THE ELDER

Brinkmann, Brodo (ed.), *Cranach* (London: Royal Academy of Arts, 2007)

Koerner, Joseph Leo, *The Reformation of the Image* (Chicago: University of Chicago Press, 2007)

Moser, Peter, *Lucas Cranach: His Life, his World and his Art*, trans. Kenneth Wynne (Bamberg: Babenberg, 2005)

• THOMAS MORE

Ackroyd, Peter, *The Life of Thomas More* (London: Chatto & Windus, 1998)

Guy, John Alexander, *Thomas More* (London: Arnold, 2000)

Marius, Richard, *Thomas More: A Biography* (Cambridge, MA: Harvard University Press, 1999)

More, Thomas, *Utopia*, trans. Paul Turner (Harmondsworth: Penguin, 1965)

Moynahan, Brian, *God's Bestseller: William Tyndale, Thomas More, and the Writing of the English Bible – A Story of Martyrdom and Betrayal* (New York: St. Martin's Press, 2002)

• MARTIN LUTHER

Daudert, Charles (ed. and trans.), *Off The Record with Martin Luther: An Original Translation of the Table Talks* (Kalamazoo, MI: Hansa-Hewlett Publishing, 2009)

Marty, Martin E., *Martin Luther* (New York: Viking Penguin, 2004)

Oberman, Heiko A., *Luther: Man Between God and the Devil*, trans. Eileen Walliser-Schwarzbart (New Haven, CT: Yale University Press, 1989)

• BARTOLOMÉ DE LAS CASAS

MacNutt, Francis Augustus, *Bartholomew de las Casas: His Life, his Apostolate, and his Writings* (New York: New York & Co., 1909; repr. New York: AMS Press, 1972)

Vickery, Paul S., *Bartolomé de las Casas: Great Prophet of the Americas* (Mahwah, NJ: Paulist Press, 2006)

• TITIAN

Ferino-Pagden, Sylvia (ed.), *Late Titian and the Sensuality of Painting* (Venice: Marsilio, 2008)

Humfrey, Peter, *Titian: The Complete Paintings* (Ghent: Ludion Press, 2007)

Ilchman, Frederick (ed.), *Titian, Tintoretto, Veronese: Rivals in Renaissance Venice* (Boston, MA: MFA Publications, 2009)

Rosand, David, *Painting in Sixteenth-Century Venice: Titian, Veronese, Tintoretto* (Cambridge: Cambridge University Press, 1997)

• NICHOLAUS KRATZER

Ellis, Henry (ed.), *Original Letters, Illustrative of English History: Including Numerous Royal Letters: From Autographs in the British Museum, the State Paper Office, and One or Two Other Collections*, vol. 1 (London: Richard Bentley, 1846)

Gatty, Mrs lfred, *The Book of Sun-Dials*, 4th edn, rev. H. K. F. Eden and Eleanor Lloyd (London: Bell, 1900)

Weir, Alison, *Henry VIII: The King and his Court* (New York: Ballantine Books, 2001)

• BERNARD VAN ORLEY

Campbell, Thomas P., *Tapestry in the Renaissance: Art and Magnificence* (New Haven, CT: Yale University Press, 2002)

Delmarcel, Guy, *Flemish Tapestry*, trans. Alastair Weir (New York: Abrams, 2000)

• CRISTOFORO DA MESSISBUGO

Albala, Ken, *Cooking in Europe, 1250–1650* (Westport, CT: Greenwood Press, 2006)

Albala, Ken, *The Banquet: Dining in the Great Courts of Late Renaissance Europe* (Urbana, IL: University of Illinois Press, 2007)

Capatti, Alberto and Massimo Montanari, *Italian Cuisine: A Cultural History*, trans. Aine O'Healy (New York: Columbia University Press, 2003)

• VITTORIA COLONNA

Brundin, Abigail, *Vittoria Colonna and the Spiritual Poetics of the Italian Reformation* (Aldershot: Ashgate, 2008)

Colonna, Vittoria, *Sonnets for Michelangelo: A Bilingual Edition*, ed. and trans. Abigail Brundin (London: University of Chicago Press, 2005)

• MARGUERITE OF NAVARRE

Cholakian, Patricia F., and Rouben C. Cholakian, *Marguerite de Navarre: Mother of the Renaissance* (New York: Columbia University Press, 2006)

Navarre, Marguerite de, *Selected Writings: A Bilingual Edition*, ed. and trans. Rouben Cholakian and Mary Skemp (Chicago: University of Chicago Press, 2008)

———, *The Heptameron*, ed. and trans. P. A. Chilton (London: Penguin, 1984)

• PIETRO ARETINO

Frantz, David O., 'The Scourge of Princes as Pornographer: Pietro Aretino and the Popular Tradition', *Festum Voluptatis: A Study of Renaissance Erotica* (Columbus, OH: The Ohio State University Press, 1989), pp. 43–90

Moulton, Ian Frederick, 'Courtesan Politics: The Erotic Writing and Cultural Significance of Pietro Aretino', *Before Pornography: Erotic Writing in Early Modern England* (Oxford: Oxford University Press, 2000) pp. 119–57

Waddington, Raymond B., *Aretino's Satyr: Sexuality, Satire, and Self-Projection in Sixteenth-Century Literature and Art* (Toronto: University of Toronto Press, 2003)

• WILLIAM TYNDALE

Daniell, David, *William Tyndale: A Biography* (New Haven, CT: Yale University Press, 1994)

Moynahan, Brian, *God's Bestseller: William Tyndale, Thomas More, and the Writing of the English Bible: A Story of Martyrdom and Betrayal* (New York: St. Martin's Press, 2002)

• FRANÇOIS RABELAIS

Heath, Michael J., *Rabelais* (Tempe, AZ: Center for Medieval and Renaissance Texts and Studies, 1996)

Rabelais, François, *The Complete Works of François Rabelais*, trans. Donald M. Frame (Berkeley, CA: University of California Press, 1991)

Zegura, Elizabeth Chesney (ed.), *The Rabelais Encyclopedia* (Westport, CT: Greenwood Press, 2004)

• HANS HOLBEIN THE YOUNGER

Bätschmann, Oskar, and Pascal Griener, *Hans Holbein* (London: Reaktion, 2008)

Foister, Susan, *Holbein and England* (New Haven, CT: Yale University Press, 2004)

Wilson, Derek, *Hans Holbein: Portrait of an Unknown Man* (London: Weidenfeld & Nicolson, 1996)

• NICCOLÒ TARTAGLIA

Livio, Mario, *The Equation That Couldn't be Solved: How Mathematical Genius Discovered the Language of Symmetry* (New York: Simon & Schuster, 2005)

6. THE NEW WAVE

• INTRODUCTION

Lindberg, Carter, *The European Reformations*, 2nd edn (Malden, MA: Wiley-Blackwell, 2010)

• POPE PAUL IV

Fragnito, Gigliola, *Church, Censorship and Culture in Early Modern Italy*, trans. Adrian Belton (Cambridge: Cambridge University Press, 2001)

• EMPEROR CHARLES V

Elliott, John Huxtable, *Imperial Spain: 1469–1716* (London: Edward Arnold, 1963)

Maltby, William S., *The Reign of Charles V* (Basingstoke: Palgrave, 2002)

Reston, James, *Defenders of the Faith: Charles V, Suleyman the Magnificent and the Battle for Europe, 1520–1536* (London: Penguin, 2009)

• BENVENUTO CELLINI

Cellini, Benvenuto, *My Life*, trans. Julia Conway Bondanella and Peter Bondanella (New York: Oxford University Press, 2002)

Cole, Michael W., *Cellini and the Principles of Sculpture* (Cambridge: Cambridge University Press, 2002)

• ST FRANCIS XAVIER

Maynard, Theodore, *The Odyssey of Francis Xavier* (New York: Longmans, Green, 1936)

• ANDREA PALLADIO

Ackerman, James S., *Palladio* (Harmondsworth: Penguin, 1974)

Boucher, Bruce, *Andrea Palladio: The Architect in his Time* (New York: Abbeville Press, 1998)

Rybczynski, Witold, *The Perfect House: A Journey with Renaissance Master Andrea Palladio* (London: Scribner, 2003)

• JEAN CALVIN

Gordon, Bruce, *Calvin* (New Haven, CT: Yale University Press, 2009)

Greef, Wulfert de, *The Writings of John Calvin: An Introductory Guide*, expanded edn, trans. Lyle D. Bierma (Louisville, KY: Westminster John Knox Press, 2008)

Witte, John, and Robert M. Kingdon, *Sex, Marriage, and Family Life in John Calvin's Geneva: Vol. 1, Courtship, Engagement, and Marriage* (Grand Rapids, MI: Eerdmans Publishing, 2005)

• GRACIA MENDES NASI

Birnbaum, Marianna D., *The Long Journey of Gracia Mendes* (Budapest: Central European University Press, 2003)

Brooks, Andrée Aelion, *The Woman Who Defied Kings: The Life and Times of Doña Gracia Nasi, a Jewish Leader During the Renaissance* (New York: Paragon House Publishers, 2003)

Roth, Cecil, *The House of Nasi: Doña Gracia* (Philadelphia: Jewish Publication Society of America, 1948; repr. 2001)

• ANDREAS VESALIUS

Cuir, Raphaël, *The Development of the Study of Anatomy from the Renaissance to Cartesianism: Da Carpi, Vesalius, Estienne, Bidloo* (Lewiston, NY: Edwin Mellen Press, 2009)

Saunders, J. B. de C. M. and Charles D. O'Malley, *The Illustrations from the Works of Andreas Vesalius of Brussels* (New York: Dover Publications, 1950; repr. 1973)

Sawday, Jonathan, *The Body Emblazoned: Dissection and the Human Body in Renaissance Culture* (London: Routledge, 1995)

• ST TERESA OF AVILA

Mujica, Barbara, *Teresa de Avila, Lettered Woman* (Nashville, TN: Vanderbilt University Press, 2009)

Teresa of Avila, *The Life of Saint Teresa of Avila by herself*, trans. J. M. Cohen (London: Penguin, 1957; repr. 1987)

• CATHERINE DE' MEDICI

Frieda, Leonie, *Catherine de Medici: Renaissance Queen of France* (London: Weidenfeld & Nicolson, 2003; repr. New York: Harper Perennial, 2006)

Holt, Mack P., *The French Wars of Religion, 1562–1629* (Cambridge: Cambridge University Press, 2005)

Kruse, Elaine, 'The Blood-Stained Hands of Catherine de Médicis', in *Political Rhetoric, Power, and Renaissance Women*, ed. Carole Levin and Patricia A. Sullivan (Albany, NY: State University of New York Press, 1995), pp. 139–55

Tomas, Natalie R., *The Medici Women: Gender and Power in Renaissance Florence* (Aldershot: Ashgate, 2003)

• LOUISE LABÉ

Jones, Ann Rosalind, 'Literary Cross-Dressing in the Defense of Women in Louis Labé and Veronica Franco', *The Currency of Eros: Women's Love Lyric in Europe, 1540–1620* (Bloomington, IN: Indiana University Press, 1990), pp. 155–200

Labé, Louise, *Complete Poetry and Prose: A Bilingual Edition*, ed. and prose trans. Deborah Lesko Baker, poetry trans. Annie Finch (Chicago: University of Chicago Press, 2006)

• ELEANOR OF TOLEDO

Eisenbichler, Konrad (ed.), *The Cultural World of Eleonora di Toledo, Duchess of Florence and Siena* (Aldershot: Ashgate, 2004)

Langdon, Gabrielle, *Medici Women: Portraits of Power, Love and Betrayal in the Court of Duke Cosimo I* (Toronto: University of Toronto Press, 2006)

7. THE FRAMING OF MODERNITY
• INTRODUCTION

Rabb, Theodore K., *The Last Days of the Renaissance and the March to Modernity* (New York: Basic Books, 2006)

• LAURA BATTIFERRA AMMANNATI

Battiferra Ammannati, Laura, *Laura Battiferra and her Literary Circle: An Anthology*, ed. and trans. Victoria Kirkham (Chicago: Chicago University Press 2006)

Kirkham, Victoria, 'Sappho on the Arno', *Strong Voices, Weak History: Early Women Writers and Canons in England, France, and Italy*, ed. Pamela Joseph Benson and Victoria Kirkham (Ann Arbor, MI: University of Michigan Press, 2005)

• PIETER BRUEGEL THE ELDER

Gibson, Walter S., *Pieter Bruegel and the Art of Laughter* (Berkeley, CA: University of California Press, 2006)

Michel, Emile, and Victoria Charles, *The Brueghels* (New York: Parkstone Press, 2007)

Woollett, Anne T., *Rubens and Brueghel: A Working Friendship* (Los Angeles: J. Paul Getty Museum, 2006)

• DICK TARLTON

Lawrence, William John, 'On the Underrated Genius of Dick Tarleton', *Speeding up Shakespeare: Studies of Bygone Theatre and Drama* (London: Argonaut Press, 1937), pp. 17–38

Otto, Beatrice K., *Fools are Everywhere: The Court Jester Around the World* (Chicago: University of Chicago Press, 2001)

• GIOVANNI PIERLUIGI DA PALESTRINA

Boyd, Malcolm, *Palestrina's Style: A Practical Introduction* (London: Oxford University Press, 1973)

Jeppesen, Knud, *The Style of Palestrina and the Dissonance*, 2nd edn (New York: Dover, 1970)

• GIUSEPPE ARCIMBOLDO

Craig, Diana, *The Life and Works of Arcimboldo: A Compilation of Works from the Bridgeman Art Library* (Bristol: Parragon, 1996)

Ferino-Pagden, Sylvia (ed.), *Arcimboldo 1526–1593* (Milan: Skira, 2007)

• SOFONISBA ANGUISSOLA

Ferino-Pagden, Sylvia and Maria Kusche, *Sofonisba Anguissola: A Renaissance Woman* (Washington, DC: National Museum of Women in the Arts, 1995)

Jacobs, Fredrika H., *Defining the Renaissance Virtuosa: Women Artists and the Language of Art History and Criticism* (Cambridge: Cambridge University Press, 1997)

Perlingieri, Ilya Sandra, *Sofonisba Anguissola: The First Great Woman Artist of the Renaissance* (New York: Rizzoli, 1992)

Pizzagalli, Daniela, *La signora della pittura: Vita di Sofonisba Anguissola, gentildonna e artista nel Rinascimento* (Milan: Rizzoli, 2003)

• MICHEL DE MONTAIGNE

Cave, Terence, *How to Read Montaigne* (London: Granta, 2007)

Frame, Donald M., *Montaigne: A Biography* (San Francisco: North Point Press, 1984)

Hartle, Ann, *Michel de Montaigne: Accidental Philosopher* (Cambridge: Cambridge University Press, 2007)

Montaigne, Michel de, *The Complete Essays*, ed. and trans. M. A. Screech (London: Penguin, 1991)

• ARCANGELO TUCCARO

Cox, J. Charles, and J. R. Allen, 'Tumblers', *The Reliquary and Illustrated Archaeologist*, vol. 9 (Harvard University, 1903), pp. 186–202

McClelland, John, *Body and Mind: Sport in Europe from the Roman Empire to the Renaissance* (New York: Routledge, 2006)

Zeigler, Earle F., *Sport and Physical Education in the Middle Ages* (Bloomington, IN: Trafford Publishing, 2006)

• EDMUND CAMPION

Kilroy, Gerard, *Edmund Campion: Memory and Transcription* (Aldershot: Ashgate, 2005)

Waugh, Evelyn, *Edmund Campion: A Life* (London: Longmans, Green, 1935; repr. San Francisco: Ignatius Press, 2005)

• CATENA

Polverini Fosi, Irene, *La società violenta: Il banditismo dello stato pontificio nella seconda metà del Cinquecento* (Rome: Atneo, 1985)

• VERONICA FRANCO

Franco, Veronica, *Poems and Selected Letters*, ed. and trans. Ann Rosalind Jones and Margaret F. Rosenthal (Chicago: University of Chicago Press, 1998)

Jones, Ann Rosalind, 'Literary Cross-Dressing and the Defense of Women in Louis Labé and Veronica Franco', *The Currency of Eros: Women's Love Lyric in Europe, 1540–1620* (Bloomington, IN: Indiana University Press, 1990), pp. 155–200

Rosenthal, Margaret F., *The Honest Courtesan: Veronica Franco, Citizen and Writer in Sixteenth-Century Venice* (Chicago: University of Chicago Press, 1993)

• TYCHO BRAHE

Christianson, John Robert, *On Tycho's Island: Tycho Brahe, Science, and Culture in the Sixteenth Century* (Cambridge: Cambridge University Press, 2003)

Ferguson, Kitty, *Tycho and Kepler: The Unlikely Partnership that Forever Changed our Understanding of the Heavens* (New York: Walker & Co., 2002)

North, John David, 'The New Empiricism', *Cosmos: An Illustrated History of Astronomy and Cosmology* (Chicago: University of Chicago Press, 2008), pp. 321–98

• GIORDANO BRUNO

Bruno, Giordano, *The Expulsion of the Triumphant Beast*, 2nd edn, ed. and trans. Arthur D. Imerti (Lincoln, NE: University of Nebraska Press, 2004)

Rowland, Ingrid D., *Giordano Bruno: Philospher/ Heretic* (Chicago: University of Chicago Press, 2009)

• ISABELLA ANDREINI

Andreini, Isabella, *Selected Poems of Isabella Andreini*, ed. Anne MacNeil, trans. James Wyatt Cook (Lanham, MD: Scarecrow Press, 2005)

MacNeil, Anne, *Music and Women of the Commedia dell'Arte in the Late Sixteenth Century* (Oxford: Oxford University Press, 2003)

Sources of Quotations

1. OLD TRADITIONS AND NEW IDEAS:
Introduction, 'one of the saddest chapters...':
Ludwig Pastor, *The History of the Popes, from the
Close of the Middle Ages* (London: Paul, Trench
& Trübner, 1891), p. 165. Christine de Pizan,
'And I who was formerly a woman...': C. de
Pizan, *The Selected Writings of Christine de Pizan*,
ed. and trans. R. Blumenfeld-Kosinski, (New
York: W. W. Norton, 1997), p. 91. 'inclination to
learning...girlishness': C. de Pizan, *The Book of
the City of Ladies*, rev. edn, trans. E. J. Richards
(New York: Persea Books, 1998), pp. 154–55.
'crumbs I gathered from my father's table':
Pizan, *Selected Writings*, p. xii. 'stupid looks from
some fat drunkard': Pizan, *Selected Writings*,
p. 190. 'When I saw the flood of tribulations...':
Pizan, *Selected Writings*, p. 188. 'duties common
to married women...': Pizan, *Selected Writings*,
p. 192. 'I closed my doors...': Pizan, *Selected
Writings*, p. 193. 'spoil for others...': Pizan,
Selected Writings, p. 129. 'The realm [has been]
elevated...': Pizan, *Selected Writings*, p. 257.
'abandoned all feminine tasks...study': Pizan,
Selected Writings, p. 137. Leonardo Bruni, 'with
the coming of Chrysoloras...': Michele Scherillo,
Le origini e lo svolgimento della letteratura italiana,
6 vols (Milan: Hoepli, 1919–26), vol. 1, p. 25
(trans. Robert C. Davis). 'There are plenty of
teachers...': Scherillo, *Le origini*, vol. 1, p. 25
(trans. Robert C. Davis). 'the foundation of all
true learning...exhibited': William Harrison
Woodword, *Vittorino da Feltre and Other Humanist
Educators* (Toronto: University of Toronto
Press, 1996), p. 124. 'The noblest intellects...':
Woodword, *Vittorino da Feltre*, p. 127. 'the careful
study of the past...': Woodword, *Vittorino da
Feltre*, p. 128. Jan Hus, 'more wretched than
dogs...without complaint': J. Hus, *The Letters
of John Hus*, ed. and trans. Herbert B. Workman
and R. Martin Pope (London: Hodder and
Stoughton, 1904), p. 7. 'dung': Jan Hus, *De
ecclesia: The Church*, ed. and trans. David Schaff
(New York: Charles Scribner's Sons, 1915), p. 140.
'laying aside pomp, avarice, and luxury': Hus,
De ecclesia, trans. Schaff, p. 184. 'follies of the
Unlearned': Hus, *De ecclesia*, trans. Schaff, p. 130.

'decry and overthrow the spiritual estate': Hus,
Letters, p. 217. St Bernardino of Siena, 'God has
given the instrument...': Cynthia L. Polecritti,
*Preaching Peace in Renaissance Italy: Bernardino
of Siena and his Audience* (Washington, DC:
Catholic University of American Press, 2000),
p. 23. 'strong as a lion': Polecritti, *Preaching Peace*,
p. 23. Have you understood me?...': Polecritti,
Preaching Peace, p. 192. 'the father [who is] the
enemy of the son...': Polecritti, *Preaching Peace*,
p. 192. 'Like Jerusalem...each one to the other!':
Polecritti, *Preaching Peace*, pp. 195–96. 'punished
by fire or fines': Polecritti, *Preaching Peace*,
p. 61. Cosimo de' Medici, 'among buildings,
alms and taxes...': *Lives of the Early Medici as
Told in their Correspondence*, ed. and trans. Janet
Ross (Boston: R. G. Badger, 1911), p. 155. 'For
fifty years...': Francis H. Taylor, *The Taste of
Angels: A History of Art Collecting from Rameses
to Napoleon* (Boston, MA: Little, Brown, 1948),
pp. 65–66. Masaccio, 'about worldly affairs...
details of art': Giorgio Vasari, *The Lives of the
Artists*, trans. Julia Conaway Bondanella and Peter
Bondanella (Oxford: Oxford University Press,
1991), pp. 102–3.

2. EUROPEANS AT PEACE: Luca della Robbia,
'calculated how much time...': Giorgio Vasari,
The Lives of the Artists, trans. Julia Conaway
Bondanella and Peter Bondanella (Oxford:
Oxford University Press, 1991), p. 69. 'he made
up his mind...': Vasari, *Lives of the Artists*, p. 69.
'all earned a great deal more...': Vasari, *Lives
of the Artists*, p. 70. Leon Battista Alberti, 'could
in the great cathedral...climbing mountains':
Leon Battista Alberti, *Autobiografia* (1438) trans.
Antonio Muratori; cited in Will Durant, *The
Renaissance: The Story of Civilization*, vol. 5 (New
York: Simon & Schuster, 1980), p. 107. 'some of
his [own] relatives...': Leon Battista Alberti, *On
Painting*, ed. and trans. John R. Spencer (New
Haven, CT: Yale University Press, 1956), p. 43.
'possesses a divine power...': Leon Battista
Alberti, *On Painting*, ed. Martin Kemp, trans.
Cecil Grayson (London: Penguin, 1991), p. 60.
Lorenzo Valla, 'certain great writers...drag me

to punishment!': Lorenzo Valla, *The Treatise of Lorenzo Valla on the Donation of Constantine: Text and Translation into English*, trans. C. B. Colema of Constantine, p. 23. Alessandra Strozzi, 'made up the way you like them': Alessandra Strozzi, *Selected Letters of Alessandra Strozzi*, ed. and trans. Heather Gregory (Berkeley, CA: University of California Press, 1997), p. 73. 'particularly one who didn't desert…': Strozzi, *Selected Letters*, p. 147. 'When she goes out…': Strozzi, *Selected Letters*, p. 31. '[You and Filippo will] both be unmarried…': Strozzi, *Selected Letters*, p. 153. 'it seemed to me from looking at her face…': Strozzi, *Selected Letters*, p. 155. 'is not soiled merchandise': Ann Crabb, *The Strozzi of Florence: Widowhood and Family Solidarity in the Renaissance* (Ann Arbor, MI: University of Michigan Press, 2000), p. 189. 'good meat with lots of flavour': Gene Brucker, *Living on the Edge in Leonardo's Florence: Selected Essays* (Berkeley, CA: University of California Press, 2005), p. 161. 'so are the rest of us': Strozzi, *Selected Letters*, p. 217. Isotta Nogarola, 'an eloquent woman is never chaste': Isotta Nogarola, *Complete Writings: Letterbook, Dialogue on Adam and Eve, Orations*, ed. and trans. Margaret L. King and Diana Robin (Chicago: University of Chicago Press, 2004), pp. 68–69. 'dare to engage so deeply…': Nogarola, *Complete Writings*, pp. 68–69. 'women are ridiculed by men': Nogarola, *Complete Writings*, p. 53. 'I see that you are unmoved…': Nogarola, *Complete Writings*, p. 53. 'manly soul': Nogarola, *Complete Writings*, pp. 42–43. 'greater understanding and knowledge of truth': Nogarola, *Complete Writings*, p. 151. 'libidinous way of life…uncorrupted ornament': Nogarola, *Complete Writings*, p. 123. Lucrezia Tornabuoni, 'the vilest repute': Natalie R. Tomas, *The Medici Women: Gender and Power in Renaissance Florence* (Aldershot: Ashgate, 2003), p. 31. 'I am sending you several trout': Tomas, *Medici Women*, p. 49. 'manly heart': Lucrezia Tornabuoni de' Medici, *Sacred Narratives*, ed. and trans. Jane Tylus (Chicago: University of Chicago Press, 2001), p. 145. Gentile Bellini, 'no less acquainted with naval warfare…': Giorgio Vasari, *The Lives of the Painters, Sculptors, and Architects*, vol. 3, trans. A. B. Hinds (London: J. M. Dent, 1900), p. 42. 'wondering how a mortal man…': Vasari, *Lives of the Painters*, pp. 46–47. 'had been assisted by some divine spirit': Vasari, *Lives of the Painters*, p. 47. Mehmet II, 'He is mine.

He is the one…': Nancy Bisaha, *Creating East and West: Renaissance Humanists and the Ottoman Turks* (Philadelphia: University of Pennsylvania Press, 2004), p. 163. 'No one doubts that you are emperor of the Romans': Halil Inalcik, 'The Policy of Mehmed II toward the Greek Population of Istanbul and the Byzantine Buildings of the City', *Dumbarton Oaks Papers*, vol. 23/24 (1969–70), pp. 229–49 at p. 233. 'a city of ruins, poor, and largely uninhabited': Inalcik, 'The Policy of Mehmed II', p. 231. 'When the Sultan…the city repopulated': Inalcik, 'The Policy of Mehmed II', p. 236. 'Here in the land of the Turks…': Israel Zinberg, *A History of Jewish Literature: The Jewish Center of Culture in the Ottoman Empire*, 13 vols, trans. Bernard Martin (Cleveland, OH: Case Western University Press, 1972), vol. 5, p. 14.

3. THE EMERGING NATIONS: William Caxton, 'To eschew sloth and idleness': George D. Painter, *William Caxton: A Biography* (New York: G. P. Putnam's Sons, 1977), p. 39. 'my pen is worn…': Painter, *William Caxton*, p. 53. 'He asked after eggs…': W. F. Bolton, *A Living Language: The History and Structure of English* (New York: Random House, 1982), p. 173 [quotation modernized]. 'over curious terms…old and homely': Bolton, *A Living Language*, p. 173 [quotations modernized]. 'sugared eloquence': Charles W. Eliot (ed.), *Prefaces and Prologues to Famous Books*, vol. 39, Harvard Classics (New York: P. F. Collier & Son, 1910), p. 18. 'princes, lords, barons, knights…all the common people': Yu-Chiao Wang, 'Caxton's Romances and their Early Tudor Readers', *Huntington Library Quarterly*, vol. 67, no. 2 (2004), p. 177. Heinrich Kramer, 'more given to fleshly lusts…carnal filthiness': Heinrich Institoris, *The Malleus maleficarum*, ed. and trans. P. G. Maxwell-Stuart (Manchester: Manchester University Press, 2007), p. 75. 'move about in order to eat oats and fodder': Heinrich Institoris, *Malleus maleficarum*, pp. 152–53. Felix Fabri, 'that whether I was asleep…': Felix Fabri, *The Book of the Wanderings of Felix Fabri*, trans. Aubrey Stewart (London: Palestine Pilgrims' Text Society, 1892), p. 3. 'alarmed, and feared for my life…': Fabri, *Book of the Wanderings*, p. 3. 'stale bread, biscuit full of worms…': Fabri, *Wanderings*, p. 29. 'we did not spend more than nine days…': Fabri, *Wanderings*, pp. 23–24. 'frequently [writing] as I sat…': Fabri,

Wanderings, p. 56. 'so that they also, in mind…':
Fabri, *Wanderings*, p. 58. 'several times…more
valuable than before': Fabri, *Wanderings*, p. 93.
'dull-minded and slow of understanding': Fabri,
Wanderings, p. 2. 'of some small learning…':
Fabri, *Wanderings*, p. 2. Antonio de Nebrija, 'to
overthrow the [intellectual] barbarity…': Joseph
R. Jones, 'The Six-Hundredth Anniversary of
the Founding of the Spanish College at Bologna
by Don Gil de Albornoz', *Hispania*, vol. 50, no. 3
(1967), pp. 555–58 at p. 557. 'What do I want a
work like this for…': quoted in *Prosofagia: Revista
literaria*, vol. 7 (2010), p. 26 (trans. Robert C.
Davis). 'Not only the enemies…Navarres [of
northern Spain]': Antonio de Nebrija, *Gramática
castellana*, trans. Claudio Véliz (Madrid: Junta
del Centenario, 1946), p. 5. 'Your highness, the
language is…': Antonio de Nebrija, *Gramática
castellana*, p. 11 (trans. Robert C. Davis). Matthias
Corvinus, 'glorious struggle to stamp out
Mohammedanism': Marcus Tanner, *The Raven
King: Matthew Corvinus and the Fate of his Lost
Library* (New Haven, CT: Yale University Press,
2008), p. 51. 'Matthias is dead…': Tanner, *The
Raven King*, p. 141. Luca Pacioli, 'with the most
astute…': Robert Emmett Taylor, *No Royal Road:
Luca Pacioli and his Times* (New York: Arno
Press, 1980), p. 256. 'happy times…': Martin
Kemp, *Behind the Picture: Art and Evidence in
the Italian Renaissance* (New Haven, CT: Yale
University Press, 1997), p. 249. 'that constitutes
the measure…be called certainties': Taylor, *No
Royal Road*, p. 256. 'to the uneducated…it will
seem like a miracle': Taylor, *No Royal Road*,
p. 267. Sandro Botticelli, 'beyond all other work
in Italy': Laurence Kanter, 'Alessandro Filipepi,
called Botticelli', in Laurence Kanter, Hilliard T.
Goldfarb and James Hankins, *Botticelli's Witness:
Changing Style in a Changing Florence* (Boston,
MA: Isabella Stewart Gardner Museum, 1997)
p. 22. Leonardo da Vinci, 'This man will never
do anything…': Giorgio Vasari, *Lives of the
Artists*, vol. 1, ed. and trans. George Bull (London:
Penguin, 1988), p. 269. 'instead of [wasting time]
defining…': Codex Atlantico, Milan, Biblioteca
Ambrosiana, folio 119v (trans. Robert C. Davis).
'I well know how…': Codex Atlantico, folio 119v.
Antonio Rinaldeschi 'seeming to almost be…':
William J. Connell and Giles Constable, *Sacrilege
and Redemption in Renaissance Florence: The
Case of Antonio Rinaldeschi* (Toronto: Centre for

Reformation and Renaissance Studies, 2005), p. 17
(trans. Robert C. Davis).

4. SUDDEN SHOCKS: Introduction, 'beggared
his own country…': quoted in Heinrich Graetz,
Popular History of the Jews, trans. A. B. Rhine,
6 vols (New York: Hebrew Publishing Company,
1919), vol. 4, p. 225. 'Now we are in the
power…': quoted in James Reston, Jr, *Dogs of
God: Columbus, the Inquisition, and the Defeat
of the Moors* (New York: Anchor Books, 2006),
p. 287. Christopher Columbus, 'since Genoa
was Genoa…': Felipe Fernández-Armesto,
Columbus (Oxford: Oxford University Press,
1991), pp. 103–4. 'the most beautiful island…':
Christopher Columbus, *Diario de a bordo de
Cristóbal Colón, primer viaje* (Barcelona: Editorial
Arcadia, 1957), entry for 28 October 1492. 'the
Isles of India beyond the Ganges': quoted in
C. D. Warner (ed.), *Library of the World's Best
Literature, Ancient and Modern: Index Guide*
(New York: Peale and Hill, 1899), p. 229. 'as
many idolatrous slaves…': John Boyd Thacher,
*Christopher Columbus: His Life, his Works, his
Remains: As Revealed by Original Printed and
Manuscript Records* (New York: Putnam, 1903),
vol. 1, folio letter 25. John Cabot, 'of heathens
and infidels': 'The First Letters Patent Granted
by Henry VII to John Cabot, 5 March 1496', cited
in H. B. Biggar (ed.), *The Precursors of Jacques
Cartier, 1497–1534: A Collection of Documents
Relating to the Early History of the Dominion of
Canada* (Ottawa: Government Printing Bureau,
1911), p. 8. 'discovered, 700 leagues off…':
Lorenzo Pasqualigo, letter sent from London,
23 August 1497, in Clements Markham (ed. and
trans.), *The Journal of Christopher Columbus
(during his first voyage, 1492–93), and Documents
Relating to the Voyages of John Cabot and Gaspar
Corte Real* (London: Hakluyt Society, 1893),
p. 201. 'Great honours are done…': Markham,
Journal of Christopher Columbus, p. 202. Girolamo
Savonarola, 'so pulled down by every vice…':
Lauro Martines, *Fire in the City: Savonarola and
the Struggle for the Soul of Renaissance Florence*
(Oxford: Oxford University Press, 2006), p. 11.
'What are you crying about, you blind ones?':
Martines, *Fire in the City*, p. 14. Jakob Fugger,
'Once the coin…': James Kittelson, *Luther the
Reformer: The Story of the Man and his Career*
(Minneapolis, MN: Augsburg Fortress Publishing

House, 1986), pp. 103–4. Desiderius Erasmus, 'the nature of a woman…': Desiderius Erasmus, *The Praise of Folly*, ed. and trans. Clarence H. Miller, 2nd edn (New Haven, CT: Yale University Press, 2003), pp. 88–89. 'everything by the book': Desiderius Erasmus, *The Praise of Folly and Other Writings*, ed. and trans. Robert M. Adams (New York: W. W. Norton, 1989), p. 62. 'make frightful scenes…fixed to the same spot': Erasmus, *Praise of Folly and Other Writings*, p. 62. 'anything except to be spared…to know nothing': Erasmus, *Praise of Folly and Other Writings*, p. 43. 'Erasmus is an eel…grab him': *Luther and Erasmus: Free Will and Salvation*, ed. and trans. E. Gordon Rupp and Philip S. Watson (Philadelphia: Westminster Press, 1969), p. 2. 'laying the egg that Luther hatched…very different feather': Desiderius Erasmus, *The Correspondence of Erasmus: Letters 1356 to 1534*, ed. James M. Estes, trans. R. A. B. Mynors and Alexander Dalzell, vol. 10 of *The Collected Works of Erasmus* (Toronto: University of Toronto Press, 1992), p. 464. Niccolò Machiavelli, 'oblige citizens to love…': Niccolò Machiavelli, *The Art of War*, trans. Ellis Farneworth, rev. Neal Wood (Cambridge, MA: Da Capo Press, 2001), p. 12. 'the wonderful examples…': Niccolò Machiavelli, *The Prince and The Discourses*, trans. Luigi Ricci, with an introduction by Max Lerner (New York: Random House, Modern Library, 1950), p. 104. 'the lack of a real…': Machiavelli, *The Prince and The Discourses*, p. 104.'when there is combined…': Machiavelli, *The Prince and The Discourses*, p. 115. Albrecht Dürer, 'in need of instruction…': Judith Bell, 'Drawings of the German Renaissance', *World and I* (April 2000), p. 98 ('Educator's Reference Complete' website at http://www.worldandi.com/specialreport/2000/april/Sa19075.htm, accessed 1 June 2010). 'Art is rooted in Nature… has it': Jane Campbell Hutchison, *Albrecht Dürer: A Biography* (Princeton, NJ: Princeton University Press, 1990), p. 69. 'much praise but little profit… handle colours': Hutchison, *Albrecht Dürer*, p. 93. Cesare Borgia, 'one to be imitated…': Niccolò Machiavelli, *Il principe*, ed. L. Arthur Burd, (Oxford: Clarendon Press, 1891), p. 227 (trans. Robert C. Davis). Michelangelo Buonarroti, 'the man whose amazing art…': Laura Battiferra Ammannati, *Laura Battiferra and her Literary Circle: An Anthology*, ed. and trans. Victoria

Kirkham (Chicago: University of Chicago Press, 2006), p. 287. 'When the work was thrown…': Giorgio Vasari, *Lives of the Artists*, ed. and trans. George Bull (London: Penguin, 1988) vol. 1, p. 361. 'restor[ed] light to a world…': Vasari, *Lives of the Artists*, vol. 1, p. 354. Baldassare Castiglione, 'conceals all artistry…': Baldassare Castiglione, *The Book of the Courtier*, ed. and trans. George Bull (London: Penguin, 1988), p. 65. Raphael, 'delighting much in women…': Giorgio Vasari, *The Lives of the Most Excellent Painters, Sculptors, and Architects*, ed. Philip Jacks, trans. Gaston du C. de Vere (New York: Modern Library Classics, 2006), p. 289.

5. THE COLLAPSE OF THE OLD ORDER: Introduction, 'There is nothing harder…': Niccolò Machiavelli, *Il principe*, ed. L. Arthur Burd (Oxford: Clarendon Press, 1891), p. 210 (trans. Robert C. Davis). Thomas More, 'Good Catholyke Realme': Peter Ackroyd, *The Life of Thomas More* (London: Chatto & Windus, 1998), p. 303. 'To breake a little winde…': quoted in Michelle O'Callaghan, *The English Wits: Literature and Sociability in Early Modern England* (Cambridge: Cambridge University Press, 2007), p. 95. 'not precisely beautiful': Desiderius Erasmus, letter to Ulrich von Hutten, 23 July 1519, in *Erasmus and Cambridge: The Cambridge Letters of Erasmus*, trans. Douglas Ferguson Scott Thomson (Toronto: University of Toronto Press, 1963) p. 113. 'diametrically opposed to ours': Thomas More, *Utopia*, trans. Paul Turner (Harmondsworth: Penguin, 1965), p. 108. 'great matter': Thomas More, 'To Thomas Cromwell, March? 1534', *The Last Letters of Thomas More*, ed. Alvaro de Silva (Grand Rapids, MI: W. B. Eerdmans, 2001), p. 38. 'Pluck up thy spirits… do thine office': Ackroyd, *Life of Thomas More*, p. 406. 'my neck is very short': Ackroyd, *Life of Thomas More*, p. 406. Martin Luther, 'This is the sort of thing…': Roland Bainton, *Here I Stand: A Life of Martin Luther* (Nashville, TN: Abingdon Press, 1978) p. 235. 'Hans is cutting his teeth…': Bainton, *Here I Stand*, p. 229. Bartolomé de Las Casas, 'humble, patient, and peaceable…': Tzvetan Todorov, *The Conquest of America: The Question of the Other* (Norman, OK: University of Oklahoma Press, 1999), p. 164. 'into this sheepfold…': Todorov, *Conquest of America*, p. 165. 'no one with a clear conscience…': Bartolomé de las Casas,

An Account, Much Abbreviated, of the Destruction of the Indies, with Related Texts, ed. Franklin W. Knight, trans. Andrew Hurley (Cambridge, MA: Hackett Publications, 2003), p. xxiii. Vittoria Colonna, 'driven by a frenzy...': Irma B. Jaffe with Gernando Colombardo, *Shining Eyes, Cruel Fortune: The Lives and Loves of Italian Renaissance Women Poets* (New York: Fordham University Press, 2002), p. 59 (trans. Robert C. Davis). 'a sweet style...': Katharina M. Wilson (ed.), *Women Writers of the Renaissance and Reformation* (Athens, ga: University of Georgia Press, 1987), p. 22. 'cursed century and evil harpies...': Vittoria Colonna, *Sonnets for Michelangelo: A Bilingual Edition*, ed. and trans. Abigail Brundin (Chicago: University of Chicago Press, 2005), p. 125. Marguerite of Navarre, 'marry a man who is...': Patricia F. Cholakian and Rouben C. Cholakian, *Marguerite de Navarre: Mother of the Renaissance* (New York: Columbia University Press, 2006), p. 25. 'having neither read nor studied...': Cholakian and Cholakian, *Marguerite de Navarre*, p. 28. 'How vexing it is...': Cholakian and Cholakian, *Marguerite de Navarre*, p. 157. Pietro Aretino, 'live by the sweat of my ink': quoted in Luba Freedman, *Titian's Portraits Through Aretino's Lens* (University Park, pa: Pennsylvania State University Press, 1995), p. 11. 'I have made every Duke...': quoted in Raymond B. Waddington, *Aretino's Satyr: Sexuality, Satire and Self-Projection in Sixteenth-Century Literature and Art* (Toronto: University of Toronto Press, 2004), p. 58. William Tyndale, 'process, order, and meaning': David Daniell, *William Tyndale: A Biography* (New Haven, CT: Yale University Press, 1994), p. 83. François Rabelais, 'joyfully rubbing their bacon together': François Rabelais, *The Histories of Gargantua and Pantagruel*, ed. and trans. John Michael Cohen (London: Penguin, 1955) p. 46. 'digging tool[s]...': François Rabelais, *Gargantua and Pantagruel*, trans. Burton Raffel (New York: W. W. Norton, 1990) p. 136. 'hypocritical codpieces...the feminine sex': Rabelais, *Gargantua and Pantagruel*, p. 24. Hans Holbein the Younger, 'the arts are freezing...': Derek Wilson, *Hans Holbein: Portrait of an Unknown Man* (London: Pimlico, 2006), p. 120. 'a wonderful artist': Wilson, *Hans Holbein*, p. 130. 'he deceived those to whom...': Roy Strong, *Holbein: The Complete Paintings* (London: Granada, 1980), p. 4. 'since he saw it he has been...': Wilson, *Hans*

Holbein, p. 255. 'If I had two heads...': Wilson, *Hans Holbein*, p. 256.

6. THE NEW WAVE: Pope Paul IV, 'I have never conferred...': quoted in Michael Walsh, *The Conclave: A Sometimes Secret and Occasionally Bloody History of Papal Elections* (Lanham, md: Roman & Littlefield, 2003), p. 118. 'Even if my own father...': quoted in Leonard Shlain, *The Alphabet Versus the Goddess: The Conflict between Word and Image* (London: Penguin, 1999), p. 358. Benvenuto Cellini, 'that was the name they decided on': Benvenuto Cellini, *Autobiography*, ed. and trans. George Bull (London: Penguin, 1998), p. 6. 'I hated every minute...': Cellini, *Autobiography*, p. 7. 'all men of every sort...': Cellini, *Autobiography*, p. 1. 'tried to persuade me to join...': Cellini, *Autobiography*, p. 116. St Francis Xavier, 'whether [he] sends us among...': from the *Formula* of Ignatius Loyola (1540), quoted in Mark Rotsaert, S. J., 'Obedience in the Life of the Society of Jesus', *Review of Ignatian Spirituality*, vol. 40 (2009), pp. 26–36, at p. 32. 'a plentiful harvest [of souls]': Henry James Coleridge (ed. and trans.), *The Life and Letters of St Francis Xavier*, 2 vols (London: Burns and Oates, 1876), vol. 2, p. 345. 'the place is very dangerous...': James Brodrick, *San Francesco Saverio: Apostolo delle Indie e del Giappone, 1506–1562*, trans. L. Marzollo and O. Fochesato (Parma: Edizioni Missionarie, 2006) p. 246 (trans. Robert C. Davis). 'led by reason in everything...': Coleridge, *Life and Letters of St Francis Xavier*, vol. 2, p. 338. 'We have decided at all costs...': quoted in Gianni Colzani, 'San Francesco Saverio missionario: La nascita di una nuova figura ecclesiale e il suo servizio', *Euntes Docete*, vol. 60 (2007), pp. 23–45, at p. 39 (trans. Robert C. Davis). Jean Calvin, 'live henceforth according to...': Alister E. McGrath, *A Life of John Calvin: A Study in the Shaping of Western Culture* (Oxford: Basil Blackwell, 1990), pp. 94–95. Andreas Vesalius, 'How many often absurd things...': Andrea Vesalio, *De humani corporis fabrica*, Book 7, ch. 12 (Basel: Ioannis Oporini, 1543) (trans. Robert C. Davis). St Teresa of Avila, 'I was very adroit...': St Teresa of Avila, *The Autobiography of St Teresa of Avila: The Life of St Teresa of Jesus*, ed. Benedict Zimmerman, trans. David Lewis (Charlotte, NC: TAN Books, 2009), p. 9. 'to make much of dress...': St Teresa

of Avila, *Autobiography*, p. 7. 'the fear of God...':
St Teresa of Avila, *Autobiography*, p. 10. Catherine
de' Medici, 'showed valour in their joust': quoted
in Leonie Frieda, *Catherine de Medici: Renaissance
Queen of France* (New York: Harper Perennial,
2006), p. 46. 'the greatest match in the world':
Frieda, *Catherine de Medici*, p. 31. 'the protruding
eyes...': Frieda, *Catherine de Medici*, p. 28.
'merchant's daughter': Frieda, *Catherine de Medici*,
p. 31. 'The girl has been given to me stark naked!':
Frieda, *Catherine de Medici*, p. 48. 'What could the
woman...grasping the crown': quoted in Pierre
de Bourdeille Brantôme, *Illustrious Dames of the
Court of the Valois Kings*, trans. Katharine Prescott
Wormeley (New York: The Lamb Publishing
Co., 1912), p. 88. Louise Labé, 'Kiss me again...':
Louise Labé, *Complete Poetry and Prose*, ed. and
prose trans. Deborah Lesko Baker, poetry trans.
Annie Finch (Chicago: University of Chicago
Press, 2006), Sonnet 18, p. 207. 'Ladies, I beg
you...': Louise Labé, *French Women Poets of Nine
Centuries: The Distaff and the Pen*, ed. and trans.
Norman R. Shapiro (Baltimore: Johns Hopkins
University Press, 2008), Sonnet 24, p. 157. 'men's
harsh laws...to be in command': Labé, *Complete
Poetry and Prose*, p. 43. Eleanor of Toledo, 'a
young man on a marvellous horse': quoted in
Michael Levey, *Florence: A Portrait* (Cambridge,
MA: Harvard University Press, 1998), p. 324.

7. THE FRAMING OF MODERNITY: Laura
Battiferra Ammannati, 'musician and familiar':
Laura Battiferra Ammannati, *Laura Battiferra
and Her Literary Circle: An Anthology* (*The Other
Voice in Early Modern Europe*), ed. and trans.
Victoria Kirkham (Chicago: University of
Chicago Press, 2006), p. 17. 'docile, obedient,
benevolent...': Battiferra Ammannati, *An
Anthology*, p. 18. 'I would go contemplating...':
Battiferra Ammannati, *An Anthology*, p. 143.
'cultured intellects': Battiferra Ammannati,
An Anthology, p. 119. Dick Tarlton, 'un-dumpish
her...all of her Physicians': Thomas Fuller,
The History of the Worthies of England (1662, 1811
edn), vol. 2, p. 312; quoted in Beatrice K. Otto,
*Fools Are Everywhere: The Court Jester Around the
World* (Chicago: University of Chicago Press,
2001), p. 90. 'happy unhappy wit': Alexandra
Halasz, '"So beloved that men use his picture
for their signs": Richard Tarlton and the Uses
of Sixteenth-Century Celebrity', in Leeds Barroll

(ed.), *Shakespeare Studies*, vol. 23 (Madison, NJ:
Fairleigh Dickinson University Press, 1995),
p. 21. 'more of her faults...': Fuller, *Worthies
of England*, in Otto, *Fools Are Everywhere*,
p. 90. 'like a drummer...': George Wilson, *The
Commendation of Cockes and Cock-Fighting* (1607),
quoted in E. K. Chambers (ed.), *The Elizabethan
Stage*, vol. 2 (Oxford: Oxford University Press,
2009), p. 345. Giovanni Pierluigi da Palestrina,
'lascivious or impure': Craig A. Monson, 'The
Council of Trent Revisited', *Journal of the
American Musicological Society*, vol. 55 (Spring
2002), pp. 1–37, at p. 11. Giuseppe Arcimboldo,
'various oddities': Thomas DaCosta Kaufmann,
'Arcimboldo's Imperial Allegories', *Zeitschrift
für Kunstgeschichte*, vol. 39 (1976), pp. 275–96,
at p. 275. Sofonisba Anguissola, 'among the
exceptional painters of our times': Daniela
Pizzagalli, *La signora della pittura: Vita di
Sofonisba di Anguissola, gentildonna e artista nel
Rinascimento* (Milan: Rizzoli, 2003), p. 196 (trans.
Robert C. Davis). 'her age is 96...': Pizzagalli,
La signora della pittura, p. 231 (trans. Robert C.
Davis). Michel de Montaigne, 'the slavery of the
court...': Michel de Montaigne, *The Complete
Works of Montaigne*, trans. Donald M. Frame
(Stanford, CA: Stanford University Press, 1957),
p. ix. 'like a runaway horse...ashamed of itself':
Montaigne, *Complete Works*, p. 21. 'fully boated
with all sorts...poverty and hunger': Montaigne,
The Complete Essays, ed. and trans. M. A. Screech
(London: Penguin, 1991), pp. 240–41. 'every man
calls barbarous...': Montaigne, *Complete Essays*,
p. 231. 'keeps our souls constantly exercised...':
Montaigne, *Complete Essays*, p. 1101. 'I know what
I am escaping...I am looking for': Montaigne,
Complete Essays, p. 1100. 'almost as much as
from Montagnié': Ben Jonson, *Volpone*, Act III,
Scene 2, line 90, in Ben Jonson, *Volpone and Other
Plays*, ed. Michael Jamieson (London: Penguin,
2004), p. 104. 'the marrow of the man...': Ralph
Waldo Emerson quoted in Jane Kramer, 'Me,
Myself, and I' in *New Yorker* (7 September 2009),
p. 40. Arcangelo Tuccaro, 'autres choses plus
dangereuses': Catherine de Médicis, *Lettres de
Catherine de Médicis*, vol. 2: *1563–1566*, ed. Hector
La Ferrière-Percy, et al. (Paris: Imprimerie
Nationale, 1885), letter of 8 September 1563,
p. 95. 'proportions stipulated by mathematical
measurement': Tuccaro quoted in John
McClelland, *Body and Mind: Sport in Europe from*

the Roman Empire to the Renaissance (New York: Routledge, 2007), p. 135. Edmund Campion, 'one of the diamonds of England': Alice Hogge, *God's Secret Agents: Queen Elizabeth's Forbidden Priests and the Hatching of the Gunpowder Plot* (New York: HarperCollins, 2005), p. 67. 'condemned all [their] own...': Leanda de Lisle, *After Elizabeth: The Rise of James of Scotland and the Struggle for the Throne of England* (New York: Ballantine Books, 2007), p. 20. 'to test the truth of his creed': Evelyn Waugh, *Edmund Campion* (Boston, MA: Little, Brown & Co., 1946), pp. 230–31. Catena, 'I'm bold and ready...I am Catena!': Processi criminali, Tribunale del Governatore, Rome, Archivio di Stato, *busta* 169, *filza* 28, folios 684*v*–685*r* (trans. Robert C. Davis). 'a famous thief and bandit...': Michel de Montaigne, *The Complete Works: Essays, Travel Journal, Letters*, ed. and trans. Donald M. Frame (London: Everyman, 2003), p. 1148. 'acting the spy for our enemies': Processi criminali, folio 691*v*. 'we also hamstrung upwards...': Processi criminali, folio 694*r*. 'You should know that...': Processi criminali, folio 694*v*. 'who go behind the sheep': Processi criminali, folio 714*r*. '8 or 10 braids longer...': Romolo Allegrini, 'Memorie di Perugia', *Cronache della città di Perugia*, 5 vols, ed. Ariodante Fabretti (Turin, 1894), vol. 5, pp. 1–148, at p. 50 (trans. Robert C. Davis). 'as long as we don't annoy...': Processi criminali, folio 720*v*. 'a great crowd of people...': Montaigne, *The Complete Works*, p. 382. 'showing no emotion...': Montaigne, *The Complete Works*, p. 1148. Veronica Franco, 'principal and most illustrious Venetian courtesans': Ann Rosalind Jones, 'City Women and their Audiences: Louise Labé and Veronica Franco', in *Rewriting the Renaissance: The Discourses of Sexual Difference in Early Modern Europe*, ed. Margaret W. Ferguson, Maureen Quilligan and Nancy J. Vickers (Chicago: University of Chicago Press, 1986), p. 303. 'So sweet and delicious...a nail in hard wood': Veronica Franco, *Poems and Selected Letters*, ed. and trans. Ann Rosalind Jones and Margaret F. Rosenthal (Chicago: University of Chicago Press, 1998), Capitolo 2, p. 69. 'a cow that could satisfy the entire Ghetto': Elizabeth Horodowich, *Language and Statecraft in Early Modern Venice* (Cambridge: Cambridge University Press, 2008), p. 103. 'made up their minds...': Franco quoted in Irma B. Jaffe with Gernando Colombardo, *Shining Eyes, Cruel Fortune: The Lives and Loves of Italian*

Renaissance Women Poets (New York: Fordham University Press, 2002), p. 355. Tycho Brahe, 'a long-term project...': Paul Murdin, *Full Meridian of Glory: Perilous Adventures in the Competition to Measure the Earth* (New York: Springer, 2008), p. 2. Giordano Bruno, 'to put together a bit of cash...': Anacleto Verrecchia, *Giordano Bruno: La falena dello spirito* (Rome: Donzelli, 2002), p. 58 (trans. Robert C. Davis). 'a jackass': Verrecchia, *Giordano Bruno*, p. 90. 'that wretched little Italian...': Verrecchia, *Giordano Bruno*, p. 118. 'perpetual foreigner, exile, fugitive...': Verrecchia, *Giordano Bruno*, p. 177. 'an academic with no academy': Verrecchia, *Giordano Bruno*, p. 108. Isabella Andreini, 'I began [it] almost as a joke': Isabella Andreini, *La mirtilla*, ed. and trans. Julie D. Campbell (Tempe, AZ: Arizona Center for Medieval and Renaissance Studies, 2002), p. 1.

Sources of Illustrations

Index